Albuquerque Academy
6400 W
Albuquerque

D0792103

It was Caesar, after all, who christened it 'the Province', and at first its shifting contours, expanding and contracting in response to wars and migrations, seemed to encompass a land-mass which included Geneva on the one hand and Toulouse on the other: an improbably vast territory. But over the years its outlines hovered and retraced themselves until it assumed the outlines of our modern Provence which comprised Montélimar in the north, Nice in the east and Béziers or Narbonne in the south . . .

Lawrence Durrell

Caesar's Vast Ghost

ROBERT CARRIER

FEASTS
of
PROVENCE

RIZZOLI
NEW YORK

There is the first time we go abroad, and the first time we go to Provence. For me they almost coincided, and it would be hard to express what I felt that evening in the garden above the Papal Palace. The frogs croaked, the silver Rhône flowed underneath, the Mediterranean spring was advancing.

I have been back so many times to that place, to Hiély's restaurant with its plate-glass windows, to the Greek theatre at Arles, the hills of Les Baux, the ruins of Saint Rémy, to the Rhône with its eddies and islands, and the cypress hedges where the cicadas charge the batteries of summer, that I can no longer remember what they looked like for the first time. I only know that they are sacred places.

Cyril Connolly

Enemies of Promise

641.59449
CAR

For Pelote and France who taught me warmth and love and kindness *à la française*; for Raymond who opened the doors to French thought, French writing and French theater for me ... and finally for Fifine, who summer after summer in her small kitchen in St Tropez taught me the essence of her art.

Contents

The spring of 1989 signaled the beginning of this book. I went to stay with a friend in Provence, in a small hilltop house just outside one of those villages in the Var which seem to be made up of a cluster of houses, a church and a wine co-operative, where the only excitement each week is the arrival of the fish van on Fridays so that villagers who are not able to get into nearby Lorgues for the market can make their purchases for the weekend.

All around the little village there were hills of pine and scrub and wild herbs, and then further on other villages – Entrecasteaux with its lovely old château; Le Thoronet with its austere abbey, Flayosc, Villecroze and Tourtour. Nearby lay Cotignac, one of the prettiest villages in the Var, with its charming open square and fountain. To me this is one of the loveliest areas in all France.

After a week of enjoying the calm and peace of the house, with its view over a magnificent valley, and wandering to my heart's content through the neighboring villages, I drove across the Massif des Maures, through the villages of Grimaud and Vidauban to my old stamping ground: the little fishing port of St Tropez, hidden at the tip of the peninsula which separates the port and its surrounding hill villages, Gassin, Grimaud and Ramatuelle, from the rest of France.

I was curious to see St Tropez again after the many years that I had been away; anxious to see if the quiet fishing village that I had known so well just after the Second World War had been spoiled by its years of success. It was Easter and the sleepy little town had just begun to open its shops and restaurants to welcome the first visitors of the season. I walked all round the town, street by street, and if anything – except for the new bans on parking on the Port, the one-way system and the parking lot as you enter the town – it is better now than it ever was.

The two houses I had owned there at one time or another and where I had spent so many happy summers and winters

were both still there, safely rooted in the very heart of the old town, as were one or two of my favorite restaurants and the cafés on the Port. I found it was only I who had changed: I was no longer the eager twenty-two-year-old who had voyaged down with friends in a beat-up little Renault, the minute that gas rationing had eased enough to let us speed down *autoroute numéro sept* from Paris. I was older, more settled, more experienced. No longer willing to dance the night away in the *boîtes* of St Tropez, or drink pastis or a *coup de rouge* in the

Café du Port at seven in the morning. But I found I appreciated even more the warm, luxurious light; the markets and the sun-dappled crooked streets. And I fell in love once again with the brilliantly colored fruits and vegetables fresh from the markets, the fish that could be caught that morning and be on the grill for lunch or dinner, whether in a restaurant or at home, the wines that could be obtained at reasonable prices anyone could afford . . . and the wild game, wild mushrooms and even truffles that were there for the asking.

I The Good

HERBS, SPICES, SAUCES AND BUTTERS OF PROVENCE

Hillsides full of the overwhelming scent of wild thyme, rosemary and summer savory, and fields of purple lavender stretching as far as the eye can see, are the natural riches of the countryside behind the coast. And even in St Tropez a short and aromatic walk up by the citadel on a sun-drenched morning, just after the early morning dew has dissipated, will fill your mind with visions of herb-sprigged legs of lamb roasting before the open fire, and of Mediterranean vegetables sprinkled with Provençal herbs simmering on the back of the stove.

Wild or cultivated, fresh or dried, the traditional herbs of Provence are in abundant supply. The rule for pungent herbs, according to the experts, is the lighter the rainfall, the more concentrated the aromas. And here the sun is apt to shine for 300 days a year. Another benefit bestowed by these fields of aromatic herbs is the local cottage industry producing those specially flavored honeys – thyme, lavender and acacia – to be found in every village market or in the series of attractive little shops called 'Goût' (Taste) that dot the villages of Provence. And no, the beekeepers do not add distillations of the herbs or blossoms to the honey, as a friend once told me, nor do they inject the bees: they just bring the

14

Seasonings

hives out into the fields at the appropriate season and the bees do the rest. The same is true of course for almond-flavored honey, one of the great specialities of the region, produced by setting the hives out among the almond trees at blossom time.

Fresh herbs of Provence

In Provence herbs are used medicinally as much as they are in cooking. It has always pleased me to know that I am adding health to my casseroles as I take advantage of the wonderful herbs available in the region: sage, good for fatigue and asthma and problems of the liver, and wonderful with pork, is the perfect additive for conserves of meats, games and vegetables (see *thon de lapin* on page 209), and is surprisingly good with fish. Provençal cooks also use sage in casseroles of game, and it is of course one of the two principal ingredients for *aïgo boulido* (sometimes known as *soupe à la sauge*). But because of its strong, bold flavor when dried it should be used with great care – especially in stuffings for ravioli, chicken, duck and goose, where it is apt to swamp other more delicate flavors.

Rosemary, the second of the herbs of the Provençal hills, has a fresh, sweet, pinewoods flavor when newly picked. I like to use it to add a fragrant, herby taste to sauces, stews and creamed soups, and a sprinkling will complement the flavor of young lamb and kid and stews of Mediterranean vegetables. Use fresh sprigs of rosemary, in conjunction with thin strips of garlic and anchovy, to bring out the flavor of roasts of lamb and grills of fresh sea bream. And try it with steaks of beef or veal, using the finely chopped leaves of this fragrant herb as you would pepper for a *steak au poivre*, and no other seasoning.

A distillation (a tea, really) of fresh rosemary makes a wonderful refresher for the digestion and the liver. Traditional Provençal medicinal lore has it, too, that this fresh-tasting herbal tea helps to clear the complexion.

The seeds, dried stalks and feathery sprigs of fennel are used extensively in cooking by the Mediterranean French. This pale green herb, which looks something like dill, is excellent in fish sauces and salad dressings. Fennel seeds – famous for their use in liqueurs such as anisette or Provence's own Ricard and Pernod – can add a subtle flavor and texture to breads and pastries, but my favorite use for them is to lend an exotic touch to saffron- and tomato-based sauces for poultry and fish. Indeed, one of the simplest and best Provençal sauces for grilled or poached fresh fish is a combination simply of equal parts of melted butter and

lemon juice with chopped fresh tarragon and two or three fennel seeds.

Dried fennel stalks are used in Provence for flaming *loup de mer* (sea bass) and as an aromatic in bouillabaisse and *soupe de poissons*.

Another herb which is familiar in Provence, and yet which has not been much used here since the nineteenth century, is *sarriette* or summer savory. The perfect accompaniment to goat's cheese, this herb is lightly peppery in flavor, as its old Provençal name, *lou pebre* or *pebre d'ail*, suggests. It is also one of the dried *herbes de Provence* used, along with thyme, rosemary, fennel and lavender flowers, for grills of meats, fish and poultry and for marinades. Little pottery containers of the dried *herbes de Provence* can be found in gourmet shops, but this aromatic mix is also outstandingly good when used fresh.

My own herb mix from
the garden combines
rosemary, thyme, fennel,
dill, sage, summer savory,
bay and lavender flowers:
the essence of Provence
in a basket.

Provençal seasonings

In the nineteenth century, classic Provençal cuisine made use of special seasoning mixes to give extra depth and savor to daubes and ragouts of meats and poultry, salmis of game, fish sauces and even *brouillades* and omelets. Many of these pungent flavoring aids combined equal quantities of dried thyme and rosemary, crumbled bay leaf, cracked mignonette pepper and coarsely grated nutmeg with a little cayenne pepper, to taste, and blended the pungent mix with sea salt before pounding it in a mortar to a fine powder. The seasoning salt was passed through a fine sieve and kept in a tightly closed jar in the kitchen to use as required for the wonderfully flavored dishes of old Provence.

Les herbes de Provence
Classic Provençal dried herb mixture

The best Provençal herb mix I know combines equal quantities of dried herbs and spices plus dried lavender flowers and dried orange peel for its special Provençal flavor. It is so easy to make: just pound the mixture in a mortar; sieve it carefully and pack it in tightly covered little jars to keep for your own cooking and to give to friends.

2 tbsps garden thyme	2 tbsps crumbled bay leaves
2 tbsps wild thyme	
2 tbsps summer savory	1 tbsp ground cloves
2 tbsps lavender	1 tbsp dried orange peel
2 tbsps rosemary	1 tbsp ground nutmeg

Dry the fresh herbs carefully on the lowest setting. Add the dried herbs and spices and pound them all to a fine powder in a mortar. Pass the powder through a fine sieve. Keep in a tightly closed jar.

Le sel épicé du Cuisinier Durand

—

In the nineteenth century, Charles Durand, a famous Provençal cook and author of *Le Cuisinier Durand*, published in 1830 and the first book devoted to Mediterranean cooking, created a delicious seasoning salt to give depth and flavor to his very personal dishes. According to Durand, each and every grain of spice must be sieved, for this recipe is the 'fruit of thousands of tastings and fifty years of experience'.

1 cup coarse salt	1½ tbsps dried basil
¼ cup black peppercorns	1 tbsp ground mace
2 tbsps ground cloves	1½ tbsps coriander seeds
1 tbsp ground nutmeg	3 bay leaves
1 tbsp ground cinnamon	

Pound the salt and spices in a large mortar (or process them in a food processor) until finely ground. Pass the ground seasoning through a fine sieve. Store in hermetically sealed jars.

PROVENÇAL SEASONING SALT

I like to keep a small jar of Provençal seasoning salt – French sea salt spiked with a mixture of equal amounts of dried thyme and rosemary, cracked pepper, cayenne pepper and finely crumbled bay leaf – to give added flavor to grills of poultry, veal, pork, lamb and even oven-grilled potatoes.

¼ tsp dried thyme	¼ tsp cracked pepper
2 bay leaves, crumbled finely	¼ tsp cayenne pepper
¼ tsp dried rosemary	4 tbsps sea salt

Pound all the ingredients except the sea salt in a mortar to a fine powder. Pass through a fine sieve. Add the sea salt and pass through a fine sieve again. Keep in a tightly closed jar to use as required.

J.-B. Reboul's 'poudre aromatique' and 'poudre friande'

—

In his charming book *La Cuisinière provençale*, first published in 1895 and still on sale in bookshops throughout France, J.-B. Reboul, another celebrated cook, gives two seasoning mixes – *poudre aromatique* and *poudre friande* – the latter being a mix of pounded sun- and oven-dried button mushrooms, morels, *mousserons* and black truffles. These fascinating recipes give some idea of the lengths to which the professional cooks of Provence were willing to go to flavor their dishes.

POUDRE AROMATIQUE

1 tbsp crushed red pepper flakes	1½ tbsps dried summer savory
2 tbsps crumbled bay leaves	1 tbsp ground mace
1½ tbsps dried marjoram	1 tbsp ground cinnamon
1½ tbsps dried basil	1 tbsp ground nutmeg
1½ tbsps dried sage	1 tbsp ground cloves

Pound the dried herbs and spices to a fine powder in a mortar and then pass through a fine sieve. Keep in a tightly closed jar to use as desired.

POUDRE FRIANDE

⅓ cup button mushrooms	⅓ cup black truffles of Provence
⅓ cup morels	
⅓ cup *mousserons*	

Clean the mushrooms and truffles carefully, being sure to remove all sand. Slice them thinly and spread them out on a flat tile to dry in the sun for 2 to 3 hours. Then place them, according to the original recipe, in a '*four de boulanger complètement tombé*' (a baker's oven that has been allowed to go out).

When they are dry enough to crumble (*cassants*), pound them in a mortar to a fine powder. Pass the powder through a fine sieve and keep in a closed jar to use as required.

Mayonnaise sauce and variations

The cold emulsion sauce known as mayonnaise is one of the most useful sauces I know. In the Provençal kitchen it is often used to dress salads of sliced red tomatoes, or to bind chilled salads of saffron rice sparked with diced red and green pepper, sliced celery and halved little black olives from Nice. A little mayonnaise spiced with the cold saffron-flavored jelly from yesterday's bouillabaisse makes a festive 'binder' for leftover pieces of fish from the same bouillabaisse, especially when piled into hollowed-out ripe tomatoes or horizontally cut halves of brilliant green peppers. Try mayonnaise subtly flavored with a little finely chopped garlic (no, not a true *aïoli* sauce ... but that is delicious, too) as the accompaniment to a sliced cold *gigot* of lamb; mix it with equal parts of puréed watercress for a fresh-tasting green foil for cold sliced rare roast beef; and use the same idea, pairing equal quantities of thick mayonnaise with puréed black olives (you can buy olive purée now in supermarkets across the country) to enliven a first course of cold poached fish.

Mayonnaise is so easy to make. I can remember my first attempts at a one-egg mayonnaise as a boy, my only aids one of those shallow saffron-colored earthenware soup plates found everywhere in Provence and a fork. The secret then, as it is now, was to mix a little mustard with the egg yolk and a pinch of salt, and then to add the olive oil, literally drop by drop, whisking it into the mustard and yolk mixture as carefully as if one's life depended on it. And then, as the emulsion began to hold and one could feel the eggy sauce begin to take on resistance to the fork, to add the olive oil in the thinnest of all possible streams, beating all the while with the fork until a smooth, creamy, golden emulsion began to take shape before my delighted eyes. It was then that I first realized that cooking could be magic, and that with a plate and a fork and an egg yolk as starters one of the world's greatest sauces could be created. Today, I lazily start off with two egg yolks, a deep porcelain bowl and a rotary whisk. The sauce is as delicious as ever but the magic has gone.

Traditional Provençal flavors – puréed tomatoes, finely chopped garlic, thinly slivered fresh basil leaves, powdered saffron, chopped black olives and a dollop of anise-flavored Ricard or Pastis – play their part in mayonnaise just as they do in practically every other dish in the cuisine of the sun. Let tomato-flavored mayonnaise with basil bring out the best in a cold poached or grilled fish; dress a salad of cold poached zucchini with a Ricard or Pastis-flavored mayonnaise; set the rustic flavors of spicy Catalan mayonnaise (tomato paste, paprika and cayenne) against the firm moist whiteness of poached squid and conger eel; dress a salad of mussels from Bouzigues in the Camargue with a mayonnaise to which you have added finely chopped onion and a glorious hint of saffron. Let a cold Niçoise sauce (mayonnaise flavored with tomato paste, saffron, cayenne pepper and chopped black olives) lend color and interest to a platter of little red mullet or mixed vegetables. You will find that the choices are legion.

Sauce mayonnaise

2 egg yolks
salt and ground
 black pepper
½ level tsp
 Dijon mustard
lemon juice
1¼ cups olive oil

Add garlic or basil to mayonnaise for authentic Provençal variations.

Place the egg yolks (make sure the gelatinous thread of the egg is removed), salt, freshly ground black pepper and mustard in a bowl. Twist a cloth wrung out in very cold water around the bottom of the bowl to keep it steady and cool. Using a wire whisk, fork or wooden spoon, beat the yolks to a smooth paste. Add a little lemon juice (the acid helps the emulsion), and beat in about a quarter of the oil, drop by drop. Add a little more lemon juice to the mixture and then, a little more quickly now, add more oil, beating all the while. Continue adding oil and beating until the sauce is of a good thick consistency. Correct the seasoning, adding more salt, pepper and lemon juice as desired. If you are making the mayonnaise a day before using it, stir in 1 tablespoon boiling water when it is of the desired consistency. This will keep it from turning or separating.

Note: If the mayonnaise should curdle, break another egg yolk into a clean bowl and gradually beat the curdled mayonnaise into it. The mayonnaise will begin to 'take' immediately.

If the mayonnaise is to be used for a salad, thin it down considerably with dry white wine, vinegar or lemon juice. If it is to be used for coating meat, poultry or fish, add a little liquid aspic to stiffen it.

If the sauce is to be kept for several hours before serving, cover the bowl with a cloth wrung out in very cold water to prevent a skin from forming on the top. 19

Albuquerque Academy
Library
6400 Wyoming Blvd. N.E.
Albuquerque, N.M. 87109

Provençal variations on mayonnaise

—

SAUCE TOMATE FROIDE AU BASILIC
Tomato-flavored mayonnaise with basil

To 1 bowl of mayonnaise add 2 tablespoons tomato paste, ½ clove garlic, finely chopped, and 8 fresh basil leaves, thinly sliced.

SAUCE ANIS FROIDE
Anise-flavored mayonnaise

To 1 bowl of mayonnaise add half a bowl very firm whipped cream flavored with 1–2 tablespoons Ricard or Pastis and 2 tablespoons chopped fresh fennel or dill.

SAUCE CATALANE FROIDE
Catalan mayonnaise

To 1 bowl of mayonnaise add 1 tablespoon tomato paste, ¼ teaspoon paprika and ⅛ teaspoon cayenne pepper.

SAUCE NIÇOISE FROIDE
Cold Niçoise sauce

To 1 bowl of mayonnaise add 1 tablespoon tomato paste, 1 pinch each powdered saffron and cayenne pepper and 2 tablespoons chopped black olives.

Provençal green sauces

Provençal green sauces and butters based on chopped green herbs – chervil, Italian (flat-leaf) parsley, chives and tarragon, with a few young spinach leaves added for color – are famous around the world. I have chosen a green sauce from Martigues and a green butter from Montpellier. The green sauce is excellent with poached and grilled fish; and both the sauce and the butter make a fine addition to grilled and sautéed white meats: veal, lamb and pork. Try a pat of Montpellier butter, too, with grills of beef, lamb and calves' kidneys.

I found I appreciated even more the warm, luxurious light of the Mediterranean; the markets and sun-dappled crooked streets of the towns. And I fell in love once again with the brilliantly colored fruits and vegetables from the market.

Sauce verte de Martigues

Green sauce from Martigues

1 good handful each of chervil, Italian (flat-leaf) parsley, chives and tarragon, chopped coarsely

6–8 young spinach leaves, chopped coarsely

2 tbsps capers

3 tbsps gherkins, chopped

10 anchovy fillets in oil, drained and chopped

½ cup butter, diced

yolks of 2 hard-boiled eggs, sieved

½ – ⅔ cup extra-virgin olive oil

salt and ground black pepper

lemon juice (optional)

TO PREPARE THE HERBS FOR COLORING

Wash, dry and chop the herbs and spinach leaves. Place them in a small saucepan; add cold water to cover and bring gently to a boil. Remove from the heat; drain and squeeze dry.

TO MAKE THE SAUCE

Combine the prepared greens in a mortar and pound until smooth; add the capers, chopped gherkins and anchovies and pound again. Then add the butter and sieved hard-boiled egg yolks and pound again until smooth.

Drop by drop, and then in a steady trickle, as if you were making a mayonnaise, add extra-virgin olive oil until the sauce is smooth and thick. Taste, and add salt, freshly ground black pepper and a little lemon juice, if desired.

Beurre de Montpellier

Green butter from Montpellier

SERVES 6

1 cup softened butter	6 sprigs Italian (flat-leaf)
2 hard-boiled eggs, sieved	parsley
2 tbsps olive oil	2 shallots, chopped
1–2 cloves garlic, mashed	2 tbsps capers
12 young spinach leaves	½ tsp Dijon mustard
6 dark green (outer)	lemon juice
lettuce leaves, white	salt and ground black
parts removed	pepper
6 sprigs watercress	

Place the softened butter, sieved hard-boiled eggs, olive oil and mashed garlic in the bowl of a food processor and process until creamy. Add more oil if the mixture seems too dry.

Blanch the spinach leaves (with stems removed), green lettuce leaves, watercress, parsley and chopped shallots. Drain well and press dry. Chop the herbs finely and add to the butter mixture with the capers and mustard and process again. When well blended add lemon juice, salt and black pepper to taste.

Spoon a fat strip of green herb butter onto a piece of aluminum foil or plastic wrap and roll it up to form a sausage shape about 1–1½ inches thick. Chill until ready to serve.

'Moutarde' à la provençale

Provençal 'mustard'

SERVES 4

Provençal 'mustard' is not a mustard at all but a traditional tart-flavored, breadcrumb-thickened fish sauce to serve with boiled fish.

2 cloves garlic, cut in	4 tbsps fresh
quarters	breadcrumbs
salt	well-flavored fish stock
2 egg yolks	lemon juice or wine
½–⅔ cup	vinegar
extra-virgin olive oil	

In a mortar, combine the garlic cloves with a little salt and pound until smooth. Stir in the egg yolks until well blended, and then, drop by drop and then in a thin trickle, as if you were making a mayonnaise, whisk in the extra-virgin olive oil until the sauce is thick and smooth.

Moisten the fresh breadcrumbs with 2–3 tablespoons of well-flavored fish stock. Squeeze them dry and add them to the sauce. Mix well. Then add several drops of lemon juice or wine vinegar and mix well again.

When ready to serve, moisten the thickened sauce with hot fish stock, added drop by drop, until the sauce is smooth and creamy.

Sauce aux anchois pour viandes

Quick and easy anchovy sauce for roasts and grills

Any broiled, sautéed or roast lamb, beef or pork dish can be given a Provençal accent by making a well-flavored anchovy sauce from the pan juices.

6–10 anchovy fillets, finely	water or dry white wine
chopped	lemon juice
2 tbsps finely chopped	ground black pepper
parsley	

Roast the meat in the usual way; remove the roast from the oven and transfer it to a heated serving dish. Keep warm.

Skim the excess fat from the pan juices in the roasting pan and stir in the chopped anchovy fillets and parsley. Add a little water or dry white wine to the pan juices and, with a wooden spoon, stir in all the crusty bits from the bottom of the pan. Add lemon juice and freshly ground black pepper to taste, and simmer the liquid over a medium heat for 2–3 minutes. Pour into a heated sauce bowl and serve with the roast.

Glace de viande à l'ancienne

Traditional meat glaze

Classic *glace de viande* (a dark essence of meat, poultry and vegetables, made by the careful reduction of bouillon to a syrupy state) sets to a thick rubbery jelly when allowed to cool. In the nineteenth century, this jelly was packed into a scrubbed sausage skin and kept in a cold larder to use bit by bit (the cook would slice off an inch or so of the 'sausage' as needed) to add intense flavor and substance to a sauce created from the pan juices of roast or broiled meats or poultry.

Today, of course, rather than packing it into a sausage skin, the modern chef keeps *glace de viande* in little jars in the refrigerator, to use as required. Take a leaf out of the books of the nineteenth-century kitchen and keep *glace de viande* in your refrigerator to create instant sauces and soups. It is also good when added to a little melted butter to make a quick sauce for vegetable dishes and even pasta.

2 lb shin of beef (or half shin of beef and half stewing beef), cut into 6 or more pieces
2 lb veal shank, cut into pieces

1 stewing hen, cut into quarters
7 cups (or more) beef stock
6 carrots
6 leeks, white parts only
2 large yellow onions

In a large soup pot or casserole, combine the pieces of beef, veal and chicken. Add the beef stock and bring to a boil. Skim off any impurities and add the carrots, leeks and onions. Bring to a boil again; skim off any impurities that may have risen to the surface of the stock and reduce the heat to a low simmer. Cover the pot or casserole and, skimming from time to time, simmer very gently over very low heat (or in a very low oven) for 3 hours, then remove from the heat. Do not add salt, pepper or any other seasoning. Remove the meats and vegetables from the bouillon and reserve for other use.

Strain the bouillon into a large clean bowl and allow it to cool. When cool, skim all the fat off the surface of the stock and pour the stock into a clean bowl through a muslin-lined sieve. Allow to cool completely. Refrigerate overnight, and your *glace de viande* will have set to a thick slightly rubbery consistency.

On the following day, skim off any congealed fat that may have risen to the surface.

Keep in covered jars in the refrigerator.

Glace de viande à l'ancienne adds its own intense flavor and substance to meat, poultry or game recipes such as this rabbit dish.

Tomato sauces

Provençal cooks rely heavily on the tomato for flavoring their sauces for meats and poultry, fish and shellfish, and as a base – along with onion, garlic, fennel and saffron – for fish soups, *soupe de poissons* and bouillabaisse. Niçois dishes in particular are often tomato-based, as are the special dishes of the gipsies and *gardianes* of the Camargue. *Sauce vierge* (a combination of raw finely chopped tomatoes, onion, garlic and fresh herbs blended with extra-virgin olive oil) is often found in Provençal kitchens today, as are the cooked tomato preparations *coulis de tomates* and *sauce tomate*.

Sauce vierge

—

Raw tomato sauce

—

This smooth raw sauce is excellent with grilled tuna and swordfish, poached John Dory or ocean perch.

8–10 medium, ripe tomatoes, peeled, seeded and chopped	**6 black olives, pitted and finely chopped**
8 tbsps extra-virgin olive oil	**salt and ground black pepper**
3 tbsps lemon juice	**1 tbsp each finely chopped tarragon, chives and Italian (flat-leaf) parsley**
2 cloves garlic, finely chopped	

In a medium-sized bowl, combine the tomatoes, olive oil, lemon juice and garlic, and add salt and freshly ground black pepper to taste. Set aside for 2 hours to allow flavors to blend. Just before serving stir in the chopped black olives and herbs.

Coulis de tomates

—

Fresh tomato coulis

—

A *coulis de tomates* is a compote of tomatoes, served hot and produced without any thickening agent other than the emulsion created by the combination of the acid of the tomatoes and the extra-virgin olive oil. A little finely chopped shallot, onion or garlic simmered for a moment in olive oil is the only aromatic used, with the addition of a little salt, ground pepper and sugar to bring out the flavors of the ripe tomatoes.

Use *coulis de tomates* to add extra savor to a sauce or vegetable soup, or toss noodles or macaroni in a little oil or butter and add a few tablespoons of *coulis* and top with grated cheese. Steam open little Provençal shellfish – *palourdes, praires* or *tellines* – in a little finely chopped onion and some *coulis de tomates*, and mix with cooked rice.

1 small shallot, finely chopped (or 1 clove of garlic or 1 tbsp finely chopped onion)
2 tbsps extra-virgin olive oil
8–10 medium, ripe tomatoes, peeled, seeded and chopped
1 *bouquet garni* (1 sprig thyme, 2 sprigs tarragon, 2 sprigs parsley and 1 bay leaf)
salt and ground black pepper
sugar
2 tbsps diced butter

In a medium-sized saucepan sauté the finely chopped shallot (or garlic or onion) in the olive oil until the vegetable is transparent. Add the peeled, seeded and chopped tomatoes and *bouquet garni* and cook, covered, over a medium heat for about 20 minutes. Season with salt, freshly ground black pepper and a pinch of sugar. Remove the saucepan from the heat; remove the *bouquet garni* and beat in the diced butter.

Fondue de tomates

—

Fresh tomato sauce

—

Fondue de tomates is a summer standby in many Provençal kitchens. This simple sauce simply takes the *coulis de tomates* one step further, simmering it for another 20 minutes, stirring it from time to time to make sure the sauce does not stick to the bottom of the pan. The *fondue* can be kept in a jar in the refrigerator for about 10 days. Its uses are many: several tablespoons of fondue can be used to garnish an omelet or make a sauce for poached eggs, vegetables or fish; and with light stock or milk added it can make a refreshing summer soup in a matter of minutes, needing only a swirl of cream or olive oil and a sprinkling of fresh herbs to make a delicious first course.

Classic poivrade sauce

A highly flavored pepper-based sauce called *poivrade* is one of the great standbys of Provençal cuisine where game is concerned, or when a gamey flavor is sought to give more emphasis to roast lamb or beef. This wine-based marinade for rabbit, hare or venison is part of the classic Provençal repertoire.

Classic poivrade sauce

½ cup ground raw beef (and any raw bones and trimmings you may have from a chicken, *carré* of lamb, rabbit, hare or game)	1 leek
	1 *bouquet garni* (parsley, thyme, bay leaf, green of leek)
2 tbsps peanut oil	12 black peppercorns
2 cloves garlic, chopped	12 juniper berries
½ tsp dried thyme	2–4 cloves
1 bay leaf	1 bottle full-bodied red wine of Provence
4 carrots	chicken or beef stock
2 onions	2 tbsps diced butter
2 ribs celery	cracked black pepper

Chop the bones and trimmings (if you have them) coarsely with a cleaver. In a large heat-proof casserole, sauté the chopped bones and ground beef in peanut oil with the garlic, thyme and bay leaves. Add the carrots, onions, celery, leek, *bouquet garni* and spices and cook over medium heat, stirring from time to time, for 20 minutes.

Add the red wine; bring to the boil; skim off impurities and cook over high heat until the sauce is reduced to one quarter of the original quantity, about 20 minutes.

Add enough chicken or beef stock to cover meat and bones (if available) and the aromatics. Cook for 2 minutes to amalgamate the flavors. Then strain the sauce through a fine sieve into a clean saucepan; return to the heat and reduce the sauce to the desired consistency.

Remove saucepan from heat and whisk in the diced butter, piece by piece. Add cracked black pepper, to taste.

Serve with roast hare, rabbit, venison or meat.

Simple poivrade sauce

1 bunch Italian (flat-leaf) parsley, finely chopped	¼ tsp salt
1 bunch chives, finely chopped	¼ tsp cracked black pepper
¼ large yellow onion, finely chopped	1¼ cups tomato *coulis* (see page 24) or well-flavored beef stock thickened with a roux
1 bay leaf, crumbled	
6 tbsps red wine vinegar	

In a small saucepan, combine all the ingredients except the *coulis* or stock and cook, stirring, until the liquid has evaporated to about 1 tablespoon. Add the *coulis* or stock and stir over high heat until the sauce has taken on the *poivrade* flavors.

The flavored butters of Provence

In many of the little restaurants of the Provençal interior you will be offered appetizers of slices of grilled bread, brushed with garlic and olive oil and topped with any number of simple spreads and butters. The recipes are legion – a few are given below – and the method is simplicity itself. Just blend the ingredients of each butter in a mortar; season as indicated and then add a few teaspoons of olive oil to 'smooth' the mixture. Pack into small ramekins or jars and chill until ready to use.

Beurre à l'ail
Garlic butter

½ cup butter	salt and ground black pepper
2–4 cloves garlic, crushed	
1 tbsp finely chopped parsley	olive oil, to smooth
1–2 tbsps lemon juice	

In a mortar, pound the butter with crushed garlic and finely chopped parsley. Season to taste with lemon juice, salt and freshly ground black pepper. Add a little olive oil, to smooth.

Flavored butters (clockwise from left): anchovy, saffron, red pepper, black olive and fresh basil.

Beurre au safran

Saffron butter

½ cup butter   olive oil, to smooth
salt and cayenne pepper
¼ tsp powdered saffron
   dissolved in 1 tbsp
   lemon juice

In a mortar, pound the butter with salt, cayenne pepper and powdered saffron, dissolved in lemon juice. Add olive oil, to smooth. Chill.

Beurre aux olives

Black olive butter

black olives, pitted   ½ cup butter
salt and cayenne pepper   olive oil, to smooth

In a mortar, pound the pitted black olives with salt, and cayenne pepper, to taste, until smooth. Add the butter and cream until well blended. Add a little olive oil, to smooth. Chill.

Beurre aux anchois

Anchovy butter

24 anchovy fillets   ground black pepper
½ cup butter   olive oil, to smooth

In a mortar, pound the anchovy fillets with butter until well blended. Add freshly ground black pepper, to taste, and a little olive oil to smooth.

Beurre au basilic

Fresh basil butter

fresh basil leaves   ½ cup butter
salt and cayenne pepper   olive oil, to smooth

In a mortar, pound the fresh basil leaves with salt until smooth; add the butter and cayenne pepper, to taste, and cream until well blended. Add a little olive oil, to smooth. Chill.

Beurre aux poivrons rouges

Red pepper butter

½ red pepper, thinly sliced   salt and cayenne pepper
1–2 tbsps lemon juice   olive oil, to smooth
½ cup butter

In a mortar, pound the sliced red pepper with lemon juice and salt until well blended. Add the butter and cream until smooth. Season with cayenne pepper; add a little olive oil, to smooth.

2 The Gift of

OLIVES AND OLIVE OIL:
THE ESSENCE OF PROVENCE

If you are not a full-blooded, dyed-in-the-wool olive aficionado, forget your prejudices. The little black wrinkled olives from the upper slopes of Haute Provence will make you change your mind – especially those of the Colombale variety, which are black, almost dry and have lost their bitterness. The secret, according to the famous French food writer and gastronome J.-P. Pudlowski, lies in the fact that the olive growers allow the olives to freeze, to soften their acid, bitter flavor, before sautéing them in a little water and extra-virgin olive oil from the preceding harvest. The olives are then allowed to cool, and remain in their fragrant cooking bouillon until they are ready to be consumed.

The olive is one of the perennial symbols of Mediterranean cookery. Not only does it provide the basic oil in which everything else is cooked in Provence, but it is also the chief ingredient of the dressings in which many raw foods and all salads are served. The olive trees of Provence – said to have been introduced by the Greeks over 2,500 years ago – today produce many varieties of the fruit: small and relatively dry and hard, medium-sized and moist, or large, soft and juicy.

Provençal olive oil is made from olives crushed to a pulp, from which is pressed the fruity- flavored, golden-colored virgin oil, *l'huile extra-vierge*, which adds so much to Provençal cookery and salads. Cold water is added to the remaining pulp after this first pressing to produce a second pressing, called *fine* or *extra-fine*, more bland in flavor but usually clearer in color. A third pressing for manufacturing processes,

the Olive

or for the farmer's own use, is sometimes made with the addition of warm water to the almost dry olive pulp. Further pressings produce oil for use in soaps and fertilizers.

In Provence I like to serve a plate of wrinkled black olives – scooped from a giant barrel with a black-stained olive-wood scoop – or green preserved olives flavored with orange peel and fresh herbs as a simple accompaniment to a glass of chilled rosé or white wine. They make a wonderful prelunch appetizer. Richly flavored *tapenade*, a savory mixture of pounded black olives, anchovy fillets, tuna fish and olive oil flavored with capers, mustard and a little cognac, also makes a delicious hors d'oeuvre when served with hard-boiled eggs or crusty pieces of French bread.

Fragrant, golden oil has been the foundation of Provençal cookery since time immemorial. Today Provençal cooks use olive oil to sauté meats, poultry and game for ragouts and daubes; to sauté vegetable main courses and to make healthy, light dressings for salads of cooked and raw vegetables; to moisten *tians* (vegetable gratins) and pâtés; and to tenderize meats, poultry and game for roasting, casseroling or grilling. In Provence all foods grilled in the open air – a cooking method much loved in the traditional Provençal kitchen as well as in the more modern recipes of the *haute cuisine* chefs now

working in the major cities of Provence – are always brushed with olive oil before and during cooking to moisten and tenderize them; and olive oil is used in making the wonderful breads and even some of the pastries of Provençal cuisine.

Les frottés d'ail

One of the simplest of my Provençal pleasures when I first came to live in St Tropez was the *frotté d'ail* – a slice of day-old French bread rubbed with a cut clove of garlic, drizzled with a few drops of extra-virgin olive oil and sprinkled with coarse salt – brought to my excited attention by the writings of Colette, who spent many summers in the sun-washed flatlands behind St Tropez, overlooking the bay of Pampelonne, in a house called 'La Treille Muscat'. It was here that she wrote *Le Paradis terrestre* (Earthly Paradise) and *La Naissance du jour* (Birth of Day) based on her experiences of Provence: tales of sensual pleasures in the sun, of wonderful foods and wines, of gardens and cats and the delights of living in the far-away little fishing port, cut off from the rest of France at that time by the Littoral.

Preserved green olives are delicious served as a simple aperitif. It is the wrinkled black olives that are crushed to yield the golden, fragrant olive oil of Provence.

Colette's *frottés d'ail* – literally 'garlic rubs' – were so novel and tempting to my young palate (I was twenty-two at the time) that we used to exult in their sexy, homespun flavors and would serve them at sun-down on the terrace with glasses of the delicious chilled dry white or rosé wines of Provence after a long, hot day at the beach.

From there we went on to discover other ways to make this simple canapé even more appealing. I used to make a sauce of chopped garlic, salt and olive oil in which to soak wrinkled little black olives until they became fat and filled with the magic oil of Provence. This fragrant dish of oil, garlic and plumped-up olives was then served in little hors d'oeuvres dishes so that each guest could take a thin slice of fresh French bread, cut on the diagonal, and with a teaspoon top it with a fat black olive and a little of the heady chopped garlic and oil. Another favorite canapé was made of a thin flute of crisp French bread, split down the center and with all its soft interior scraped out. (No, of course we didn't waste it: we set it aside to make fresh breadcrumbs to top a dish of broiled tomatoes *à la provençale*, or to use in a garlic and herb-flavored vinaigrette dressing for a 'gazpacho-like' salad of sliced tomatoes, cucumbers, green peppers and red onion.) We rubbed the insides of the hollowed-out crusts with a cut clove of garlic (you might need two), drizzled a little olive oil over them, sprinkled them with a little coarse salt and topped them with a thin slice or two of ripe tomato and a leaf or two of fresh basil or arugula, or a few bits of mashed anchovy. Perfect fare when cut up into manageable portions and served with a chilled rosé wine.

Or try thin rounds of crisp French bread spread with *tapenade* (see page 38) topped with a thin round of fresh goat's cheese and a sprinkling of paprika; or spread with *tapenade* topped with a slice of ripe tomato and a sprinkling of chopped fresh basil; or garlic-rubbed, oven-baked croûtons of French bread spread with *brandade de morue* (see page 41) and topped with a sprinkling of chopped black olives.

It was perhaps these simple rustic touches that I liked best about the cooking of Provence when I first came to live there. It seemed so right, the dishes were so easy to prepare, the local ingredients so fresh and appealing, the open markets so pleasant to shop in. It was indeed paradise, Colette's *Paradis terrestre.*

31

La fougasse aux olives

———

Outside the perimeters of Provence few people know the pizza-like flat bread called *fougasse*. A classic inherited from the time of the early Ligurians and a kissing cousin of Tuscan *focaccia*, which it most resembles (though more decorative with its long oval shape and airy cutouts), *fougasse* is a much-loved standby in the hill towns of Provence. Every little bakery has its own tasty versions: simple, flavored with a hint of garlic and a sprinkling of dried rosemary or sage, or dried *herbes de Provence*; or more robust, with chopped anchovies, or even sun-dried tomatoes and flakes of dried salt cod. But of all the garnishes, my favorite combines the little black olives of Nice, coarsely chopped, and a generous sprinkling of dried *herbes de Provence*.

Even though most cooks in Provence are content to purchase their *fougasses* ready-made from the local baker, it is possible to make a delicious homemade *fougasse* using a plain bread or yeast dough.

Fougasse aux olives, an inheritance from the early Ligurians and a more decorative cousin of Tuscan *focaccia*, is a much-loved standby in the hill towns of Provence. In Cotignac (opposite) as elsewhere, every little bakery will have its own tempting version, each with a subtly different filling.

Makes 1 loaf

FOR THE YEAST DOUGH

1 package active dry yeast	**3½ cups flour**
1 tsp honey	**1 tsp salt**
1⅓ cups warm water	**3 tbsps olive oil**

FOR THE BLACK OLIVE AND HERB GARNISH

8 small black olives, pitted and chopped	**1 tsp dried *herbes de Provence***
ground black pepper	**1–2 tbsps olive oil**

In the bowl of an electric mixer, combine the yeast, honey and warm water. Fit the paddle attachment and proof the yeast at a low speed until the mixture is foamy, about 5 minutes.

Remove the paddle attachment and attach the dough hook; add the flour, salt and 2 tablespoons of the olive oil and knead the dough for 5 minutes, or until the dough is soft and slightly sticky.

Brush a warmed mixing bowl with the remaining tablespoon of oil. Form the dough into a ball; transfer it to the bowl; turn the dough to coat it with oil and let it rise, covered with plastic wrap, in a warm place for 1½ hours, or until it has doubled in bulk.

On a floured board, roll or pull out the dough to a sheet measuring 10 × 12 inches. Scatter chopped black olives and dried *herbes de Provence* over half the dough, leaving ½ inch of pastry uncovered on the three outside edges; drizzle the olive and herb filling with a little olive oil and season with freshly ground black pepper to taste. Fold over the other half of the dough, pressing down the edges all around to seal the dough. Then with a sharp kitchen knife cut diagonal slits (about 1½ inches long) in two rows down the length of the dough, making sure you cut right through the dough, and opening up the slits by rolling and/or pulling out the dough.

Carefully transfer the *fougasse* to a floured baking sheet and let it rise, covered loosely, in a warm place for 1 hour, or until it is almost double in bulk.

Note: Make sure that the slits remain open by gently prying the dough apart.

WHEN READY TO BAKE

Pre-heat the oven to 375°F. Brush the *fougasse* with olive oil. Then place the *fougasse* on its baking sheet in the bottom third of the oven and bake for about 30 minutes, or until it is golden brown. Transfer the *fougasse* to a cake rack and let it cool. Serve warm or at room temperature.

Le pain aux olives

Olive bread

MAKES 1 LARGE LOAF, OR 2 SMALL ONES

1 package active dry yeast	olive oil
1 tsp honey	8 small black olives, pitted and chopped
3 tbsps warm water	½–1 tsp dried *herbes de Provence*
3½ cups whole-wheat flour	flour for kneading
1 tsp salt	oil for greasing
4 tbsps cracked wheat	

In a small bowl mix the yeast, honey and warm water, stirring until the yeast and honey are dissolved; then cover the bowl with plastic wrap and leave in a warm place until the yeast is foaming, about 20 minutes.

Sift the whole-wheat flour and salt into a large warmed mixing bowl. Beat in the yeast mixture and enough warm water (about 1⅓ cups) to make a fairly soft, sticky dough.

Transfer the dough to a floured board and knead it vigorously until it becomes smooth and elastic and no longer sticks to the board or your fingers, about 15 minutes. Cover it with a damp cloth and leave it to rise in a warm place until doubled in bulk, about 1½–2 hours.

While the dough is rising, heat 2 tablespoons olive oil in a small skillet over medium heat; add the olives and *herbes de Provence* and continue to cook, stirring, until the olives are well coated with the oil and herb mixture. Remove from the heat and reserve.

Punch down the dough and knead in the olives with the oil and herbs in which they were cooked. Knead the dough until the olives are evenly distributed through it.

WHEN READY TO COOK

Shape the dough into a ball and transfer it to an oiled baking sheet. Pull the ball out at each end, shaping it into a more conventional loaf shape. Cover and leave to rise in a warm place until doubled in bulk (50–60 minutes). Heat the oven to 375°F.

Bake the loaf for about 1 hour or until golden brown. Remove it from the baking sheet at once and cool it on a cake rack so that air can reach the undersides. It is best 2 hours after baking.

L'huile d'olive givrée

Frozen olive oil

This is an invention of the famous Marseillais chef Maurice Brun, whose restaurant, Chez Maurice Brun (Aux Mets de Provence), on the quai Rive-Neuve was famous in the thirties and forties. The restaurant – a Provençal classic – is still there, run now by the great chef's widow, son and daughter-in-law, who carry on his imaginative innovations on classic Provençal cooking. His gargantuan thirteen-course feast is still presented every night except Sunday, featuring (after a series of little Provençal appetizers) fish, cooked within hours of being caught from the sea with its scales and innards intact, grilled without salt (or seasoning of any kind) over an open fire in the restaurant dining room. The charred skins and innards are removed before serving and the fish, in all its original splendor, is a masterpiece of firm texture and fresh sea flavor. This recipe can only be followed when the fish is fresh from the sea, otherwise

L'huile d'olive givrée.

the unseasoned, ungutted fish might be dull or even unpleasant in flavor.

L'huile d'olive givrée is simplicity itself to prepare: just fill little soufflé ramekins with the best extra-virgin olive oil you can find and set them in the freezer overnight. Just before serving, with a teaspoon or large melon baller scoop out balls of frozen olive oil, set them on fresh slices of crisp French bread and serve immediately. You will find the frozen golden oil a complete surprise in both texture and flavor.

Anchoïade

*A*nchoïade – like so many dishes in the classic repertoire of Provençal cooking – is both a sauce and the name of a dish, as well as being the essential secret ingredient that gives so many other Provençal dishes their authentic rustic savor.

In its purest form *anchoïade* is basically a sauce – or paste – made of anchovies, garlic and olive oil. Some

cooks add a few capers or pounded tuna and/or a few drops of lemon juice, cognac or *marc de Provence* to bring out the potent flavor. I personally add a final dollop of red wine vinegar and a sprinkling of dried *herbes de Provence* to the mix, as I was taught when I first came to Provence at the tender age of twenty-two. But no one has gone as far as the bon vivant, French culinary authority and prolific compiler of mammoth cookbooks in the early part of this century, Comte Austin de Croze, a great friend of Armand Sailland (known to all France as Prince Curnonsky, the elected 'prince' of French gastronomes). Sailland/Curnonsky and de Croze became the undisputed 'gurus' of the French culinary/literary scene in the early twenties, writing many great cookbooks and a stream of regular cookery articles vaunting the delights of French regional cooking. Together the two friends all but created French gastronomy as we know it today. Their jointly authored books and articles on the traditional cooking of the French provinces did much to bring the simple country dishes of provincial France, and especially Provence, to the attention of a delighted Parisian public, professional chefs and home cooks alike.

Austin de Croze's *anchoïade de gastronome* (see over) must be the ultimate in exaggeration: a sumptuous, poetic, slightly mad version of the basically simple peasant dish which has always been a comforting and elegant snack when spread on crusty farm bread and toasted over an open fire. De Croze's wildly imaginative version includes pounded almonds, dried figs, finely chopped onion and *fines herbes*, hot red pepper and a dash of orange flower water for a spectacular *anchoïade* which he termed a 'quintuple essence' of all things Provençal.

René Jouveau, a distinguished octogenarian who lives in Antibes, gives his recipe for a cooked *anchoïade* that is simplicity itself in his delightful book *La Cuisine provençale de tradition populaire*:

'Take a [salted] anchovy or two per person; wash them; remove the backbones and put them in a *platet d'Aubagne* [heat-proof glazed earthenware dish]; moisten them with good olive oil and a good vinegar and leave them on the corner of the stove [over a very low heat] until all the ingredients have melted and formed a sauce.' Delicious.

In Provence, *anchoïade* is served with hard-boiled

eggs, on toast grilled over an open fire, as a hot sauce for *bagna caudo* (raw and cooked vegetables with a dipping sauce), and as a cold sauce for raw celery, raw cardoons and raw green peppers.

L'anchoïade du gastronome

Comte Austin de Croze's anchoïade

MAKES 12 ROLLS

The first Provençal cookbook that I ever owned was a tattered blue-covered early edition of a remarkable old tome entitled *La Cuisinière provençale*, given to me by my dear friend Fifine, self-taught *cuisinière* and restaurateur of St Tropez, who started me out on the long road to gastronomic delights with this simple gift, written over a hundred years ago by the

Provençal chef J.-B. Reboul. It was in this old book that I first discovered all the culinary treasures of the region that has become my spiritual home, including a delicious recipe for *anchoïade*. Another great classic of Provençal cooking, *La Véritable Cuisine provençale et nicoise* by Jean-Noël Escudier (1964) gives this facinating variation.

12 **salted anchovies**	1 **sprig fennel, finely**
12 **anchovy fillets, in oil**	**chopped**
12 **almonds**	3 **dried figs, stems**
6 **walnuts**	**removed**
2 **cloves garlic, quartered**	1 **tbsp orange flower water**
1 **small onion, quartered**	**extra-virgin olive oil**
1 **small hot red pepper**	12 **little oval rolls, made of**
2 **sprigs each Italian (flat-**	**brioche dough**
leaf) parsley, basil,	
tarragon and chervil,	
finely chopped	

TO PREPARE THE ANCHOVIES

Wash the salt off the salted anchovies under running water. Remove any bones and place the anchovies in a large shallow bowl under gently running cold water. Allow them to 'desalt' in this way for 2 hours. Drain and pat dry with a paper towel. Remove canned (or bottled) anchovies from oil and place in a sieve to drain. Pat dry with a paper towel.

TO MAKE THE ANCHOÏADE

Process the almonds and walnuts in a food processor. Add the garlic, onion and small hot red pepper and process again. Transfer the mixture to a bowl; add the finely chopped herbs and mix well.

Add the dried figs to the food processor and process until the figs are finely ground. Add the figs to the nut and herb mixture. Add the orange flower water and just enough olive oil to make a spreadable mixture.

Cut the rolls in half lengthwise. Spread the cut sides of the rolls with *anchoïade* and re-form the rolls. Brush the tops of the rolls with a little olive oil; place the rolls in a pre-heated fairly hot oven (400°F) and heat for 5 minutes. Serve immediately.

Refrigerate any remaining *anchoïade* mixture for another occasion.

Anchoïade.

Anchoïade

1 2 oz can anchovy fillets in oil	**1 tbsp softened butter**
1 large clove garlic, crushed	**pinch dried *herbes de Provence***
1 tbsp olive oil	**ground black pepper**
few drops lemon juice, cognac or red wine vinegar	**4–6 thick slices white bread**

Combine the anchovy fillets, crushed garlic, olive oil and softened butter in a mortar, and pound to a smooth paste. Season to taste with a few drops of lemon juice or cognac and a little freshly ground black pepper, or a dollop of red wine vinegar and a pinch of dried *herbes de Provence*.

Slice the bread in half; toast on one side only and, while still hot, spread *anchoïade* paste on the untoasted side, pressing the paste well into the bread. Toast in a hot oven or under the broiler for a few minutes just before serving.

Les petits pains frits à l'anchois

Fried anchovy fingers

FOR THE CANAPÉS

1 loaf white bread	**oil for frying**
milk	

Cut six slices of white bread ¹⁄₂ inch thick. Trim off the crusts and cut each slice in half to make 12 canapés. Soak in milk. Drain off excess moisture on a cake rack. Heat the oil in a deep-fryer. Cook the canapés in hot oil until they are crisp and golden brown on all sides.

Drain again. Spread each canapé with a layer of *beurre d'anchois* (anchovy butter).

FOR THE *BEURRE D'ANCHOIS*

¹⁄₂ cup softened butter	**1 shallot, finely chopped**
8 canned anchovy fillets, chopped	**2 tbsps finely chopped parsley**
1 clove garlic, finely chopped	**ground black pepper**

In a small bowl, combine the softened butter, chopped anchovies, finely chopped shallot and garlic and finely chopped parsley. Season generously with freshly ground black pepper. Mix well. Chill until ready to use.

Tapenade, anchoïade and *frottés d'ail.*

Tapenade

*T*apenade – which takes its name from the Provençal dialect word *tapeno*, meaning caper – is one of the most useful of the classic Provençal sauces or spreads. Even though it owes its name to capers, the sauce is mainly based on chopped or puréed black olives, to which finely chopped garlic, capers and onions are added before the sauce is pounded with olive oil and a little wine vinegar or *marc de Provence*.

Like *anchoïade*, it can be used in many different ways: as a creamy black sauce for *oeufs mollets* or hard-boiled eggs; or a spread for grilled or toasted country bread; or a delicious filling for miniature tart shells.

I also like to use *tapenade* as a pungent dark sauce to enliven toasted open sandwiches of sliced chicken or

spread soft cheese, topped with slices of ripe tomato and leaves of basil or arugula. But perhaps better than all of these is the idea of using *tapenade* as a garnish for braised sea bass, as served at La Bonne Etape restaurant in Château Arnoux by the father-and-son cooking team Pierre and Jany Gleize (see page 171); or, more coarsely chopped this time, as a distinctive accompaniment to roasted chicken or guinea fowl (see page 139).

Twin swirls of *tapenade* and *rouille* (see page 62) also make flamboyant accents for broiled or poached fish or broiled baked potatoes.

Tapenade

2 tbsps pitted ripe olives in oil	about ¼ cup olive oil
	cognac
8–10 anchovy fillets in oil	ground black pepper
1 tbsp tuna fish in oil	hard-boiled eggs or red
2 tbsps capers	peppers, chopped
Dijon mustard	(optional)

In a mortar, pound the pitted ripe olives, anchovy fillets and tuna fish to a smooth paste with the capers and Dijon mustard (to taste), adding the olive oil gradually as you would for a mayonnaise. Season to taste with cognac and freshly ground black pepper and force the mixture through a fine sieve. The *tapenade* mixture keeps well in a jar.

Note: If you are going to use the *tapenade* as a highly flavored topping for broiled or poached fish or broiled chicken or guinea fowl, or to fill chopped hard-boiled eggs, do not sieve the mixture. Use it as it is, or add chopped hard-boiled eggs or chopped red pepper to the mixture.

Brandade de morue

Brandade de morue – literally a 'shake up' of dried salt cod, blended with olive oil and milk or cream – is one of the truly great classics of Provençal cuisine. In the old days it was primarily a winter dish in the hill towns and the little villages of the flatlands, perfect for rustic meals far from the sea when fresh fish was not available.

Salt cod has been used in the south of France since the time of the early Romans, when Breton sailors would bring the hard sticks of salted fish to the south of France to exchange them for the precious salt from the marshes around the ancient city of Aigues-Mortes in the Camargue. It was used primarily as a winter staple – the hard dry sides of codfish would keep indefinitely – and the old Provençal cookbooks were full of simple recipes for salt cod, soaked overnight and then breadcrumbed and fried and served with Swiss chard (still a tradition for Christmas Eve feasts throughout Provence); *au gratin* (flaked poached salt cod, chopped leeks, onions and chard or spinach, baked in a creamy sauce flavored with chopped anchovies and garnished with hard-boiled eggs); *en beignets* (flaked poached salt cod deep-fried in batter); *en fleurs de courgette* (pounded poached salt cod stuffed inside zucchini flowers, dipped in batter and deep-fried); and, after the advent of the tomato, in many mixtures in which the *pomme d'amour* played an essential role: *en raïto* (a rich red sauce from the Camargue which simmers chopped onions, tomatoes, garlic and walnuts in olive oil and a reduction of red wine); *à la marseillaise* (diced salt cod simmered with potatoes in a sauce flavored with chopped onion, tomato and green olives); and *à la bouillabaisse* (a poor man's mix of all the ingredients for a bouillabaisse except the fresh fish: salt cod plays the starring role).

Legend has it that it was a Nîmoise housewife who was the first to pound the flesh of the pre-soaked salt-dried fish with milk and olive oil to make the creamy emulsion that we know today. But legend does not tell who was the first to accompany the creamy *brandade* with its golden snippets of crisp-fried bread, or who added the first finely chopped black truffles or black olives to the majestic dish that is now served in the world's greatest restaurants.

Suffice it to say that Nîmes is always credited with the creation of this great dish: *brandade de morue à la nîmoise* is the name usually used on menus to describe it. Today *brandade* is back in fashion, served as a creamy first course or used as a savory filling for the pointed little red peppers of Provence, for baked potatoes or for zucchini flowers fried in batter; and as a savory topping for party canapés of great distinction.

Brandade de morue.

Brandade de morue

Brandade of salt cod

SERVES 4–6

1 lb salt cod fillets	juice and grated peel
2 cloves garlic, crushed	of ½ lemon
6 tbsps heavy cream	ground black pepper
⅔ cup olive oil	toast triangles, fried in
	olive oil or butter

Soak the cod fillets in cold water for at least 12 hours, changing the water often. Place the drained fillets in a saucepan, cover with cold water and bring gently to a boil. Remove from the heat; cover the saucepan and let the cod steep for 10 minutes. Drain, remove the bones and skin, and flake with a fork.

Place the cod flakes in a food processor with the crushed garlic, 2 tablespoons cream and 4 tablespoons olive oil and process, adding the remainder of the cream and olive oil alternately from time to time, until they are completely absorbed and the *brandade* has the consistency of creamy mashed potatoes.

WHEN READY TO SERVE

Simmer the mixture until heated through in a *bain-marie*, or in a saucepan over simmering water; stir in the lemon juice and peel and add pepper to taste.

Brandade de morue may be served hot or cold. If serving hot, place it in a mound on a heated serving dish and surround it with toast triangles fried in olive oil or butter. If it is too salty, blend in 1 or 2 boiled potatoes and add a little more cream and olive oil. When serving the *brandade* cold, beat in a little more olive oil and/or lemon juice and pipe it into hollowed-out tomato cases or on to canapés of fried bread.

Brandade aux pommes de terre

Brandade de morue in baked potato shells

Brandade de morue is delicious served in baked potato shells. Bake the potatoes in the usual way; slice each baked potato in half lengthwise; scoop out the flesh and blend it with the *brandade de morue* mixture, adding a little more cream if necessary. Pile the mixture into the potato halves; brush with olive oil and bake in a fairly hot oven (375°F) until heated through.

Brandade aux poivrons rouges

Brandade de morue in baked red pepper cases

The little pointed red peppers of Provence make an unusual hot hors d'oeuvre when filled with a little *brandade* mixture and baked in the oven.

Cut off the tops of small medium-hot red peppers and remove the seeds; fill with the *brandade* mixture and bake until tender. Serve with a sauce made of heavy cream spiked with 1 tablespoon white wine vinegar.

Outside Provence, choose the smallest red peppers in the market and cut in half lengthwise. Remove seeds and stems and pre-bake the pepper shells in a fairly hot oven for 10 minutes.

Remove the pepper shells from the oven, fill with the *brandade* mixture, brush with olive oil and bake in the oven until completely tender. Serve with ivory-tinted cream sauce, as above.

OPPOSITE Brandade aux pommes de terre.

LEFT Brandade aux poivrons rouges.

Aïoli

If bouillabaisse (see page 60) vies with *bourride* and its lesser-known cousin *le revesset* along the southern coast from Sète to Menton, *aïoli* is the undisputed star of the *arrière-pays*, the herb-scented backlands that separate the famed pleasure ports of the Riviera from the austere mountain villages behind.

Aïoli traces its pungent history back some 2,000 years. To garlic lovers, now as then, it is one of the most enjoyable feasts in the world. In its essentials, *aïoli* is the simplest thing one can imagine: simple to prepare and deceptively simple to eat. The only difficulty I find is that it is just impossible to resist taking a few more succulent mouthfuls.

This extravagant dish is a whole meal in itself when it consists of a great platter of cooked vegetables served hot – a choice of green beans, zucchini, artichokes, potatoes, sweet potatoes and carrots (the sweetness of the potatoes and the carrots goes splendidly with the fiery richness of the *aïoli* sauce) – accompanied by poached salt cod or fresh fish, a

Each new season brings a fresh pressing of extra-virgin olive oil, always eagerly awaited.

squid or two, and sometimes mussels or snails. Raw vegetables, too, play their part – raw tomatoes, baby fava beans, lettuce hearts and sprigs of fresh basil and Italian (flat-leaf) parsley are heaped on the platters with all the ingenuity that cooks can muster. A well-presented *aïoli*, with its clumps of brilliantly colored vegetables and fresh herbs surrounding the fish, scattered as it used to be in the old times for festive occasions with a few snails, mussels or periwinkles, is a sight to remember.

The star of this generous spread is the *aïoli* itself, an unctuous mayonnaise sauce plentifully endowed with the magic fire of pounded fresh garlic. Indeed, so popular in the region is this pungent pommade that it is known as *le beurre de Provence*.

Aïoli is the dish for true enthusiasts, definitely not to be recommended for those with fastidious appetites or for those who fear that the strong aroma of garlic will inhibit them socially for life. It is at its best when served for lunch out of doors, with great quantities of Provençal white wine, followed by a selection of cooling sorbets, or perhaps a lemon or orange tart (see page 181) or a *tarte tropézienne* (see page 184).

Fifine's aïoli

SERVES 6

1 lb salt cod	6 large ripe tomatoes
6 potatoes	lettuce leaves and large
6 small sweet potatoes	sprigs of fresh herbs
6 zucchini	(Italian [flat-leaf]
1 lb small carrots	parsley, basil, *pourpier*
1 lb green beans	or purslane, dill, etc.)
6 hard-boiled eggs	

FOR THE *AÏOLI* SAUCE

4 fat cloves garlic per serving	salt and ground black pepper
1 egg yolk per two servings	lemon juice
olive oil	

Soak the cod overnight in cold water. Boil the fish and each vegetable – white and sweet potatoes in their jackets, whole zucchini and carrots and topped-and-tailed green beans – separately. All of them should be tender but still quite firm, and on no account overcooked. Serve the hot vegetables, hard boiled eggs in their shells and raw tomatoes on large serving dishes decorated with lettuce and sprigs of fresh

herbs. Place the fish in the center. For best effect, group the well-drained vegetables by color. Serve with the *aïoli* sauce which gives the dish its name.

Note: Fifine also serves fresh red snapper, John Dory or other Mediterranean fish as well as a slice or two of conger eel or squid instead of the traditional salt cod. Some cooks add snails or mussels to the dish on feast days.

TO MAKE THE *AÏOLI* SAUCE

Crush the garlic to a smooth paste in a mortar with a little salt; blend in the egg yolks until the mixture is a smooth, homogeneous mass. Now take the olive oil and proceed (drop by drop at first, a fine trickle later) to whisk the mixture as you would for a mayonnaise. The *aïoli* will thicken gradually until it reaches the proper stiff consistency. The exact quantity of oil is, of course, determined by the number of egg yolks used. Season to taste with additional salt, a little ground black pepper and lemon juice. This sauce is served chilled in a bowl for guests to help themselves throughout the meal.

Vegetables with aïoli sauce

The same recipe for *aïoli* sauce can also be used to make simple and delicious vegetable first courses: just poach little new potatoes, trimmed zucchini or topped-and-tailed green beans separately in a saucepan of lightly salted boiling water until they are just tender. Drain and serve either hot or cold with *aïoli* sauce. Garnish each serving with ripe red tomato wedges, sprigs of fresh basil and black olives. Or serve this recipe for vegetables with *aïoli*.

6 new potatoes	6 ripe tomatoes
6 zucchini	salt and ground black
1 lb baby carrots	pepper
1 lb green beans	*aïoli* sauce, see above

Peel the potatoes and cut them into ½-inch cubes; slash and cut the zucchini, baby carrots and green beans into ½-inch lengths. Boil each vegetable until just tender.

Seed large fresh tomatoes and cut them into ½-inch cubes. Arrange the vegetables in colorful clusters on a large shallow serving dish; sprinkle with salt and freshly ground black pepper and serve with *aïoli* sauce.

43

Deep in the cellars of
the seventeenth-century
Château d'Entrecasteaux
lies the perfect Provençal
kitchen, its great tiled
hotte, deep pottery
braziers and capacious
fireplace making the ideal

setting for a traditional
Christmas Eve feast
of salt cod, sea bream,
mussels, tomatoes, hard-
boiled eggs and country
vegetables. Centerpiece
of the generous spread
is a bowl of pungent,
garlic-scented *aïoli*,
often called the 'butter
of Provence'.

45

FEAST

Christian Millo
L'Auberge de la Madone, Peillon

On the map it looked so easy. But then it always does. Just a few minutes' drive and we'd be there in time for lunch, in one of the highest, most magical hill towns of the entire coast, perched on a rocky crag far above Nice, or was it Monte Carlo? That's what they had told us ... and there was always the map. Anyway, it was easy. We'd start by leaving the *autoroute* at the sign for Roquebrune. Roquebrune, after all, was a delightful hill village – we'd been there often – and then from Roquebrune, we'd just take any of the little roads going up into the mountains until we saw one signposted to Peillon.

But when we reached Roquebrune there didn't seem to be any little roads. To anywhere. So back we headed; and then we saw a tiny sign for Ste Agnès-de-Peille. Peille – Peillon? It couldn't be far. 'The highest village of the Littoral', said the sign, as French signs do. It was half past one when we arrived in Ste Agnès-de-Peille, and we decided we'd better stop, and not risk missing lunch at Peillon. It was a lovely sunny day when we got out of the car and entered the little Vieille Auberge de Ste Agnès.

Sunday lunch at the little village inn was an unbelievable 110 francs and there was just one table left, right in front of the window. So we took it, bemused but not too unhappy to try the *pissaladière* or the *tourte Agnésoise* (an open tart of greens *à la niçoise*) followed by a huge platter of *jambon de montagne* accompanied by a *salade* Vieille Auberge. And then *raviolis grandmère*, '*faits par la patronne*'. I could see *la patronne* right there in her little yellow kitchen, so that was all right. And then the main course: a choice between *coquelet royal, sauce aux champignons frais* (a wonderful appellation evoking simultaneously the long-forgotten etiquette of the royal court and the musky, earthy flavor of field mushrooms) and *lapin aux herbes* (sautéed rabbit with aromatic herbs). The rabbit won hands down. Then it was time for *salade*

Peillon – twenty minutes behind Nice on the straight road and up to four hours if you follow the breath-taking mountain route – is a fortified mountain village with tall houses clinging perilously over the gorge, the whole topped by the ochre-tinted tower of the little parish church.

mesclun and *fromage*, followed by dessert. A delicious coffee and we were back in the car and on our way.

But now it was almost four o'clock and everything seemed changed. We were in a London fog, thick, gray, worrying, but shot with light as no London fog has ever been: a magic mist in which to travel the winding, narrow roads to Peillon and the long-sought Auberge de la Madone.

Filled with the elusive happiness that only a bottle of red Côtes de Provence and a Marc de Myrtilles can bring, we set off up the mountain in the wrong

direction and on the wrong side of the road . . . Then, with a quick and forceful decision at the next little signpost, on to Peille (eleven kilometers). Could Peillon be far? Suddenly the mist began to clear. We were above the cloud at last and the way became easy. Altitude 870 meters, the sign said. But then the road began to descend sharply again and we were rocketing down and around hairpin bends, along narrow tunnels cut through white rock, down again into the mist, across magical sun-shot glades . . . and down again. It was perhaps the most beautiful road,

through the most beautiful mountains that I have ever seen.

Then suddenly we were back at 700 meters again and on a plain; the mist was gone and the late afternoon sun was shining. It was five o'clock. One sign said fourteen kilometers to the *autoroute*. The other that we had just passed the Col de la Madone: was it she who had protected us, brought us safely to the plain? Around another bend, in the shadow of the mountain, and there was Peille: '*le plus curieux village des Alpes Maritimes*', said the sign. Peille was a simple

47

little village full of the scent of woodsmoke. Nice seemed to be only twenty-two kilometers away.

From Peille and going in the direction of La Grave, we arrived suddenly in a tiny village called Le Moulin, *commune de* Peillac (no mention of Peillon). Then a sharp left at a sign saying 'Peillon only 3 km' and up again into the hills, through a tiny village called Les Sept Lacets (the Seven Shoelaces), and there straight ahead of us was a pink and white and gray village on the tip of a mountain top. On, round a sharp bend, and then up the ever-turning single track road straight into the Middle Ages: Peillon is a fortified mountain village with four-

Christian Millo's *tourton des pénitents*.

and five-story houses clinging on perilously over the gorge, the whole topped by the ocher-tinted tower of the parish church. And there, at the foot of the village, just where it should be, were the saffron and rose-tiled rooftops and cozy brown shutters of the Auberge de la Madone at Peillon, with Christian Millo and his wife Carine, and the warm scent of daube of beef with wild mushrooms and the haunting fragrance of wild thyme and orange.

'Where have you been? We expected you at lunch. We told you it was only twenty minutes from Nice.'

The Auberge de la Madone has been a family-run business for three generations, ever since Augustine and Aulaine Millo opened a little two-room inn and food shop for the village. Today, under the inspired direction of forty-five-year-old Christian Millo and his mother and sister, Marie Josée, the little inn tucked away in the mountains has caught the attention of international gourmets, food writers and food-loving locals, who happily make the twenty-minute trip up the mountains for a superb lunch on the sunny terrace overlooking the old hill village, or for a tranquil weekend away from

the cares of the world. I can't imagine a more perfect place for a writer to work in peace and comfort, sure in the knowledge that the muse would be fed sublimely on the natural flavors and country cooking of Christian and his mother Aimée, who incidentally looks so young that at first I thought she was his wife or his sister.

Dinner at La Madone might begin with fine, fat spears of lightly poached local asparagus, with a few leaves of wild dandelion dressed simply with extra-virgin olive oil from the old mill at Peillon, and topped with a spoonful of *tapenade*; or with the famous *tourton des pénitents* (an incredibly light, soufflélike flat omelet with chopped fresh green herbs and pine nuts, served on a bed of tomato *coulis* and *sauce verte*); or a simple platter of local ham with white melon.

The main course has to be Christian's earthy *daube de boeuf aux cèpes et à l'orange*, a long-simmered combination of meats from the chuck and the upper leg of beef with a special cut that Milo calls the *canard* (duck), found where the upper leg joins the body; the whole simmered in red wine and aromatics with wild mushrooms and dried orange peel. The daube is served in the classic manner with *raviolis de blettes* (Swiss chard and herb-filled ravioli flavored with the meats and juices of the daube). On my first visit these delicious little ravioli were made for me by Christian's mother in the form of the old *lous crous* of classic Provençal country cuisine. That is to say that the green-flecked ravioli filling, wrapped in the thinnest of homemade pasta doughs, was rolled into long sticks of dough which were divided into ¾-inch pieces, each side of which was then gently pinched or teased with the fingertips into a little winged 'ear'. In the old days, I am told, the cooked puréed chard and green herbs were sometimes incorporated into the dough itself, creating an attractive green-flecked pasta similar in type to Italian green gnocchi.

These simple but delicious country-style pastas became very popular in the early nineteenth century, replacing the comforting vegetable soups and ragouts of vegetables which were the normal fare of the back country. And they are still served to this day in Provence, with a sauce of tomatoes, onion and garlic, or sometimes with just a bit of the water in which the pasta was cooked (or water in which chestnuts or chick-peas have been cooked), seasoned with salt, freshly ground black pepper and a few leaves of fresh sage. Chopped walnuts and a drop or two of precious walnut oil were sometimes added, or a combination of sage, rosemary and summer savory, moistened with the cooking juices left over from last Sunday's daube of beef.

Ravioli 'made in Madone', as they are called in Peillon, take time, but are wonderful examples of the love and care that Provençal cooks will put into the simplest ingredients to create a memorable feast.

On another visit, this time for lunch, I enjoyed the best fricassee of rabbit I have ever tasted, served with homemade tagliatelle tossed in a little of the sauce of the fricassee, in the traditional manner of Provence, where almost all pasta dishes are dressed simply with the pan juices of a daube or fricassee of meats, poultry or game. There is no magic ingredient here, just the best possible produce. Rabbits bred by the local farmers; vegetables from the market gardens nearby; herbs gathered from the hillsides; and the care and attention that goes into the cooking of the simple recipes.

The cuisine of Christian Millo is family cooking at its very best: the noble yet simple heritage of his mother and his grandmother, and generations of mountain cooks behind them, imbued with the classic traditions of old Piedmont and Provence. I love the simplicity and rightness of his flavors; the understated way he has of giving a dish just the right amount of sauce, a skill given only to born cooks. I love his *duo de cailles aux raisins sur canapé de polenta* (a pair of quail from the neighboring village of Lucéram with grapes, served on a crêpe of polenta): again the country (and Italian) touch of polenta with the sophistication of the grape- and wine-infused sauce. And his country-style 'griddled' lamb chops served with a *poêlée* of tiny new potatoes, zucchini, mushrooms, diced peppers and green onions. After a meal of such simple perfection, what could be better than a platter of little local cheeses and a fresh peach, or a basket of ripe figs or apricots, or one of La Madone's country sweets? My favorite is *le gratin de pomme au miel de lavande et sa croûte aux amandes*.

Le bouquet d'asperges à la tapenade et son voile d'huile d'olive de Peillon, garni de pissenlits

—

Poached asparagus with tapenade

—

SERVES 4

20–24 fat asparagus spears	**4 tbsps *tapenade* (home-**
1 cup wild dandelion	**made or bought)**
leaves	**salt and ground black**
½ cup extra-virgin olive	**pepper**
oil	

Peel the asparagus spears and put them in a pot of lightly salted boiling water; when the water comes to a boil again, cook the asparagus for 15 minutes. Drain and allow to cool on a clean kitchen towel to absorb any remaining moisture. They should be served slightly warm.

Wash and dry the dandelion leaves. Arrange the leaves on 4 salad plates. Place 5–6 asparagus spears in a fan on each bed of dandelion leaves; spoon over olive oil and season with salt and ground black pepper. Just before serving, garnish each plate with a nut of *tapenade*.

Tourton des pénitents

Christian Millo's soufflé omelet

SERVES 4

Christian Millo serves this delightfully named first course – a fluffy, herb-flavored soufflé omelet – on a bed of complementary green herb and red tomato sauces. If you would like to follow his example, I recommend *sauce verte* and *coulis de tomates* (see pages 21 and 24).

8 oz fresh spinach or Swiss chard leaves	1 tbsp finely chopped mint
1 tbsp finely chopped leek	3 tbsps pine nuts
½ clove garlic, finely chopped	4 egg yolks
extra-virgin olive oil	6 tbsps *crème fraîche*
salt and ground black pepper	1 cup freshly grated Gruyère cheese
4 tbsps finely chopped chives	4 egg whites
1 tbsp finely chopped basil	tomato *coulis*
	sauce verte

Blanch the spinach or Swiss chard in lightly salted boiling water. Drain and and press dry. Chop finely.

In a medium-sized skillet, sauté the chopped leek and garlic in 2 tablespoons of extra-virgin olive oil until the vegetables are transparent, but not colored. Add the finely chopped spinach or Swiss chard and continue to cook, stirring, for 1 minute more. Season with salt and freshly ground black pepper; add the finely chopped chives, basil, mint and pine nuts and sauté, stirring constantly, for 1 minute more. Transfer the mixture to a sieve to drain off excess oil and reserve.

In a medium-sized bowl, whisk the egg yolks, *crème fraîche* and grated Gruyère until well blended. Stir in the spinach or Swiss chard mixture and reserve.

WHEN READY TO COOK

Beat the egg whites in a clean bowl until stiff; fold them gently into the creamy herb and egg mixture and pour into an oiled and buttered 10-inch skillet. Cook over a medium heat, as for a tortilla or flat omelet, adding a little more oil or butter if necessary, for 4 minutes. Place a large plate over the omelet and turn it over on the plate. Slide the omelet back into the pan and continue to cook for a few minutes more, until it is a warm golden brown on the other side.

Daube de boeuf de l'Auberge de la Madone aux cèpes et à l'orange

Daube of beef with wild mushrooms and orange, Auberge de la Madone

SERVES 4–6

3 lb beef for braising, preferably equal quantities of rump, leg and shin, cut into 1½-inch cubes	2 tbsps *marc de Provence* or cognac
	½ bottle red wine (a Bellet or a Côtes du Rhône)
2–4 carrots, cut into thick slices	extra-virgin olive oil
	2 tbsps butter
2 medium onions, coarsely chopped	3 cups *cèpes (porcini)*, *chanterelles* or other wild mushrooms
2 cloves garlic	
1 rib celery, thickly sliced	salt and ground black pepper
2 sprigs Italian (flat-leaf) parsley	1–2 tbsps tomato paste
	crushed red pepper flakes (optional)
2 sprigs fresh thyme	
2 bay leaves	2 strips dried orange peel
2 cloves	juice of 1 small orange
12 black peppercorns	

TO PREPARE THE MARINADE

One or two days before serving: in a large heat-proof earthenware, enameled or stainless-steel casserole, combine the cubes of meat, carrots, onions, garlic, celery and herbs and spices. Pour over the red wine and *marc de Provence* or cognac and 4 tablespoons olive oil; stir well to ensure that the meat is impregnated with the marinade and aromatics. Cover the casserole and allow the meats, vegetables and aromatics to marinate in the refrigerator for 24 hours, stirring the marinade once or twice during this time.

TO MAKE THE DAUBE

After one or two days, remove the meat from the refrigerator and allow it to come to room temperature. Remove the cubes of meat with a slotted spoon, pat them dry with kitchen paper and sauté them, a few at a time, in butter and oil in a large skillet until they are well browned on all sides. As they are cooked, place the meat pieces in a large clean casserole.

Pre-heat the oven to very cool (225°F).

Remove the vegetables (carrots, onions and celery) from the marinade and sauté them in the fats remaining in the skillet, stirring from time to time, until the vegetables are well browned on all sides, 5–8

Daube de boeuf de l'Auberge de la Madone aux cèpes et à l'orange.

minutes. Add to the meat in the casserole. Then add a little more olive oil to the skillet and sauté the *cèpes* (or other wild mushrooms) until golden, about 5 minutes. Season to taste with salt and freshly ground black pepper.

Pour the marinade juices into a heat-proof saucepan; add the tomato paste and bring gently to a boil; skim, lower the heat to medium and continue to cook for 5 minutes to lightly reduce the marinade juices. Pour the marinade over the meat and vegetables and cook the daube over medium heat until

the marinade juices begin to bubble gently. Cover the casserole, put it in the pre-heated oven and cook for 3–3½ hours, stirring from time to time. After the first two hours, test the meat for tenderness: a true daube should be meltingly tender.

Correct the seasoning, adding a little more salt and pepper, some red pepper flakes, or a little more *marc de Provence* or cognac if necessary. Then add the sautéed mushrooms, dried orange peel and orange juice and cook for 10–20 minutes. Serve with fresh noodles, ravioli or boiled new potatoes.

Les raviolis de la Madone

Ravioli 'made in Madone'

SERVES 6

One of the great specialities of the Auberge de la Madone is the *daube de boeuf à la provençale* served, with a loving nod to the old traditions, with a great bowl of *raviolis à la niçoise* bathed in the juices of the daube. On my first visit, the ravioli were stuffed with chopped Swiss chard, eggs and freshly grated Parmesan and formed into little square 'eared' ravioli by Aimée Millo, Christian's mother, like the traditional *lous crous* of the ancient cuisine. They were delicious. On my second visit, months later, Christian gave me his own version: the ravioli were stuffed with a *hachis* of meat from the daube, blended with chopped Swiss chard and the usual binder of eggs and freshly grated Parmesan: equally inspiring. I give you his version.

FOR THE PASTA

6 cups semolina flour	1½ tsps salt
	5 eggs, well beaten

FOR THE FILLING

2–3 cups meat from the *daube de boeuf* (see page 50), finely chopped	¼ tsp dried thyme
	¼ tsp freshly grated nutmeg
2 lb Swiss chard, green parts only, blanched and finely chopped	2 eggs, well beaten
	1¼ cups freshly grated Parmesan cheese
1 clove garlic, finely chopped	olive oil or juices from the daube
2 tbsps finely chopped onion	salt and ground black pepper

TO MAKE THE PASTA

Sift the flour and salt into a large mixing bowl. Make a well in the center and pour in the beaten eggs. Add 3 tablespoons water, and mix the flour and liquids together with your fingertips until the dough is just soft enough to form into a ball, adding 2 or more tablespoons of water to the mixture as you work the dough if the mixture seems too dry.

Sprinkle a large pastry board with flour and knead the dough on the board with the flat of your hand until it is smooth and elastic (about 15 minutes), sifting a little flour over your hand and the board from time to time.

TO ROLL OUT THE DOUGH

Divide the dough in half; using a rolling pin roll out one piece at a time into sheets ⅛ inch thick. To do

RIGHT *Les raviolis de la Madone.*

OPPOSITE *Le gratin de pomme au miel de lavande et sa croûte aux amandes.*

this, roll out the dough in one direction, stretching it as you go, and then roll it out in the opposite direction. Sprinkle with flour; fold over and repeat. The dough should be just dry enough not to stick to the rolling pin. Repeat this process of rolling, stretching and folding the dough another 2 or 3 times. Repeat with the remaining piece of dough.

TO FORM THE RAVIOLI

Cut the dough into strips 2 inches wide, and place teaspoons of filling (see below) on it at 2-inch intervals. With your finger or a small pastry brush moisten the dough between the filling with water, to seal the edges of the dough. Cover with another strip of the dough. With your finger, press the dough down around the filling. Using a pastry cutter, cut the dough into 2-inch squares. Set the ravioli aside for 2 hours, then cook as for any pasta.

FOR THE FILLING

In a large mixing bowl combine the finely chopped meat from the daube, chard, garlic and onion. Add the thyme and nutmeg, beaten eggs and grated Parmesan and salt and ground black pepper to taste. Mix well.

Note: If the mixture seems a little dry, add a few tablespoons of olive oil or juices from the daube. Use to fill the ravioli as indicated above.

Le gratin de pomme au miel de lavande et sa croûte aux amandes

Apple gratins with lavender honey and almond croûtes

SERVES 4

4 large Golden Delicious apples	3 tbsps lavender honey
butter	2 eggs

Pre-heat the oven to moderate (325°F). Butter 4 ramekins.

Peel, core and quarter the apples; cut each quarter into very thin slices.

Heat 2 tablespoons butter in a small skillet. Add the apple slices and cook over low heat, stirring from time to time, until the apples are soft, about 4 minutes. Add the lavender honey and continue to cook, stirring, until the honey has melted. Remove from heat.

In a mixing bowl, beat the eggs until light-colored; add the apple and honey mixture and mix.

Pour the mixture into the prepared ramekins and cook in the pre-heated oven for 20 minutes. Remove from the oven and allow to cool.

LA CROÛTE AUX AMANDES

3 egg whites	1 cup chopped almonds
½ cup granulated sugar	⅔ cup all-purpose flour
1 packet vanilla sugar	5 tbsps butter melted

Pre-heat the oven to hot (425°F).

In a medium-sized bowl, beat the egg whites until stiff; then gradually beat in the sugar and vanilla sugar.

With a spatula, fold in the chopped almonds, then the flour and finally the hot melted butter.

With a tablespoon, make 8 little mounds of the mixture on a buttered baking sheet; flatten each mound with a fork and bake the *croûtes* in a pre-heated oven for 10–12 minutes. When the *croûtes* are cooked, place one on each dessert plate; unmold a gratin of apples on each and then place a second *croûte* on top of each gratin. Pour a little *sauce vanille* around each croûte and serve immediately.

LA SAUCE VANILLE

2 cups milk	4 egg yolks
½ tsp vanilla extract	¼ tsp salt
4 tbsps granulated sugar	

In a medium-sized saucepan, simmer the milk for 5 minutes; stir in the vanilla extract.

In a small bowl, combine the sugar, egg yolks and salt and beat until fluffy and lemon-colored. Pour a little of the hot milk into the egg and sugar mixture; blend well and then stir into the hot milk.

In the top of a double boiler, heat the mixture slowly, stirring constantly, until it coats the back of a wooden spoon.

FISH SOUPS
AND FISH DISHES OF PROVENCE

It was by sea, along the coast from Asia Minor and ancient Greece, that the first settlers of Provence arrived to found the great cities whose names are now but pale scratchings on ancient maps in the museums of our modern cities. Their landing places on the coast were destined to open the way for the conquests of Caesar and Pompey and to provide the early foundations for the western spread of Roman civilization.

Arriving in Marseilles by boat today, sharing the perilous adventure of the remote past as we approach one of its most ancient cities from the sea, is an overwhelming experience. The harbor magically opens up, just as it did for those early adventurers, and once in the lagoon, inside the bright rectangle of water formed by the *quais*, behind the bobbing masts of the pleasure boats and the working craft, we can see the houses of the old city rise up around us in a multicolored mosaic. Above them stand the ribboned marble façade of Notre Dame de la Garde and the ample figure of *La Bonne Mère*, as the imposing statue of the Virgin is affectionately known to the Marseillais.

Marseilles still has a mythical quality – mysterious, pulsating with life, as exotic as the East and with more than a touch of the sinister. For behind the polite *quais* with their bright cafés and restaurants, behind the classical façade of the eighteenth-century town hall, lie a decadent world of noisome, narrow back streets and a claustrophobic Arab quarter.

The Marseillais display their Eastern heritage in their use of herbs and spices. A hint of nutmeg, warm and aromatic, can be discerned for instance in the *pâtes aux palourdes* (spaghetti prepared with tiny clams still in their shells) served in restaurants on the harbor; and a dish of astonishing subtlety made from tender little octopus called *supions*, and served with a dense, dark red sauce, contains no fewer than eight different herbs and spices. It is in fact a refined version of a Greek octopus stew.

the Sea

Bouillabaisse, perhaps the most famous dish of the entire coast, was reputedly born in Marseilles. Bouillabaisse lovers of modern times dispute the holder of the blue ribbon today: the three best bouillabaisses I know are those of Chez Bacon in Antibes, La Mère Terrats in Cannes and Chez Fifine in St Tropez. My own personal choice has always been Fifine, who makes it *sur commande* only, as with her other specialities, *bourride*, *aïoli* and *chapon farci*.

CHEZ FIFINE

Chez Fifine is a tiny restaurant on the rue Cepoun Martin, just behind the open-air fish market which opens onto the harbor, its only sign a signature 'Chez Fifine' on the awning. On the first floor are a

kitchen and one small room containing five tables; a slightly larger dining room lies up some narrow stairs (you have to go through the spotless kitchen), and a few tables are strategically placed outside for the inevitable overflow. Fifine does all the cooking, aided by a kitchen staff of one; the service is carried out by family and friends – on busy nights you might find Josef, ex-fisherman and local *pétanque* champion, Fifine's close companion for many years, directing the activities of a team of personable young 'cousins' who wait on table. To those who demand *la grande cuisine*, an impressive decor and impeccable service, my advice is to stay away. For here the service is friendly but often erratic;

Fifine loves and excels in the rustic dishes of Provence, which she produces using only the finest and simplest of local ingredients.

there is no *cave* of select vintage wines; no flaming *spécialités de la maison*; no fuss, no bother: just the simple, homely dishes of Provence lovingly prepared by Fifine.

Only the finest ingredients are to be found in her kitchen, and only the simplest, but the most perfect dishes are produced by this truly great cook. All Provence is her domain: fennel comes from the mountains behind the coast, wild thyme and rosemary from the neighboring hills; the town's best fishermen arrive at her door several times daily with their latest catch; the local fishmonger, one of her most fervent admirers, is at her beck and call to bring her some great sea creature from the early morning market at Marseilles if it is not available in St Tropez; tomatoes are selected with care from one special *vendeuse* in the open-air market, fresh basil from another; and eggs and vegetables are delivered daily from a nearby farm.

Fifine loves and excels in the rustic dishes of Provence and the fruits of her private sea. It was she who first taught me the pleasures of the then little-known local wines; the special richness of the pure olive oil of Provence; what fish to put in a bouillabaisse; how to make *aïoli*, a *rouille*, a *tapenade*. And the unheard-of delights of the little wild leaves of salad called *mesclun* – gathered in the fields in those days by shepherds tending their flocks, by local farmers' wives and by the gypsy women who used to come with overflowing baskets to the weekly market in the Place des Lices. Today *mesclun* is famous the world over and grown commercially in the vast kitchen gardens behind Grasse. And my first *salade niçoise* (now such a commonplace) as prepared by Fifine – with tiny raw artichoke

hearts and raw fava beans added to the more usual ingredients of sliced tomatoes, cucumbers, green pepper, hard-boiled eggs, anchovies and black olives – was a poem.

You would be lucky to get a *salade niçoise* there today, for Fifine is a good deal older now, and a little tired. She prefers to devote her energies to her famous specialities – her bouillabaisse; *bourride* so delicious that I once traveled from London to St Tropez just for the pleasure of tasting it; *chapon*

Chez Fifine.

Fifine makes her bouillabaisse from the freshest ingredients. The best fishermen in St Tropez arrive at her door several times daily with their latest catch.

farci (a huge red *rascasse* stuffed with a delicious *farce* made of the fish's huge liver blended with fresh herbs, rice and aromatics); and her *aïoli*, a fantasy of fish (both fresh and salted) and vegetables, poached separately and served, platter after platter, with a great bowl of golden, garlicky *aïoli* sauce. Each of these great works has to be ordered in advance.

These are indeed feasts of Provence, as they might have been served and enjoyed in Provençal private homes fifty years ago or more. Fifine, seventy-five years old now, is a reminder of those times. Hurry to meet her and to enjoy her food. Her years are numbered and I am sure that even as I write this she is thinking of passing on her little restaurant to her son Robert or to some younger local lady to carry on under her guidance – producing the simple yet magnificent fare that I have enjoyed so much these many years. But it won't be the same.

It was Fifine who
first taught me the
pleasures of the then
little-known local
wines; the special
richness of the pure
olive oil of Provence;
what fish to put in a
bouillabaisse; how
to make *aïoli*,
a *rouille*, a *tapenade*.

Bouillabaisse

Bouillabaisse is a meal in itself, served traditionally today in two great steaming bowls. One contains the aromatic fish bouillon, with its classic accompaniments of oven-baked, garlic-rubbed slices of French bread, grated Gruyère cheese and a fiery, rust-colored sauce called *rouille*. In the other are the poached fish, the smaller ones whole, the larger ones cut in pieces.

In Provence family feuds have been triggered by fierce debates about which varieties of fish go into a true bouillabaisse. Freshly caught local fish – *grondin* and *rascasse* (gurnard and scorpion fish), *Saint-Pierre* (John Dory) and *baudroie* (monkfish or anglerfish) – cooked in a broth made from the myriad little fishes '*pour la bouillabaisse*' sold in every port, are most often cited, though some purists claim that *rascasse* and *rascasse* alone should be used.

Another battle can ensue about whether or not potatoes should be included in the traditional recipe. And even saffron (an absolutely necessary ingredient as far as this 'Provençal' is concerned) is often omitted from the true *bouillabaisse des pêcheurs* (fishermen's bouillabaisse). A slice or two of *congre* (conger eel) is often included to enrich the bouillon and sometimes the horny-shelled little crabs called *favouilles* and a *poulpe* (squid) or two are added for extra flavor. The whole is then simmered for minutes only, with tomatoes, leeks, onions and garlic, a touch of saffron, some sticks of dried fennel, a strip of dried orange peel and sprigs of fresh parsley and basil.

The name bouillabaisse comes from two simple culinary directions: *bouille* (boil) and *baisse* (lower the heat). In old Provençal, *boui abaisso* literally means boil over a high heat for a matter of minutes and then lower the heat and continue to cook until the fish is just tender, not falling into overcooked, unattractive pieces. Sounds simple? It is. The only thing you have to watch is your watch.

La bouillabaisse des pêcheurs

—

Fishermen's bouillabaisse

—

Along the *calanques* (little inlets) to the east and west of Marseilles the original bouillabaisse was a simple fishermen's dish cooked on board their boats from the fish they had caught that day, or at a picnic on shore or a feast with their comrades in a little *cabanon* (hut) hidden in the reeds along the coast. Made in the traditional way with slices of potato, and served with a hot, potato-thickened *rouille* sauce, this was a man's dish in the old days: a short-sauced dish that he could cook in one pot and serve proudly to his friends, the highly flavored bouillon and the piquant sauce making a wondrous accompaniment to the tender fish fresh from the sea. There were probably no chic accompaniments of garlic-rubbed bread or freshly grated cheese in those older, simpler times. All that came later. The only embellishments necessary were a bowl of the fiery hot *rouille*, a loaf or two of freshly baked bread to mop up the sauce and liberal quantities of white wine to wash it down.

When making a true fishermen's bouillabaisse the fishermen in Provence use whatever is in their catch of the day: *rascasse rouge* and *rascasse grise*, *baudroie* (monkfish), *fiélas* or *congre* (conger eel), *Saint-Pierre* (John Dory) and *galinette* or *grondin* (gurnard).

SERVES 6

2 lb 4 oz fish (4 or 5 varieties chosen from the following: striped or black bass, red snapper, red mullet, ocean perch, silver mullet, monkfish or angler fish, conger eel and porgy)
4 large yellow onions, sliced
6–8 ripe tomatoes, thickly sliced
1 leek, thinly sliced
8 cloves garlic, flattened
coarse salt and ground black pepper
crushed red pepper flakes
2 bay leaves
3–4 dried fennel stalks, or a small glass of Pastis or Pernod
1 strip dried orange peel
$\frac{1}{4}$–$\frac{1}{2}$ tsp saffron
olive oil
1 potato for each serving, sliced
6–8 ripe tomatoes, sliced
water, or fish stock
garlic croûtons
rouille sauce

In a shallow heat-proof casserole, combine the sliced onions, tomatoes, leek and flattened garlic cloves (with skins intact). Place the sliced fish on top.

Pound the leftover fish heads once or twice with a pestle, or the flat of a cleaver, and add to the casserole to give the bouillon extra flavor; sprinkle with coarse salt, red pepper flakes and freshly ground black pepper to taste. Add bay leaves, dried fennel, dried orange peel and saffron and moisten with a good splash of olive oil. Stir gently to mix the flavors well, adding a little more olive oil if too dry.

Marinate the mixture in a cool place (definitely not the refrigerator) for 5 hours.

When ready to cook the bouillabaisse, peel the potatoes; slice them into $\frac{1}{4}$-inch slices and add them to the fish mixture with just enough water, or fish stock, to come within $\frac{1}{2}$ inch of the top of the fish and potatoes.

Cook the bouillabaisse, uncovered, for 10 minutes; lower the heat and cook gently for 15–20 minutes more.

Serve the bouillon separately with *croûtons d'ail* and a good *rouille* sauce. Accompany the bouillon with a platter of poached fish and sliced potatoes, moistened with a little of the bouillon.

Note: If you want to make the bouillabaisse exactly the way the fishermen did, use half the water or fish stock above, giving just enough reduced bouillon to sauce each slice. This is no longer a soup with a fish served separately, but a serving of divinely sauced fish cooked in a bouillabaisse fish bouillon, and accompanied by *rouille* (see over).

The ritual of eating a traditional bouillabaisse today is always the same. First, we place two to three slices of oven-toasted French bread which we have rubbed with garlic in the bottom of our soup plates; then we top each slice with freshly grated Gruyère or Cantal cheese and top it with a dab of *rouille*. Then and only then do we ladle in the steaming hot aromatic fish bouillon. One or two more plates of this and – with the necessary refurbishments of garlic bread, cheese and *rouille* – we can turn our attention to the fish, adding a few slices of *rascasse*, sea bass, conger eel or red mullet and some saffron-tinted potatoes; moistening the fish with a little more bouillon as we go, and cooling our palates from time to time with a sip of chilled *vin blanc de Provence*; and then perhaps a tiny mussel or two, or a crab. What a dish; what a creation; what an experience.

La rouille des pêcheurs

Rouille, a fiery sauce of hot red peppers, egg yolks, olive oil and garlic, originally thickened with boiled potato or with breadcrumbs moistened with fish bouillon, was invented by the fishermen of Martigues to give a strong, manly flavor to their homely dish of poached fish and aromatics. The middle classes did not know of its existence until the end of the nineteenth century, when it became the traditional accompaniment for bouillabaisse, first in the region of Martigues and then on the rest of the coast. Today, *la rouille* (*la rouia* in old Provençal) is served, along with grated cheese and slices of toasted French bread rubbed with garlic, as the traditional accompaniment to *soupe de poissons* and *bourride* as well as the classic bouillabaisse.

4 cloves garlic	1 medium-sized potato,
2–3 dried hot red	peeled and cooked in
peppers (*piments de*	bouillon from the
cayenne)	bouillabaisse
½ tsp salt	2–3 tbsps bouillon from
olive oil	the bouillabaisse

In a mortar, combine the garlic cloves, hot red peppers and salt. Pound until smooth. Add the peeled boiled potato and pound again until smooth. Then add olive oil, little by little at first, stirring with the pestle all the time, as you would when making a mayonnaise. Continue until the sauce is thick and smooth. Just before serving, stir in a few tablespoons of the fish bouillon from the bouillabaisse.

La bouillabaisse de La Mère Terrats

SERVES 6

The fabulous bouillabaisse served at La Mère Terrats restaurant just outside Cannes combines rare Mediterranean fish – *chapon* and *rascasse* and a live *langouste* (use lobster or rock lobster) – in a super-rich bouillon made of tiny little rockfish from the Mediterranean that are unavailable in this country: over 4½ lb of fish to make a bouillabaisse for six. No wonder a true bouillabaisse, as served in a top restaurant in any one of the little villages on the southern coast of France, is so delicious. And so expensive. For authenticity's sake I list the fish as used at the restaurant. In this country, of course, we would make our choice from the many fish now available (see page 61).

FOR THE BOUILLON

2 lb 4 oz fish for bouillabaisse	4–6 large ripe tomatoes, chopped
2 tbsps olive oil per serving (12 tablespoons)	1 *bouquet garni* (bay leaf, thyme, rosemary)
2 large yellow onions, finely chopped	½–1 tsp saffron
2 cloves garlic	2–3 small hot red peppers

FOR THE FISH

4 lb 8 oz fish (1 *chapon*, 1 *pageot*, 2 *rascasses*, 1 gurnard and 1 lobster, enough to give you 9–11 oz fish per serving)

FOR THE GARNISH

3–4 small potatoes per serving (18–24 in all), 3–4 slices stale French bread per serving (18–24 in all)

TO PREPARE THE BOUILLON

In a large heat-proof casserole, combine 4 or 5 varieties of fish from the list above, adding a thick slice of eel and a few small crabs if available.

Add 2 tablespoons olive oil per serving. Then add the finely chopped onions and sauté them in the oil until they are transparent. Add the garlic, chopped fresh tomatoes and *bouquet garni* and simmer until the vegetables are lightly browned. Then add the cleaned fish and continue to cook, stirring constantly, until the fish begin to disintegrate. Then add 17 cups salted water, saffron and hot red peppers. Bring the mixture to a boil; skim off any impurities rising to the surface; lower the heat and simmer for 20 minutes. Then remove the casserole from the heat and strain the mixture through a fine sieve into a clean casserole, pressing out all the juices from the fish and aromatics with the back of a wooden spoon.

When ready to cook the bouillabaisse, peel and slice the potatoes into ¼-inch slices. Add sliced potatoes to the casserole. Add the *chapon*, *pageot*, *rascasses*, gurnard and lobster. Place the casserole over high heat; bring to a boil and cook until the fish and potatoes are tender but still hold their shape.

TO SERVE

Arrange the potatoes on a long serving dish; place the fish and lobster pieces on top. Serve the soup separately in a large soup bowl. At La Mère Terrats they always accompany the soup with a few slices of stale French bread moistened with a little bouillon, sprinkled with freshly grated Gruyère cheese and browned in the oven. *Rouille* is the other essential accompaniment to this wonderful dish.

La sauce rouille Mère Terrats

4 cloves garlic	olive oil
1–2 dried hot red peppers (*piments de cayenne*)	¼ tsp powdered saffron
	fish bouillon (from the bouillabaisse)
3 egg yolks	

Place the garlic in a mortar with the hot peppers, egg yolks and saffron. Add the olive oil, drop by drop, strirring with the pestle all the time as you would for a mayonnaise. Continue until the sauce is thick and smooth. Just before serving, stir in a tablespoon or two of fish bouillon from the bouillabaisse.

La bouillabaisse de Fifine

SERVES 4–6

6 lb fish (see Fifine's choice below)

FOR FIFINE'S MIREPOIX:

6 carrots	1 strip dried orange peel
6 large ripe tomatoes, seeded	2 bay leaves
2 large yellow onions	4 sprigs fresh thyme
2 leeks	4 sprigs Italian (flat-leaf) parsley
4 cloves garlic	¼–½ tsp saffron
2 fennel bulbs	salt and ground black pepper
fish bouillon	
1 stalk dried fennel (or 1 small glass Pastis)	½ cup olive oil

To make bouillabaisse, Fifine first prepares a mirepoix of vegetables by slicing the carrots, large, ripe, seeded tomatoes, Spanish onions, leeks, cloves of garlic and fennel bulbs into a large heat-proof casserole. She then adds a dried fennel stalk (or failing this a small glass of pastis), a strip of orange peel dried in the sun (or in a very low oven), bay leaves, sprigs of fresh thyme, sprigs of Italian (flat-leaf) parsley and a good sprinkling of saffron, salt and freshly ground black pepper.

A ladleful of virgin olive oil is then poured over this; the fish are added – a thickly sliced *rascasse*, *girelles*, John Dory, conger eel, sea bass and red mullet – about 6 lb of fish in all to serve 4–6 hungry guests. The whole aromatic potful is stirred to amalgamate the seasonings and is then left to marinate in a cold larder – not a refrigerator – for 4–5 hours.

Twenty minutes before the bouillabaisse is due to be served, Fifine adds just enough fish bouillon (made

Fifine's bouillabaisse, with its accompaniments of fiery *rouille* sauce, croûtons and freshly grated Gruyère cheese.

with the pounded heads of the fish joined to a batch of the tiny bony rockfish used to make *soupe de poissons*) to barely cover the fish and vegetables in the pan. Sliced raw potatoes – one potato for each portion – are added to the pot along with another good pinch of saffron. It is then cooked over high heat for 7–10 minutes; the heat is turned down and the whole is then simmered for another 7–10 minutes until the fish are tender, but not so cooked that they are falling off the bones. Bouillabaisse at Fifine's is served in the traditional fashion: the broth first, accompanied by bowls of dry French bread lightly rubbed with garlic; freshly grated cheese and a bowl of fiery hot *rouille*. The fish is presented on a large platter, or perhaps two, and then is taken away to be deftly filleted, for easier service.

Le poupeton de bouillabaisse

Bouillabaisse mold

SERVES 4

It would be a shame to give the leftovers from a good bouillabaisse to the cat. For those pieces of fish remaining in bouillon which has jellied there is no problem. Just whip up the jelly; add a little finely chopped chervil, basil and tarragon; flavor the jelly with a squeeze of lemon juice and a little salt and freshly ground pepper if necessary; and spoon it over the fish pieces which you have tidied up, removing any unattractive bones, skin or flakes. Garnish each serving with two lettuce leaves, a slice or two of ripe red tomato and 2 or 3 shiny oil-cured olives from Provence.

La soupe de poissons.

I also like to stuff large, chilled tomatoes with the remains of a bouillabaisse, mixing a little of the richly flavored bouillon into a homemade mayonnaise and then tossing the fish pieces into this. Add a hint of chopped onion and capers and stuff the tomato shells with this mixture, mounding it up to make a delicious first-course salad.

But perhaps my favorite use for bouillabaisse leftovers is to make a *poupeton*.

Remove the skin and bones from $3\frac{1}{2}$ cups leftover fish pieces; place them in a mortar with 4 slices of white bread (crusts removed) which you have moistened with a little bouillon from the bouillabaisse. Pound well until the mixture is smooth; add 3 well-beaten egg yolks and 3 tablespoons freshly grated Gruyère cheese and pound again. Or, more simply, process in a food processor until the mixture is well blended. Season to taste with salt, freshly ground black pepper and cayenne and mix well.

Pre-heat the oven to 325°F. Beat 3 egg whites until stiff and gently fold them into the spicy fish mixture.

Butter a mold (or 4 individual molds); fill with the *poupeton* mixture; place the mold (or molds) in a roasting pan; add enough boiling water to come halfway up the mold(s) and bring the water to a boil again before putting it in the pre-heated oven for 20 minutes. Serve with *rouille* sauce.

La soupe de poissons

Provençal fish soup

SERVES 4–6

All recipes for *soupe de poissons* – whether cooked in a little *cabanon* in the reeds around Marseilles, in a fish restaurant in the ports along the coast, or at home in a country kitchen in Provence – seem to hold true to the same easygoing formula: lightly sauté some chopped onion in olive oil with finely chopped garlic and tomatoes; then add a bay leaf, some thyme and whatever fish heads and trimmings you have available. This creates a solid base on which the Provençal cook builds fantasies of fabulous flavors.

And whether the main ingredient of the dish consists of the little rockfish that abound in the rocky inlets along the coast (the true *soupe de poissons à la provençale*), or of sea bass, John Dory or red mullet, or even of a few slices of conger eel, or a small catch of crabs, the base is always the same.

2 lb 4 oz–3 lb fish (see note below)
2–3 tbsps olive oil per serving
1–3 large yellow onions, sliced
2–3 cloves garlic, crushed
6–8 ripe tomatoes, seeded and coarsely chopped

1 *bouquet garni* (parsley, thyme, rosemary, dried fennel stalks)
1 bay leaf
½ tsp powdered saffron
1 small dried hot red pepper
salt

ACCOMPANIMENTS

slices of day-old French bread, rubbed with garlic and grilled

freshly grated cheese
rouille

Heat the olive oil in a large, thick-bottomed, heat-proof casserole, and sauté the sliced onions in the oil until transparent. Add the garlic, chopped and seeded tomatoes, *bouquet garni* and bay leaf and simmer, stirring frequently, until lightly browned. Then add the fish (see note below) and continue to cook, stirring constantly, until the fish are soft.

Add the saffron, red pepper and salt to taste, and just enough water to cover the fish, plus 1 inch for good measure. Bring the contents of the casserole to a boil; skim and cook over fairly high heat for 20 minutes. Strain well, pressing all the fish and vegetable juices through a sieve. Re-heat and serve the soup in a large heated soup bowl, accompanied by bowls of freshly grated cheese and rounds of day-old French bread rubbed with garlic.

Note: In Provence, Fifine recommends *girelles*, *rascasses*, *roucaous*, *perches*, small crabs and a slice or two of eel. In this country I like to use a choice of small red mullet, sea bass, slices of monkfish, grouper, conger eel, brill, porgy and red or gray snapper. The smaller and bonier the fish, the better the flavor.

La soupe de congres

Conger eel soup

SERVES 4–6

Begin with the basic flavoring formula above: add 5 cups of water; season with a little saffron, salt and ground pepper to taste, and cook for 20 minutes. Strain the bouillon into two saucepans. Add the pieces of conger eel (you could substitute fillets of red

snapper, ocean perch or porgy) to one of the saucepans and poach until tender. In the meantime, cook small elbow macaroni until tender in the other saucepan of bouillon.

TO SERVE

With a slotted spoon, remove the pieces of conger eel to a serving platter. Keep warm. Combine the two bouillons with the elbow macaroni and serve in a soup tureen. Accompany with bowls of garlic-rubbed grilled bread, grated cheese and *rouille* (see page 62).

OVERLEAF The bouillon for *bourride,* served with *aïoli* and croûtons in Fifine's restaurant.

La bourride de Chez Fifine
SERVES 4–6

La bourride is one of the most delicious fish soups of the Côte d'Azur. In its simplest form, it is a fresh Mediterranean fish cooked in a well-flavored *soupe de poissons*, with perhaps a cuttlefish and a piece of monkfish or conger eel added on feast days.

Like its glamorous cousin bouillabaisse, *bourride* is a two-stage meal: the bouillon is served first and then, halfway through the meal, a platter of the fish cooked in the bouillon is served. The secret of the dish is the celebrated Provençal garlic and egg yolk sauce, *aïoli*, which is whisked into the bouillon just before serving, much as the Greek garlic and egg yolk sauce *skordalia* is whipped into the famous chicken and lemon soup, *avgolemono*: one more proof – if proof were needed – of the influence of the ancient Greeks on the cooking of Provence. *Aïoli*, and sometimes *rouille*, is also served with the *bourride* so that guests can add their own touches of extra flavor throughout the meal.

FOR THE *SOUPE DE POISSONS*

4 large fish heads (cod, halibut, brill, monkfish etc.) to give substance and flavor

2 lb fish for the soup (mullet, monkfish, ocean perch, porgy, sea bass, red or gray snapper etc.)

1 leek, sliced

2 large yellow onions, sliced

3 cloves garlic, crushed

olive oil

4 large tomatoes, peeled, seeded and chopped

2 tbsps tomato paste

¼ tsp saffron

1 *bouquet garni* (2 sprigs thyme, 1 bay leaf, 2 sprigs parsley)

coarse salt and ground black pepper

FOR THE GARNISH

1 sea bream or John Dory, cut into fillets

2 sections eel or monkfish, or both (about 8 oz each), cut into 4–6 pieces

4 tbsps *aïoli* sauce

ADDITIONAL ACCOMPANIMENTS

***aïoli* sauce (see page 42)**

fried croûtons of French bread

***rouille* sauce (optional)**

TO PREPARE THE *SOUPE DE POISSONS* BASE

In a large, heat-proof casserole, sauté the leek, onions and garlic in oil until transparent; add the tomatoes and tomato paste, saffron, *bouquet garni*, salt and freshly ground black pepper to taste, and continue to cook, stirring, for 5 minutes more.

Add the fish heads and fish for the soup. Add water to cover, and cook for 30 minutes.

Remove the fish pieces – they can be used to make a wonderful *poupeton* (see page 64). Pass this very thick soup through a fine sieve into a clean casserole, pressing down on the fish heads and trimmings to extract as much flavor as possible. Reserve until ready to prepare the *bourride*.

Note: The recipe can be made up to this point and refrigerated 24 hours ahead.

TO PREPARE THE *BOURRIDE*

Heat the fish soup over a medium heat until it just comes to a boil; add the sea bream or John Dory fillets (and eel and/or monkfish) and cook until just tender, about 10 minutes.

TO SERVE

Remove the fish pieces; drain and place on a large heated serving dish and keep warm. Place 2–4 tablespoons of *aïoli* sauce into a small bowl; add a little hot fish soup to the bowl; mix well and then incorporate this mixture into the soup by whisking over gentle heat until well blended. Do not boil or the egg yolks will curdle. Pour the soup into a heated soup tureen and serve immediately, accompanied by the platter of cooked fish and bowls of *aïoli* sauce, *rouille* sauce (optional) and slices of French bread, sautéed in garlic-flavored oil.

Sauce aïoli

4 cloves garlic, finely chopped	**1 cup olive oil**
	ground black pepper
salt	**juice of 1 lemon**
2 egg yolks	

Crush the garlic to a smooth paste with a little salt, using a pestle and mortar or pressing it on a plate with a round-bladed knife or the back of a wooden spoon. In a mortar or bowl, blend in the egg yolks until the mixture is smooth. Add the olive oil, drop by drop, as you would for mayonnaise, whisking all the time. Then continue adding the oil in a fine trickle, whisking continuously. The *aïoli* will thicken gradually until it reaches a stiff consistency. Season to taste with additional salt and freshly ground black pepper. Add the lemon juice and whisk until well blended.

La soupe aïgo-sau

Provençal fish soup with rouille

SERVES 4

2 lb cleaned white fish
  (John Dory, monkfish,
  red mullet, sea bass,
  gurnard or whiting)
1 leek, chopped
1 large yellow onion,
  chopped
4 tomatoes, peeled, seeded
  and chopped
4 yellow potatoes, cut in
  thick slices
2 cloves garlic, crushed

olive oil
2 sprigs parsley
2 sprigs thyme
2 sprigs fennel
1 bay leaf
1 strip lemon peel
salt and ground black
  pepper
boiling water (or fish stock
  made with bones and
  heads), to cover

ACCOMPANIMENTS

4–8 slices day-old French
  bread, lightly grilled
  and rubbed with garlic
2 cloves garlic, crushed

olive oil
ground black pepper
rouille

TO PREPARE THE FISH (I)

Cut the fish into pieces of the same size. Place in a large enameled iron casserole or stainless-steel sauce-pan with the leek, onion, tomatoes and potatoes. Add the garlic, parsley, fennel, bay leaf and lemon peel and season generously with salt and freshly ground black pepper.

TO PREPARE THE FISH (II)

Some cooks, using the same ingredients, marinate the fish and aromatics in the following manner: place the prepared fish pieces in an enameled iron or stainless-steel container; add the chopped leek, onion, tomatoes, potatoes and garlic. Pour over 6 table-spoons olive oil and mix well with your hands until the fish is coated with oil. Add the herbs and lemon peel and season generously with salt and freshly ground black pepper. Mix once again and let the fish marinate for 2 hours, or overnight.

TO COOK THE *AÏGO-SAU*

Cover the fish pieces with boiling water or fish stock and cook over high heat for 20 minutes, or until the fish flakes easily with a fork.

TO SERVE

Place slices of prepared French bread in a soup tureen; sprinkle with olive oil and freshly ground black pepper to taste. Strain the fish bouillon over and serve. Serve the fish pieces and potatoes in a separate dish. Accompany with *rouille* (see page 62).

Le revesset

Provençal fish soup with greens

SERVES 4–6

A sort of 'green bouillabaisse'. In Toulon they often use fresh sardines for this attractive dish. This more sophisticated version uses a choice of monkfish, red mullet, whiting, John Dory and conger eel.

FOR THE BOUILLON

2½ cups Swiss chard, chopped	crushed red pepper flakes (or ½ tsp dried thyme)
2½ cups fresh spinach leaves, chopped	2 lb fish (see above)
6–12 sorrel leaves, chopped	6 slices day-old French bread
4 tbsps butter	garlic
juice of ½ lemon	olive oil
salt and ground black pepper	

FOR THE VEGETABLES

Wash the Swiss chard and cut the white stems away from the green leaves. Wash the spinach leaves, removing any damaged or yellowed leaves. Cut off coarse stems and discard. Wash and prepare the sorrel leaves in the same manner.

Combine the green leaves of Swiss chard, spinach and sorrel and chop into 1-inch segments.

Cut the white parts of the Swiss chard into 2-inch segments, then cut the segments lengthwise into thin strips.

FOR THE FISH BOUILLON

In a large heat-proof casserole or saucepan melt the butter; add the lemon juice and the white strips of Swiss chard and simmer over low heat, stirring until tender. Add the chopped greens and continue to cook until the vegetables have wilted. Season with salt and freshly ground black pepper, and crushed red pepper flakes (or dried thyme) to taste.

Add 5 cups water and bring to a boil. Add the pieces of fish, the firmest first, and then the others 5 minutes later so that they are all tender at the same time. The fish should be cooked for 15–20 minutes in all.

In the meantime, prepare the garlic croûtons by rubbing the bread slices with a cut clove of garlic; drizzle with a little olive oil and bake until golden in a pre-heated oven (325°F).

TO SERVE

Place the prepared bread slices in a heated soup

tureen or individual heated soup plates. With a slotted spoon or spatula transfer the fish to a heated serving dish. Keep warm.

Pour the hot bouillon over the bread and arrange the coarsely chopped greens around it.

Serve the fish separately.

Grilling fish

Freshly caught fish from the gulf of Pampelonne, just a stone's throw across the sands from the open-air barbecues where they are cooked, is one of the great delights of St Tropez in the summer. Some of the little restaurants along the beach are beginning to do barbecued fish and lobster at lunch and can be tempted to carry this on to late-night suppers under the stars. Everything here is of optimum freshness. The vegetables – and even the wines served at one or two of these restaurants – come from the farms and vineyards located in the flatlands just behind the beach. A recent meal I enjoyed there began with *salade niçoise*: tiny whole artichokes sliced with celery, onions, radishes, small green peppers, tomatoes, cucumber and lettuce and garnished with black olives, quarters of hard-boiled egg, tuna fish and anchovies, dressed with a wine vinegar and olive oil dressing. This was followed by fresh sardines from the gulf, brushed with a sauce of olive oil, lemon juice and fresh herbs, grilled over charcoal and served with a dressing of melted butter, lemon juice and finely chopped tarragon. Melon and black coffee provided the cool finale to a perfect open-air meal.

Let grilled sea bass with herbs (see overleaf) or sardines grilled over the embers (see page 74) provide the focal point for a light Sunday lunch for family and friends. Accompany the fish, if you like, with small new potatoes boiled in their jackets, served with nothing but coarsely ground salt and ground black pepper and lots of fresh butter. Precede the dish with a quickly made *soupe de poissons* (see page 64), a fresh tomato salad dressed only with coarsely ground salt, freshly ground black pepper, finely chopped basil and olive oil or, more exotically, with the spiraled salad of raw *cèpes* (see page 168) which is a speciality of La Bonne Etape in Château Arnoux, one of the finest restaurants and hostelries in the area.

71

Sar piqué à l'ail: a fine fat sar, sea bream or John Dory, armored with garlic, brushed with olive oil and grilled for a few minutes, preferably over an open fire, makes a succulent main course when served with lemon butter sauce with fennel and fresh tarragon.

Loup de mer grillé aux herbes

Grilled sea bass with herbs

SERVES 4–6

2 sea bass
2–3 tbsps all purpose
flour
2–3 tbsps olive oil
salt and black pepper

3–4 sprigs each fennel,
parsley and thyme
lemon butter with fresh
basil

Flour the cleaned fish lightly; brush them with olive oil, and season to taste with salt and freshly ground black pepper. Stuff the cavities of the fish with herbs and grill for 3–5 minutes on each side, or until the fish flakes easily with a fork, basting it with olive oil from time to time. Serve the fish with hot melted butter flavored with a little lemon juice and fresh basil.

Sar, daurade ou Saint-Pierre piqué à l'ail

Sar, sea bream or John Dory armored with garlic

SERVES 4

Overcooking fish fresh from the sea is considered a crime in Provence. For best results it is either grilled, pan-grilled or baked in the oven. And to make a grilled fish absolutely perfect, it is brushed on both sides with olive oil and cooked over a fire of vine stumps or prunings to give the fish extra flavor. One old cook I know goes even further: he brushes the fish on both sides with the coral of a sea urchin. But it was his wife who taught me the neatest trick, and one which I have been using to fine effect ever since. She used to prick the fish (a fine fat sea bream or sar, or even a John Dory) all over on both sides with the

the fish well inside and out and pat it dry with a clean towel. Rub the insides of the fish with salt and freshly ground black pepper.

With a sharp pointed metal skewer, prick small holes down both sides of the fish in regularly spaced lines. Press one thin garlic strip into each hole, allowing the tops of the garlic strips to stick up about $\frac{1}{4}$ inch from the surface of the fish. Brush the fish lightly on both sides with olive oil; season with salt and freshly ground black pepper and grill over an open fire for 4–6 minutes on each side, or until the tips of the garlic strips are charred and the flesh of the fish flakes easily with a fork. The fish may be grilled indoors under a gas or electric broiler, but I am afraid the results will not be quite the same.

TO SERVE

Place the fish, charred garlic bits and all, on a heated serving platter and serve with hot lemon butter sauce.

TO MAKE THE LEMON BUTTER SAUCE

In a small saucepan, combine the butter and fennel seeds and, over a medium heat, melt the butter completely. Then stir in the lemon juice and fresh tarragon leaves and season with salt and freshly ground black pepper to taste.

point of a metal skewer. Then into each tiny hole she would insert a thin sliver of garlic before grilling the fish over the open fire. The essence of the trick was that the outsides of the garlic sticks would char and carry the intense flavor of the burned garlic down into the moist, tender flesh of the fish.

1 fresh sar, sea bream or John Dory	3–5 cloves garlic, cut into thin strips
salt and ground black pepper	extra-virgin olive oil

FOR THE LEMON BUTTER SAUCE WITH FENNEL SEEDS AND FRESH TARRAGON

$\frac{1}{2}$ cup butter	juice of $\frac{1}{2}$ lemon
3–4 fennel seeds	salt and ground black pepper
1–2 tbsps fresh tarragon leaves	

Ask the fishmonger to clean and gut the fish. Wash

Les sardines frites en 5 minutes

Quick-fried sardines

SERVES 4

12–16 fresh sardines	coarse salt
sifted all-purpose flour	lemon wedges, to garnish
olive oil	

Wash and clean the sardines; remove the scales by rubbing the fish with your fingers under running cold water, one by one. Drain and dry. Dredge with sifted flour.

Pour the olive oil into a large skillet to a depth of 2 inches. Heat the olive oil. Add the sardines and fry until they are crisp and golden brown, about 5 minutes.

Remove the sardines from the pan with a slotted spoon and transfer them to paper towels to drain off excess oil. Season generously with coarse salt and arrange on a heated serving dish. Garnish with wedges of fresh lemon and serve immediately.

73

Les sardines grillées sur les braises

Sardines grilled over the embers

SERVES 4

12–16 fresh sardines	**coarse salt**
olive oil	**crushed red pepper flakes**

Wash and clean the sardines. Dry them, then brush them with olive oil and season with coarse salt and crushed red pepper flakes.

Grill the sardines over low heat for 2–3 minutes on each side. Serve immediately accompanied by *sauce anchoïade* (see page 37).

Les sardines au vinaigre et à l'ail

Sardines with vinegar and garlic

SERVES 4

12–16 fresh sardines	**4 tbsps red wine vinegar**
4 tbsps olive oil	**coarse salt and ground**
2–4 cloves garlic, thinly	** black pepper**
** sliced**	**lemon wedges to garnish**
1 bay leaf	

Wash and clean the sardines. Remove the scales by rubbing the fish with your fingers under cold running water, one by one. Drain and dry.

Heat the olive oil in a large thick-bottomed skillet; add the sardines and fry over a medium heat for 2–3

minutes, or until golden brown. Add the thinly sliced garlic and bay leaf to the pan and, using a spatula or a slotted spoon, turn over the sardines.

Let the sardines fry for 2–3 minutes more, or until golden brown on the other side. Pour in the vinegar and season the fish generously with coarse salt and freshly ground black pepper to taste.

Remove the fish to a heated serving dish and continue to cook the pan juices, stirring, until the vinegar has evaporated completely.

To serve, pour the pan juices over the fish and serve immediately, accompanied by wedges of fresh lemon.

Les sardines à la niçoise

SERVES 6

24 fresh sardines	**2 ribs celery, chopped**
1½ lb mussels	**2 eggs, beaten**
1 lb Swiss chard	**butter**
olive oil	**4 slices white bread,**
1 clove garlic	** crusts removed, made**
salt and ground black	** into breadcrumbs**
** pepper**	**lemon wedges to garnish**

TO PREPARE THE SARDINES

Remove the heads and tails from the sardines. Clean and open them. Press them out flat.

TO CLEAN THE MUSSELS

Discard any that are opened or have shells that are cracked or broken. Then scrape the shells with a small kitchen knife, removing any barnacles or seaweed that might be clinging to them. Place the mussels in a plastic bucket or dishpan and wash them under running water, scraping them together with your hands to clean shells thoroughly. Wash until the water clears. With a small sharp kitchen knife, remove the beard from each mussel.

TO PREPARE THE MUSSEL AND SWISS CHARD STUFFING

Remove the tough white stalks from the Swiss chard (saving them to use cut into thin finger strips and braised in equal quantities of butter and water as a vegetable at another meal). Cut the Swiss chard crosswise into thin slivers.

Cook the Swiss chard in 2 tablespoons olive oil with the whole garlic clove and a little salt and freshly ground black pepper, until the liquid produced by the Swiss chard has evaporated. Transfer to a medium-sized bowl.

Combine the mussels with the chopped celery in a heat-proof casserole. Add 1 glass of water; cover the casserole and steam the mussels until the shells open, 3–5 minutes. Remove the mussels from the liquid in the pan with a slotted spoon, discarding any that have not opened. Remove the shells, being careful not to tear the mussels.

Chop the mussels coarsely and add them to the prepared Swiss chard. Strain the mussel liquid through a muslin-lined sieve into a clean jar. Allow any remaining impurities to sink to the bottom of the jar.

Add the beaten eggs and decanted mussel liquor to the Swiss chard and mussel mixture and season with a very little salt and a generous amount of freshly ground black pepper. Mix well.

TO ASSEMBLE THE DISH

Spread the flattened sardines with some of this mixture. Re-form the sardines.

Spread a layer of the remaining mixture on the bottom of a buttered heat-proof gratin dish and top with the stuffed sardines. Sprinkle with fresh bread-crumbs and a little olive oil. Bake in a pre-heated hot oven (425°F) for 5–10 minutes. Serve immediately with wedges of lemon.

Les sardines en beignets

Sardine fritters

SERVES 4

8–12 fresh sardines

FOR THE BATTER

2 eggs, well beaten	**pinch of salt**
1 cup all-purpose flour, sifted	**oil for frying**
½ – ⅔ cup warm water, beer or milk	

FOR THE GARNISH

lemon wedges	**sprigs of watercress**

Clean and scale the sardines. Open each fish from the stomach with the point of a sharp knife and remove the backbone and head.

In a medium-sized bowl, combine the beaten eggs, flour and water (or beer or milk) and beat until well mixed. Season with salt to taste.

Holding the fish by the tails, dip them in the light batter and deep-fry until golden brown. Drain off excess oil on paper towels. Serve immediately accompanied by lemon wedges and garnished with sprigs of fresh watercress.

Les farcies aux épinards

Spinach-stuffed sardines

SERVES 4

8–12 fresh sardines	**olive oil**
butter	

FOR THE SPINACH PURÉE

2 lb 4 oz young spinach leaves	**1 clove garlic, finely chopped**
2 tbsps butter	**freshly grated nutmeg**
2 tbsps olive oil	**salt and ground black pepper**
1 bay leaf	

Clean and scale the sardines. Open each fish from the stomach with the point of a sharp knife, and remove the backbone and head.

TO MAKE THE SPINACH PURÉE

Wash the young spinach leaves well and drain. Place them in a large saucepan with only the water adhering to the leaves and 2 tablespoons butter. Cook over high heat until the spinach wilts. Process the spinach leaves in a food processor (or vegetable mill), then sauté the purée in 2 tablespoons olive oil with the bay leaf, finely chopped garlic and freshly grated nutmeg, salt and freshly ground black pepper, to taste.

Spread half the aromatic spinach purée over the bottom of a well-buttered gratin dish; then divide the remainder between the sardines, spreading each fish generously. Roll up each fish, starting with the head end. Then lay the spinach-stuffed fish side by side on the bed of spinach, tails on top. Brush the fish with olive oil and bake in a 375°F oven for 10 minutes or until the fish are cooked.

Les sardines en beignets.

75

Suprêmes de rouget à la niçoise

Supreme of red mullet niçoise

SERVES 4

4 fresh red mullet or red snapper fillets	1¼ cups heavy cream
butter	4 tomatoes, peeled, seeded and diced
salt and cayenne pepper	saffron
dry white wine	
well-flavored fish stock	
white of 1 leek, cut in strips	

Pre-heat the oven to 350°F. Put the fillets of red mullet or red snapper in a well-buttered oven-proof dish; add salt and a pinch of cayenne; add equal parts of dry white wine and fish stock to just cover the fish, and bake in the pre-heated oven for 10–15 minutes, or until it flakes with a fork but is still moist.

Transfer the fish to a heated serving dish and keep warm in several spoonfuls of the pan juices.

TO MAKE THE SAUCE

Over high heat, reduce the remaining liquid in the pan to half its original quantity with a fine julienne of white of leek cooked in 2 tablespoons butter. Add the cream and continue to simmer over very low heat.

In the meantime, in a small saucepan melt 2 tablespoons butter; add the peeled, seeded and diced tomatoes and cook, stirring constantly, until reduced to a smooth purée. Add the cream and stock mixture to the tomatoes and continue to cook over medium heat, stirring, until the mixture forms a smooth creamy emulsion just thick enough to coat the back of a spoon. Stir in 2 tablespoons butter mixed with a pinch of saffron; heat well; mask the fish with the sauce and serve immediately.

Rouget en papillote, Baumanière

Red mullet en papillote, Baumanière

SERVES 4

4 small red mullet or red snapper fillets	4 bay leaves
olive oil	4 thin slices broiled bacon
salt and ground black pepper	4 slices lemon
	4 anchovy fillets
FOR THE SAUCE	
4–5 egg whites	salt and ground black pepper
1¼ cups heavy cream	
4–5 anchovy fillets, mashed	fat or olive oil for deep-frying
freshly grated nutmeg	

Leave the red mullet whole (do not gut them) and sprinkle fish (or fillets) with olive oil; season to taste with salt and freshly ground black pepper; place 1 bay leaf on one side of each fish (or fillet) and a thin slice of broiled bacon on the other side.

Cut 4 pieces of parchment paper approximately 8½ × 11 inches; fold each in half and cut in a heart shape. Open, brush with oil, and place the prepared fish with bay leaf and bacon on one half. Fold the parchment shape over and seal the edges well by crimping them together. Repeat with the other 3 fish. Sauté the *papillotes* in deep fat or olive oil for 15–18 minutes.

Arrange the *papillotes* on a dish; open each one carefully and decorate the mullet or snapper with lemon and anchovy. Serve with the following sauce:

TO PREPARE THE SAUCE

Beat the egg whites until they are stiff and whip the cream. Combine the two and add the mashed anchovy fillets. Season to taste with salt, freshly ground black pepper and grated nutmeg. Cook over boiling water, skimming constantly, until heated through. Strain and serve hot.

Loup de mer ou daurade en papillote

Sea bass or sea bream en papillote

SERVES 4

4 whole sea bass or striped bass (12 oz each), or 1 sea bream (2 lb 4 oz–3 lb)
4 tbsps extra-virgin olive oil
6 tbsps melted butter
2 large fresh tomatoes, peeled, seeded and diced
16–20 small black olives, pitted and coarsely chopped
12 fat cloves garlic, blanched and sautéed
dried *herbes de Provence*
salt and ground black pepper

Pre-heat the oven to moderate (350°F). Clean and wash the fish thoroughly; pat them dry and brush with olive oil.

Fold 4 pieces of parchment paper in half; then cut each folded piece into an oval large enough to accommodate the fish comfortably. Open up the ovals and brush the inside of each *papillote* with melted butter. Place one fish in the center of each oval.

Scatter the diced tomatoes and chopped olives over each fish. Add the garlic cloves which you have blanched and sautéed in olive oil (3 to each serving; see below). Then drizzle any remaining olive oil or melted butter over the fish. Season generously with dried *herbes de Provence*, salt and freshly ground black pepper.

Carefully fold the top of the parchment oval over the fish and crimp around the edges to seal the fish and aromatics in securely.

Place the parchment parcels on a baking sheet and bake for 15 minutes in the pre-heated oven. Cut open each parcel and serve the fish and aromatics in its opened parcel.

TO PREPARE THE GARLIC CLOVES

Blanch the garlic in two changes of boiling water. Drain, then sauté in olive oil until it begins to change color. Remove from the heat and use as directed above.

Saint-Pierre à la feuille de figue à la moelle, Le Provençal

—

Pan-roasted John Dory with beef marrow in a fig leaf

SERVES 4

—

Saint-Pierre à la feuille de figue à la moelle, Le Provençal.

For this elegant recipe you will need four fresh figs, four fig leaves and a small marrow bone or two. Fillets of sea bass, red mullet or even salmon can be substituted for the John Dory if desired. On one occasion, when no fig leaves were available, I substituted dried lotus leaves (available in Chinese supermarkets and oriental stores) to fine effect. Failing either of these, squares of aluminum foil can be used, but in this case it is necessary to add a pinch or two of dried *herbes de Provence* to each fish to supplement its flavor.

4 fillets of John Dory, 4–5 oz each	coarse salt and ground black pepper
4 ripe purple figs	4 fresh fig leaves
4 thin strips of orange peel (formed into spirals held in shape with a cocktail stick)	4–8 thin rounds of fresh beef marrow ($\frac{1}{3}$–$\frac{2}{3}$ inch diameter)
extra-virgin olive oil	lemon juice

Pre-heat the oven to very hot, 475°F.

With a sharp knife, cut each fig into a four-petalled flower shape. Then place the open fig flowers and orange-peel spirals on a baking sheet; brush them with the olive oil and roast them in the pre-heated oven for 10 minutes. Season the figs with coarse salt and freshly ground black pepper. In the meantime, brush the fig leaves on both sides with olive oil. Reserve.

TO PREPARE THE FISH FILLETS

Brush a non-stick skillet with olive oil and heat over high heat until the oil sizzles; add the fish fillets, skin side down, and sauté for 2 minutes. Season with coarse salt and freshly ground black pepper.

Place each fish fillet on a prepared fig leaf; place 1 or 2 thin rounds of beef marrow on each fillet; top with curled strips of orange peel and fold the leaf over to form a *papillote* fastening it with a cocktail stick. Cook in the oven for 3–5 minutes, or until the fish flakes easily with a fork.

TO SERVE

Remove the cocktail sticks from the fig leaves. Transfer each fish fillet (in its fig leaf) to a heated plate. Place a roasted fig on the side of the dish; pour the pan juices over the fish fillet and fig; season with coarse salt and freshly ground black pepper, add a squeeze of lemon juice and serve immediately.

Loup au four en croûte d'anis étoile, Le Provençal

Baked sea bass crisped with Chinese star anise

SERVES 4

8 small sea bass fillets, 4–5 oz each, or 4 small sea bass	coarse salt and cracked black pepper
extra-virgin olive oil	dried fennel stalks
4 star anise, ground	lemon juice

Pre-heat the oven to 475°F.

If using whole fish, scale, clean and fillet the fish, removing all bones. If using prepared fish fillets, make sure all bones are removed.

Brown the fillets, skin side down, in a large sizzling-hot non-stick pan (or 2 pans) until the skins are brown and crisp, about 2 minutes. Season to taste with salt, cracked pepper and ground star anise.

Place the fillets of sea bass (skin side down again) in a large skillet, lightly brushed with olive oil. Arrange the dried fennel stalks on each fillet and cover with another fillet (skin side up); brush with olive oil and place in the pre-heated oven for 3–4 minutes. Remove the skin and arrange it to give an impression of movement; return the skin to the oven for a minute to 'fix' the shape, then replace it on the fish; add a squeeze of lemon juice and place the sandwiched fillets on a heated plate. Spoon over the pan juices and serve with *ratatouille minute*.

Ratatouille minute

'Instant' ratatouille

SERVES 4

8 cloves garlic	1 large tomato
extra-virgin olive oil	coarse salt and cracked black pepper
½ green pepper	8 small lettuce leaves (from the heart)
½ red pepper	
½ yellow pepper	8 fresh basil leaves
1 small eggplant	lemon juice
1 zucchini	

Place the garlic cloves on a piece of aluminum foil; brush the foil with olive oil, crimp it around the edges to make a sealed packet and bake in a pre-heated oven for 10 minutes.

Cut the tops and bottoms off the pepper halves and cut each one into 15–20 thin matchsticks. Save the tops and bottoms to use finely diced as a garnish for a salad dressing. Cut segments of eggplant and zucchini the same length as the pepper sticks, then cut each segment into thin strips. Cut the top and bottom off the tomato; cut the central segment into thin slices and then cut each slice into thin strips.

Season the prepared vegetable strips with coarse salt and cracked pepper and fry in very hot oil for 5–6 minutes. Drain.

TO SERVE

Fold the small lettuce leaves and basil leaves into the fried vegetable sticks; add a squeeze of lemon juice and serve immediately.

RIGHT *Cèpes (porcini)* and sinister-looking but delicious *trompettes de la mort* are among the wild mushrooms to be found in the market in season.

OPPOSITE *Loup au four en croûte d'anis étoile*, garnished with wild mushrooms.

FEAST

Jean-Jacques Jouteux

Le Provençal,
St Jean-Cap-Ferrat

There is new life in the little port of St Jean-Cap-Ferrat, sheltering in the lee of prestigious Cap Ferrat with its great houses, its grand hotel and its botanical gardens. Jean-Jacques Jouteux, the volatile young chef from Normandy, has joined the coterie of famous French chefs who now make the French Riviera their home – Roger Vergé (Le Moulin de Mougins), Jacques Maximin (Le Diamant Rose, La Colle-sur-Loup), Guy Cibois (Gray Albion, Cannes), Alain

Ducasse (Restaurant Louis xv, Hôtel de Paris, Monte Carlo) and Dominique le Stanc (Le Chantecler, Hôtel Negresco, Nice). Jean-Jacques Jouteux's restaurant, Le Provençal, on the front overlooking the little harbor of St Jean-Cap-Ferrat, is a runaway success. In two years of operation, the casual but beautifully decorated restaurant has become a favorite eating place of the most knowledgeable and sophisticated clientele on the coast.

The main draw is the showy but sensitive cooking of the young chef, one of the unsung heroes of the new Provence: innovative in his creations, much moved by the quality of the natural products of the region, he is drunk with the sun and the freedom of the coast, and profoundly impressed by the civilization of the south and its peoples.

Cooking *chez* Jouteux is 'minimalist' in presentation, but with the maximum of robust and earthy flavor. Fish he cooks for what seems like seconds with a little extra-virgin olive oil or a little butter before finishing it off in the oven (for a matter of minutes more) in a delicate acidulated sauce strengthened by the pressed essence of black olives, truffles from the hinterlands, or the juices running from a cut fig topped by a small round of fresh beef marrow, the red 'blood' of the fig tempered by the rich moistness of the melted marrow.

On his menu there are no meats, or hardly any, but instead a clear-cut preference for the fish and shellfish that come from his bay. He refuses to change his style of cooking to please a greater number of patrons. 'I won't be cataloged as a restaurant *à la mode*,' he says. 'My cooking is not influenced by fashion. It is real.'

The success and elegance of his cooking lies in the novel and unexpected flavor combinations that we find in his quickly prepared dishes: his *pigeon au four, pâte plate, goût cannelle* is flavored with cinnamon and juniper berries, or star anise, according to the whim of the moment, and garnished with a crumpled thin sheet of pastry similar to the *warkha* paste used for Moroccan *bstilla* or *trid*. Tossed in the pan juices and arranged decoratively on the plate, it is a triumph of execution and flavor. As is his *grillé d'artichaut violet en coque demi-homard*, which presents a Provençal violet-tipped artichoke, flattened under a weight until it looks like a green-and-violet-hued sunflower, cooked *à point*, topped with a curled round of half lobster and served with an acidulated butter sauce (the leitmotif of the house) in which bitter-flavored leaves of wild salad have been wilted.

Méli-mélo d'anchois à la tarte fine de pommes de terre presents tiny fresh anchovies with their heads peeking out from under the thinnest of *galettes* of golden fried potato slices (a sort of French star-gazey pie), its sauce a mere nothing made of olive oil subtly flavored with pressed olive juice and lemon.

At Le Provençal, dessert is a never-ending farandole of tiny tastes, not – as in so many of today's great restaurants – a *fourre-tout* of different sweets on one large platter, but a series of small dishes that arrive one after the other in a dazzling array of tastes and textures, some hot, some cold, all delicious. And all prepared by René Salmon, the long-time friend and partner of Jean-Jacques Jouteux.

heat, being careful not to let them burn and re-forming the potato 'flowers' as you turn them if necessary. When cooked through, remove from the heat and keep warm.

TO PREPARE THE ANCHOVIES

Pre-heat the oven to fairly hot (400°F). Remove 2 fillets from each fresh anchovy; trim them and cut each diagonally across the middle to prevent curling up during cooking.

Arrange the anchovy fillets (or finger strips of red mullet or red snapper if fresh anchovies are not available) in a star shape on individual heat-proof dishes. Add 1 tablespoon olive oil to each dish and cook in the pre-heated oven for 2–3 minutes.

Remove the dishes from the oven; sprinkle each with a little lemon juice, a little olive juice and coarse salt and pepper to taste. Arrange a potato 'tart' on each serving of anchovies. Serve immediately.

Méli-mélo d'anchois à la tarte fine de pommes de terre

Anchovies under a thin potato 'tart'

SERVES 4

4 potatoes
12 fresh anchovies (or 24 finger strips cut from fillets of red mullet or red snapper)
4 tbsps olive oil
2 tsps lemon juice

2 tsps olive juice (made by squeezing the flesh of 1 ripe olive in garlic press into 2 tsps olive oil)
coarse salt and cracked black pepper

TO PREPARE THE POTATO TARTS

Peel the potatoes; from each potato cut 5 or 6 equal-sized, very thin slices. As thin as possible. Keep unused slices and trimmings for use in stock or soup.

In a non-stick pan, arrange the potato slices in overlapping concentric circles, like the petals of a flower. Cook the potatoes on both sides over medium

Méli-mélo d'anchois à la tarte fine de pommes de terre.

Grillé d'artichaut violet en coque demi-homard

Griddled artichoke 'stars' with half lobsters

SERVES 4

FOR THE ARTICHOKES

4 small Provençal violet-tipped artichokes

2 small lobsters

juice of 2 lemons

4 tbsps extra-virgin olive oil

coarse salt and coarsely ground black pepper

FOR THE LOBSTER JUICES

juices from lobsters and heads, upper carcasses and trimmings

1 tbsp olive oil

1 tsp finely chopped onion

½ can tomato paste

FOR THE *BEURRE NOISETTE*

4 tbsps butter

few drops lemon juice

This recipe as served at Le Provençal is only possible if you are able to procure tender young artichokes. Otherwise, it works quite well if you use large blanched Breton artichoke hearts as the base for the half-lobster curls.

TO PREPARE THE ARTICHOKES (OR ARTICHOKE HEARTS)

If using small young artichokes, remove the choke from the center of each artichoke, using a sharp-edged teaspoon or a small sharp kitchen knife. Flatten each artichoke (or heart) out by pressing it down on your working surface with the flat of your hand, or by tapping it lightly with a wooden kitchen mallet. Place the flattened artichokes on a baking sheet – open side up – so that the pointed leaves look like stars.

Brown the artichoke stars (or hearts) in a little olive oil for 2–3 minutes over medium heat. Then add the lobster juices (see directions below) and the juice of 2 lemons and continue to cook for 6 minutes more. Turn the artichokes stem side up and finish cooking for 2 more minutes. Remove the artichoke hearts from the pan juices with a slotted spoon. Drain.

TO PREPARE THE LOBSTER JUICES

Over a large bowl (to catch the juices), sever the lobster tails from the upper body. Cut off the claws, and reserve the tails and claws for later use. Chop the heads and upper bodies of the lobsters.

In a medium-sized saucepan, combine the chopped heads, legs and upper carcasses of the lobsters with 1 tablespoon olive oil and 1 teaspoon finely chopped onion and sauté, stirring, for 2–3 minutes. Add the tomato paste and water and continue to cook for 10 minutes. Remove from the heat; strain and reserve the juices.

TO COOK THE LOBSTER TAILS AND CLAWS

Cook the tails and claws in boiling salted water for 9–10 minutes. Cut the lobster tails in half lengthwise and remove the shells.

To serve, arrange 1 half lobster in a curl on each artichoke star (or heart). Garnish with a lobster claw, pour over 1–2 tablespoons each of the pan juices from the cooked artichokes and the lobster juices, and top each with a tablespoon of *beurre noisette*.

TO MAKE THE *BEURRE NOISETTE*

Melt the butter gently with lemon juice until it begins to turn a light golden brown, about 3 minutes.

Grillé d'artichaut violet en coque demi-homard.

Pigeon (ou perdreau) au four, pâte plate, goût cannelle

Arab-inspired young pigeon (or partridge) with flat pastry

SERVES 4

The Arab-inspired pasta, homemade and cinnamon-flavored, and its subtly perfumed sauce make this a fascinating dish. The soft-textured pastry takes time and patience to achieve: commercially prepared flat pasta is a possible substitute, though the result is neither so tender nor so excitingly flavored. The pigeons are also delicious served cold, glazed with their fragrant reduced sauce and accompanied by a salad of rice or couscous, garnished with diced black olives, red and yellow peppers, and a sprinkling of chopped fresh herbs and pine nuts.

4 young pigeons (9–11 oz each) or 1 partridge
extra-virgin olive oil
salt and ground black pepper
ground cinnamon

FOR THE PIGEON (OR PARTRIDGE) *FUMET*

Pigeon (or partridge) trimmings: neck, liver, heart,
  gizzard, skin, heads and feet, if available
2–4 tbsps olive oil
4 tbsps finely chopped shallots
2½ cups well-flavored chicken stock
salt and ground black pepper
½ tsp ground cinnamon
8 juniper berries

FOR THE *PÂTE PLATE*

2 cups all-purpose flour	**salt and ground black**
2 eggs	**pepper**
2 tsps olive oil	**½ tsp ground cinnamon**

FOR THE *BEURRE NOISETTE*

2–4 tbsps butter

TO PREPARE THE PIGEONS (OR PARTRIDGE)

Clean, trim and tie the birds. Brush them with a little extra-virgin olive oil and season generously with coarse salt, freshly ground black pepper and ground cinnamon. Reserve.

TO PREPARE THE *FUMET*

In a medium-sized saucepan, combine the olive oil, pigeon (or partridge) trimmings and chopped shallots, and sauté until lightly browned. Add the chicken stock and seasonings and simmer, uncovered, for about 20 minutes, or until the *fumet* has reduced to about one third of its original quantity. Remove from the heat and reserve.

TO MAKE THE *PÂTE PLATE*

Sift the flour into a large mixing bowl and make a well in the center. Put the eggs, oil, salt, pepper and cinnamon into the well and mix together with your fingertips, gradually drawing the flour into the egg mixture and kneading it together, adding a little water from time to time if the dough seems dry. Dust the work surface with sifted flour; remove the dough from the bowl and knead the dough firmly until smooth and elastic, about 10–15 minutes. Flour your hands and the work surface from time to time. Wrap the dough in wrap and set aside for about 1 hour. Clean the surface thoroughly for the next operation.

Divide the dough into 4 pieces. Using a rolling pin,

Pigeon au four, pâte plate, goût cannelle (above) is a triumph of execution and flavor. Follow it with refreshing *melon glacé* (right).

roll out the dough, one piece at a time, on a lightly floured surface. Roll it first in one direction, stretching as you go; sprinkle with flour to stop the dough sticking to the rolling pin; then turn and repeat. Continue these two processes (rolling and turning the dough) until it is paper-thin.

Sprinkle the dough lightly with flour and leave it to rest for 10–15 minutes to allow it to dry slightly, otherwise it will disintegrate when it comes to be cooked. Cut 4 even-sized circles or squares, approximately 7 inches in diameter. Reserve.

TO COOK THE PIGEONS (OR PARTRIDGE)
Pre-heat the oven to very hot (475°F) and cook the pigeons (or partridge) in the pre-heated oven for 15 minutes for quite rare, or 5 minutes more for a little more done.

In the meantime, blanch the *pâte plate* in boiling salted water. Drain immediately and 'seize' the pastry in a little *beurre noisette* (made by melting the butter gently over a very low heat until it begins to turn a light golden color, about 3 minutes), pushing it to the side of the pan and lifting it in the middle with a fork to give it a drapelike shape while still in the pan.

Skim the fat from the pan juices; add the *fumet* and cook over high heat until hot. Turn the heat to low to keep warm.

To serve, cut each pigeon into quarters; slice the breasts and arrange the birds on 4 heated dinner plates. Or cut the partridge into quarters and arrange a quarter on each plate. Garnish each dish with a portion of *pâte plate* and spoon 2–3 tablespoons of *fumet* over each serving. Serve immediately.

Melon glacé
Chilled melon flower
SERVES 4

2 small cantaloupe or	few drops of balsamic
Charentais melons,	vinegar
chilled	few drops of lemon juice
juices from melons	

Cut the chilled melons in half and scoop out the seeds. Over a bowl (to catch the juices), peel the melon halves, leaving a little rim of pale green around each half. Reserve the juices.

Using a rotary meat slicer, cut the peeled melon halves into the thinnest possible slices. If you do not have a rotary slicer, use the slicing attachment on a food processor, but this does not produce such perfect slices; or, with more difficulty, a vegetable peeler; or failing all this, your sharpest kitchen knife.

TO FORM THE MELON 'FLOWER'
Wrap the thin melon slices, slice by slice, around one of your thumbs; slip off the ring of melon slice carefully and arrange like an open flower on a chilled dessert plate. Repeat. Moisten each 'flower' with a little melon juice and a few drops each of balsamic vinegar and lemon juice.

4 Herbs and

VEGETABLE SOUPS, FIRST-COURSE SALADS AND ACCOMPANIMENTS

'Provence begins at the gap of Donzères just south of Montélimar. Otherwise its frontiers are vague for it is generally held to include Nîmes to the west with Aigues-Mortes and Lunel and even Montpellier, while to the east, it runs beyond Aix as far as Draguignan and Fréjus.' So wrote Cyril Connolly in *The Evening Colonnade* (1973). This was my literary introduction to Provence, discovered when I was already living in the little coastal town of St Tropez.

Connolly's writings colored all my feelings about the area, as did those of Colette. It was these two writers, one English and one French, who taught me that Provence, more than a geographical entity, was in fact a state of mind. For me Provence and its *arrière-pays*, or hinterland, extend even further than Connolly's widespread boundaries: I include the Maures and Esterel massifs as far as Menton. Pompey, after all, went as far as La Turbie, behind Monte Carlo. This area of hinterland and hills roughly corresponds to the northerly limits of the olive, that most Provençal of all fruits which needs the hot sun of the Mediterranean region to thrive, but copes hardily with the Mistral and the sudden frosts of the Provençal winter.

The spread throughout the region of a local fondness for *pissalat*, *pistou*, polenta, *pâtes* and ravioli,

all specialities either handed down from the Ligurians, the original inhabitants of the region whose

the Hills

influence spread from the Pyrenees to the Genoese coast of Tuscany, or adapted from the neighboring Comtat of Nice (a fiefdom of Piedmont for over 500 years) bears me out. Even though I did have a heated argument one night after a five-course dinner at Chez Maximin in Nice, when that Calais-born 'Provençal', Jacques Maximin, invited my guests and myself to the bar for a last-minute drink before closing.

Incensed by my theory that Provence – like the Provincia Romana of the ancient Romans from which Provence gets its name – extended from Sète to the Italian border, including both Nice and Haute Provence, Maximin insisted in no uncertain terms that Provence should be bounded strictly by the contours of the map as drawn today, excluding even Haute Provence and the Var.

All my arguments – and they were lively – were to no avail. But ask Pierre Gleize, genial chef-proprietor of the remarkable hostelry La Bonne Etape at Château Arnoux, just below Sisteron, whether his inn is in Provence or not and you will hear another story. One day I brought up the question again with Pierre and his son Jany. 'Of course, ' they cried almost in unison, 'Haute Provence is part and parcel of Provence!' And they should know for they were both born and brought up there.

Or go to Bruno Clément, whose restaurant Chez Bruno is located on the road from Les Arcs to Lorgues in the flatlands of the upper Var, to ask the same question. Born in the house where he has his restaurant today, and where his family has lived for three generations, Bruno talks of his beloved Provence with an accent that you could cut with a knife, and a vitality that is pure Pagnol. He immediately answers, 'We are in the very heart of Provence, the very center between Basse Provence and Haute Provence. It smells of the *garrigue*, of summer savory, of rosemary, of wild thyme, the very herbs of Provence.' And then with a Gallic shrug of his broad shoulders, 'This is Provence: we have our own dialect, our own history and our own traditions. We even have our own language, recognized as such and taught as a secondary language of choice in all the schools of the region.'

My romantic theories were thus confirmed. For me Provence remains forever a special place, with echoes of ancient Greece and Rome, with the added influence of the invading hordes from the East; with gracious undertones left by the medieval courts which brought culture, poetry and a formalized code of chivalry and love to the whole region. For if the love poems and ballads of the troubadours of Provence descended in a straight line from the courts of ancient Persia, many of these same troubadours came from as far away as the courts of Aragon and Catalonia. And all this romance, this history, this magic is found in Provence today. It is the land of Petrarch and his love, the divine Laura; of Daudet and his indomitable Tartarin of Tarascon; of warm-hearted Pagnol with his tales of Fanny, César and Florette; and of Giono, who opened a window on the whole wonderful world of the hill towns of Provence and its people. It is a special, private world of wood smoke and wild mushrooms, of fresh fish and garlic, of lamb and dried *herbes de Provence* sizzling over open fires. It is bougainvillea and mimosa. It is almond blossom and lavender. It is, quite simply, Provence.

René Jouveau, in his beautifully produced book *La Cuisine provençale de tradition populaire*, reminds us

Peppery wild asparagus from the hills.

that here in the hills behind the coast is another Provençal cuisine: one that does not coincide absolutely with the classic published repertoires of Provençal cooking, which tend to leave aside these simpler preparations that are not really recipes at all, but rather age-old culinary traditions.

Many of the simple recipes of modern Provençal cookery show traces of these ancient influences. It was probably the early Romans who were responsible for the Provençal taste for thick, earthy sauces rich with olive oil: *tapenade* and *anchoïade*, for example (see pages 37 and 35), could come straight out of an ancient Roman kitchen. *Pissalat* is another example: this potent mash of fermented anchovies used to flavor salad dressings, daubes and pasta sauces, the origin of *pissaladière* (the famous Niçois pizzalike open tart of anchovies, onions and black olives), goes back to one of the earliest of the ancient Roman condiments, *garum salarum*, a mixture of sun-dried fermented fish. *Aïoli*, too, even though we now make it with egg yolks and oil, was thickened with mashed potato in the nineteenth century and probably with ground almonds in ancient times.

THE ARAB INFLUENCE

The 300-year domination of the Arabs in Provence (during which they became so intermingled with the local population that the people of Provence turned to them for help when Charles Martel waged war against them in the eighth century) had equally important repercussions on the local cuisine. Martel and his troops routed the Saracens in 730, and to punish the Provençal separatists, sacked the important Provençal cities of Arles, Avignon and Marseilles. But in the beginning of the ninth century the Saracens took back Marseilles and Arles, and they were to dominate the rest of the region once again until 1032, when they were finally expelled.

This long Arab rule left many architectural and culinary traces along the entire coast. While the fortified hill towns boast Moorish castellated towers and fortresses, the use of spices and dried orange peel in daubes of beef and lamb speaks of Moorish Andalusia, as do the chick-pea flour, almonds, cinnamon and saffron to be found in Provençal dishes today. The presence of raisins in the traditional recipe for tiny onions *à la monégasque* hints at Arab influence, and the frequent use of raisins, almonds and pine nuts in dishes of pasta or rice in the Camargue give these dishes an authentic Middle Eastern touch. What else could have inspired nougat but Turkish delight? *Les petits farcis*, one of the mainstays of Provençal cuisine, are another great vegetable dish that owes its heritage to the Arab invasion. And *fressure*, a spicy Provençal ragout of lamb's liver, kidney, heart, lungs and tripe in a sharp, peppery sauce flavored with plenty of spices and herbs, could be straight out of Arab cuisine today.

Provençal vegetable soups

The hinterlands of Provence – that area between the sea and the mountains known as the *arrière-pays* – is a region of farmers who have always worked their own land, growing their own vegetables, tending their own orchards and vineyards, and keeping their own animals. As a result, Provençal cooks have a great respect for the raw materials of their region, and always use them with care in the kitchen.

In this beautiful land with its rolling hillsides covered with olive groves and apple, pear, peach and apricot orchards, almond groves and well-stocked

farmsteads, it is hard to realize that historically Provence was a poor country, where the peasant farmers lived mainly on vegetable soups and vegetables, with the occasional wild rabbit or hare, or a catch of little game birds, as their only luxury.

The vegetables were nearly always served plainly boiled and sprinkled with a little oil and (more recently) lemon juice or grated cheese to give them added flavor, with perhaps a sprinkling of fresh herbs in summer and dried herbs during the long winter months.

In those days, the water in which the previous night's vegetables had been cooked served as the basis for a soup, with the occasional addition of small quantities of meat or poultry and a few diced vegetables from the garden. Often a handful of pasta was added, or rice or potatoes, or sometimes a combination of all three, to give added body to the evening meal.

Soups made with chick-pea water or chestnut water, or even garlic and sage water, are found in country kitchens today, or are translated into glamorous clear consommés complete with saffron or slivers of rose petals in the leading hotels of the region. Bread-based soups like the famous *pappa de legumi* of Genoa or the *panzanilla* of the Italian quarter of Marseilles were popular too. Perhaps they were a legacy of the ancient Ligurians who were the first inhabitants of Provence, long before the ancient Greeks or the early Romans arrived on their shores; or were they part of a culinary tradition brought to the region by the Italian builders, quarriers and potters who came to work in Provence in the nineteenth century?

Pistou, the famous green-tinted soup of dried and fresh beans and diced vegetables, with its delicious flavor-garnish of pounded garlic, fresh basil leaves and olive oil, was a summer favorite. We do not need its classic addition of freshly grated cheese and pine nuts to tell us that it comes from Genoa. So richly flavored, it is so inexpensive, too, when you consider

Consommé à l'ail, à la sauge et à l'oeuf poché.

that everything except the grated cheese comes from the garden or the fields and forests near by.

I can still remember the delicious puréed soup of vegetables served to me at the Auberge de la Source, on the back road from Marseilles, by the Corsican-born father of Olympe Nahmias, famous Paris restaurateur. The soup was made of zucchini, onions, potatoes, squash, pumpkin and tomatoes, simmered in a light bouillon, with each cooked vegetable puréed into the bowl separately through a *mouli-légumes* to produce a bright mosaic of Mediterranean colors and flavors. At the table we each added a swirl of extra-virgin olive oil and a sprinkling of freshly grated cheese.

La soupe à l'ail

Provençal garlic soup

One of the great peasant soups of Provence is *aïgo-boulido* (boiled water), which, at its simplest, is really a healing broth made of boiled garlic cloves and fresh sage leaves served with a sprinkling of freshly grated cheese.

Famous as a restorative because of its garlic and herbal properties, this simple soup is one of the great classics of the Provençal repertoire. It used to be the first food given to infants when they were weaned, and a double-edged traditional saying celebrated its qualities: *L'aïgo-boulido, sauvo la vido; au bout dóu tèms, tuo li gènt* (boiled water saves lives, but in the end it kills people). *Aïgo-boulido* has many guises: chopped Swiss chard and sorrel are sometimes added; a hint of saffron or dried thyme is often recommended; and the steaming-hot bouillon may be poured over slices of day-old or oven-toasted bread – drizzled with a few drops of olive oil and rubbed with a cut clove of garlic – to give more substance and body to the soup. And on gala days one egg for each guest is poached in the bouillon.

So now we have something quite presentable: the soup is made of finely chopped greens, whole garlic cloves and fresh sage leaves; seasoned with saffron, salt, ground pepper and red pepper flakes; and served over a slice of oven-baked, garlic-rubbed *pain de campagne* on which one lightly poached egg is placed.

All this is still a far cry, however, from the amber-tinted *consommé à l'ail, à la sauge et à l'oeuf poché* served by Pierre and Jany Gleize at La Bonne Etape in Haute Provence. Here the saffron-flavored beef bouillon – holding its surprise cargo of strips of tender beef, gently poached egg, curling strands of saffron and thin slivers of red rose petals – is anything but rustic in character.

Consommé à l'ail, à la sauge et à l'oeuf poché

Garlic and sage consommé with poached egg

SERVES 4

3–4 cups well-flavored chicken (or beef) consommé (or a clear consommé from bouillon made from a clear *pot-au-feu*)	12 fat cloves garlic 12 fresh sage leaves 1 good pinch saffron stamens salt and ground black pepper

FOR THE GARNISH

4 eggs, freshly poached 16 finger strips of raw beef fillet, ¼ inch wide × 2 inches long	4 red rose petals, cut into hair-thin strips 1 carrot, cut into hair-thin strips

TO PREPARE THE GARLIC AND SAGE BOUILLON

Cook the peeled garlic cloves in 1¾ cups lightly salted water for 10–15 minutes, or until the garlic is tender. Remove the garlic from pan and reserve it for later use. Remove the pan from the heat; add the sage leaves and allow to infuse for 15 minutes.

Strain the garlic- and sage-flavored liquid into the well-flavored consommé of chicken (or beef). Add the saffron stamens; correct the seasoning, adding a little salt and freshly ground black pepper if necessary. Bring to a boil.

TO SERVE

Place 1 freshly poached egg in each heated shallow soup bowl; arrange 4 'strips' of raw beef (the boiling-hot bouillon will cook them) and 3 poached garlic cloves around each egg. Scatter with a fine julienne (hair-thin strips) of rose petals and carrots and gently spoon the boiling-hot bouillon into each bowl, being careful not to disturb the garnish.

At La Bonne Etape the garnished soup bowls are brought to the table where the boiling-hot saffron, garlic and sage-flavored bouillon is carefully spooned over.

La soupe d'épeautre, La Bonne Etape

SERVES 6

This is one of those wonderful highly flavored country-bred soups of old Provence, as served today by Pierre and Jany Gleize.

Epeautre is a kind of wild wheat with a small dark grain, much used in country recipes in the old days; cracked wheat or barley make acceptably rustic substitutes.

Pieces of wild duck and fat slices of country sausage were added on feast days. At other times, a shoulder of lamb or half a leg was used. And sometimes the *épeautre* and vegetables were passed through a fine sieve to produce a slightly thickened meaty broth with a delicious flavor.

1¼ cups *épeautre* (use cracked wheat or barley)	1¾ cups well-flavored duck stock
¼ cup chick-peas	1 *murçon* sausage (cooked French garlic sausage)
½ cup pumpkin flesh (or rutabaga or turnip)	salt and ground black pepper
1 medium-sized carrot	6 wild duck thighs
2 ribs celery, sliced	olive oil
2 tbsps salt pork, diced	chopped Italian (flat-leaf) parsley

The evening before you are going to cook the soup, place the cracked wheat and chick-peas in two separate bowls. Add water to cover and soak overnight.

The following day, peel the pumpkin (or rutabaga or turnip) and carrot and cut into large dice. Slice the celery.

In a large soup pot, combine the prepared vegetables and salt pork, duck stock, 4½ cups water and sausage and bring to a slow boil. Add salt and freshly ground black pepper to taste.

Lower the heat; skim the stock and simmer gently over low heat, skimming from time to time, for 2 hours, adding a little more stock or water as necessary. Add the duck legs and cook for 1 hour more.

Serve piping hot, with a dash of olive oil and a sprinkle of finely chopped fresh parsley.

Soups at La Bonne Etape: *soupe d'épeautre* (left), *soupe de potiron* (right) and *consomme à l'ail, à la sauge et à l'oeuf poché*.

97

La soupe de potiron, La Bonne Etape

Pumpkin soup baked in its shell

1 large pumpkin (6–7 lb)	salt and ground black
2 cups day-old French	pepper
bread (cut into croûtons	freshly grated nutmeg
and oven-toasted)	12 sprigs Italian (flat-leaf)
2 cloves garlic, cut in half	parsley, blanched
6¼ cups milk	(optional)
6¼ cups light cream	12 pale green celery leaves,
⅔ cup reduced chicken	blanched (optional)
stock	

TO REMOVE THE 'LID' OF THE PUMPKIN

Carefully make a diagonal cut all around the pumpkin about 2 inches from the top. Remove the top, then with a tablespoon remove the seeds and discard. With a sharp knife, remove all the flesh, being careful not to pierce the shell (it will be the serving dish). Cut the pumpkin flesh into large cubes.

Rub croûtons of oven-toasted bread on all sides with cut cloves of garlic. In a large saucepan, combine the diced pumpkin flesh with the milk, cream, reduced chicken stock (for extra flavor), and croûtons, and season generously with salt, freshly ground black pepper and freshly grated nutmeg. Bring the soup gently to a boil; skim; cover the saucepan and cook over medium heat for 20 minutes, or until the pumpkin is tender.

Transfer the contents of the saucepan to the bowl of a food processor and process until smooth and creamy, adding a little more hot milk if the mixture is too thick. Correct the seasoning, adding a little more salt, pepper or nutmeg if desired.

In the meantime, heat the pumpkin shell and lid in the oven.

TO SERVE

Place the pumpkin shell on a large serving dish; fill with the puréed pumpkin soup and garnish if desired with coarsely chopped blanched Italian (flat-leaf) parsley and pale green celery leaves. Replace the top of the pumpkin and serve immediately.

Note: If the pumpkin shell does not sit comfortably and securely on the serving dish, place it on a folded damp kitchen towel to keep it firmly in place.

La soupe au pistou

Provençal vegetable soup

SERVES 4–6

2 cups dried haricot beans	2 leeks, sliced
1 lb green beans	9 cups boiling water
2 zucchini, sliced	salt and ground black
4 medium-sized carrots	pepper
2 potatoes, diced	grated Parmesan cheese

FOR THE *PISTOU* SAUCE

8 large cloves garlic	8 tbsps grated Parmesan
8 sprigs fresh basil	cheese
olive oil	

Soak the dried haricot beans overnight. Cut the green beans into ³⁄₄-inch slices and put them, with the haricot beans, sliced zucchini, carrots, potatoes and leeks, into 9 cups of boiling water. Season to taste with salt and freshly ground black pepper, and let them cook fairly quickly. When the vegetables are cooked, add the *pistou* sauce and cook gently for 5 minutes more. Serve this hearty soup with grated Parmesan.

TO MAKE THE *PISTOU* SAUCE

Mash the garlic cloves in a mortar; add the fresh basil and mash it with the garlic. Add a glass of olive oil, little by little, to this sauce and blend thoroughly. Then add the grated Parmesan and pound smooth.

The *arrière-pays* is a region of farmers who have always worked

their own land, growing their own vegetables and tending their own orchards

and vineyards. As a result, Provençal cooks have a great respect

for the raw materials of the region, and always

use them with care in the kitchen.

The perfect Provençal lunch is a refreshing Provençal salad – a *salade niçoise*, perhaps, of quartered tomatoes and eggs, sliced sweet onions, celery and green pepper, black olives, tuna fish and anchovies, bathed in a rich dressing of Provençal olive oil and wine vinegar made from the robust red wines of the Var. Or perhaps a simpler Niçois vegetable combination: Escoffier advises equal quantities of diced boiled potatoes, cooked green beans and quartered raw tomatoes, with not a black olive in sight.

There are as many recipes for *salade niçoise* as there are cooks in Provence. Originally a first-course salad from the family kitchens of Nice, it has become a regional favorite which can be found in every village restaurant of Provence as well as on the menus (in more dressed-up versions) of the great restaurants of the world.

From simple beginnings – a tasty combination of chunks of tomato, cucumber, potato and green beans, dressed with extra-virgin olive oil, flavored only with salt and freshly ground black pepper, and garnished with anchovy fillets and black olives – this homely salad has seen many variations on its basic theme. A block of canned white tuna fish is often added, as are additional sliced vegetables, celery, tiny violet artichokes, baby fava beans and chopped fresh herbs. *Salade niçoise* is almost indestructible: it is delicious no matter what the exact mix of its ingredients, as long as they are fresh and the salad is prepared minutes before it is served and dressed with extra-virgin olive oil. And to be at its fragrant best, *salade niçoise* must be served only during the late summer months, when tomatoes have a real flavor of what they are.

Salade niçoise

4 tomatoes, seeded and quartered	4 ribs celery, sliced
½ red onion, sliced	1 6½ oz can tuna fish
1 sweet green pepper, sliced	8 anchovy fillets
8 radishes	2 hard-boiled eggs, quartered
2 lettuce hearts	8 ripe olives

FOR THE SALAD DRESSING

2 tbsps wine vinegar or lemon juice	salt and ground black pepper
6 tbsps extra-virgin olive oil	12 leaves fresh basil, coarsely chopped

Combine the prepared vegetables in a salad bowl, placing the tuna fish, anchovies and quartered eggs neatly on top. Dot with the olives. Mix the salad dressing and sprinkle over the salad.

Salade niçoise (top right), *salade aixoise* (top left) and a simple *salade frisée aux frottés d'ail*, without the hard-boiled eggs and anchovies that are often added.

Salade aixoise
SERVES 4–6

This fresh-tasting salad from the old city of Aix-en-Provence makes the most of the pure, fragrant olive oil of the countryside. Often served in Aix and the surrounding area, it is a delicious alternative to the better-known *salade niçoise* as a first course, and is sometimes served as a vegetable accompaniment for poached or broiled fish or cold roast meats.

For color and flavor contrast I sometimes add tiny sprigs of watercress or *mâche* (known as corn salad or lamb's lettuce in this country) or the bitter red note of slivered leaves of radicchio.

4 medium-sized red-skinned or yellow-fleshed potatoes
4 fresh artichoke hearts (or 6–8 canned artichoke hearts)
8 oz very fine green beans, topped and tailed
4 medium-sized tomatoes, seeded and quartered
1 large green pepper, cut into strips the size of the beans
FOR THE DRESSING
6–8 tbsps extra-virgin olive oil
2–3 tbsps red wine vinegar
1 clove garlic, finely chopped
2 tbsps finely chopped Italian (flat-leaf) parsley
salt and ground black pepper
FOR THE GARNISH
8–12 anchovy fillets, in oil
8–12 small black olives, in oil
leaves from 1–2 sprigs fresh tarragon

Boil the potatoes in their skins and, in a separate saucepan, the fresh artichoke hearts until tender, about 15–20 minutes. Choose beans that are bright green and as small and as slender as possible. Boil them separately until just tender but still a little firm, 5–7 minutes. Cool the vegetables under cold running water; drain and dry on absorbent paper.

Just before serving, peel the potatoes and slice them about ¼ inch thick. Cut the artichoke hearts in halves or quarters and put them in a large bowl with the potatoes, tomatoes, strips of green pepper and beans.

Whisk the salad dressing ingredients together; spoon over the salad and mix well.

Garnish the salad with anchovy fillets and olives and sprinkle with tarragon leaves. Serve immediately.

Salade de mesclun

In Provence, any meal would seem incomplete without a salad of varied and bitter herbs – tiny leaves of lettuce and *escarole* and the darker green of cos (romaine), pale sprigs of *salade frisée* and a few peppery leaves of *pissenlit* or *dent-de-lion* (lion's tooth),

a close cousin of the dandelion. To these tender shoots are added feathery sprigs of chervil, wild chicory and the red-tinged leaves of oak-leaf lettuce.

This is the famous Provençal salad called *mesclun* (or more rarely *mesclum*). *Mesclun* is the old Provençal for the verb to mix: *mesclun* is a 'mixture' of tender young salad shoots gathered daily in the market

gardens of Provence and shipped forthwith to the markets. It is a refreshing sight to come across a display of these brightly colored little leaves in a sun-dappled open-air market in one of the little cross streets of old Nice.

To the above mix Roger Vergé, patriarch of the restaurateurs currently working on the French Riviera, adds tiny sprigs of fat-leafed *pourpier* (purslane) and the peppery leaves of nasturtium and *roquette* (arugula) which he grows in the garden of his restaurant, Le Moulin de Mougins, behind Cannes. And to Pierre and Jany Gleize at La Bonne Etape *mesclun* is almost a religion. Every day, before lunch and before dinner, one of them can be found foraging in the garden behind the hotel for young shoots to accompany a salad of thinly sliced fresh *cèpes (porcini)*, or a fat slice of terrine of young lamb from the neighboring hills of Sisteron.

It was from these chefs that I learned that the young shoots of *mesclun* are very fragile and must not be too heavily dressed with vinaigrette sauces; nor must the salad be tossed too energetically. Just a hint of salt and the best olive oil you can find is enough to bring out the true, fresh flavors of these delicate leaves when served on their own – with perhaps just one brief grind of the peppermill. No harsh vinegars and, as far as I am concerned, not even a drop of lemon juice should be permitted.

Of course, the '*mesclun*' we now find in our supermarkets is usually just a mixture of fully grown leaves of *escarole*, *frisée*, *trevisano* and other salads cut up into pieces, with perhaps a little chervil thrown in – nothing to do with the true *mesclun* of Provence.

Years ago at Hintlesham Hall I grew my own *mesclun* in the eighteenth-century kitchen garden I created there: tiny dark green leaves of baby cos (romaine) lettuce, the tender inner leaves of light-colored *frisée*, whole sprigs of chervil, green and purple basil and tarragon, clusters of purslane with their fat green leaves, arugula and lamb's lettuce. I called it the Nine Herb Salad of Hintlesham, but it was really *mesclun* at its optimum best: freshly picked, flavorful … and, for England at the time, a revolution.

Salade de mesclun aux foies de volaille

Mesclun salad with chicken or duck livers

SERVES 4

fresh *mesclun* salad (mixture of young salad leaves)

4 chicken or duck livers

salt and ground black pepper

2 *cèpes* (*porcini* or other wild mushrooms), sliced

2 tbsps olive oil

FOR THE GARLIC VINAIGRETTE DRESSING

6 tbsps extra-virgin olive oil

2 tbsps red wine vinegar

1–2 tsps each finely chopped Italian (flat-leaf) parsley, basil and tarragon

1 small clove garlic, finely chopped

salt and ground black pepper

1–3 drops Worcestershire sauce

TO PREPARE THE SALAD

Wash and dry the salad, removing any crushed or damaged leaves. Arrange the salad leaves in a salad bowl and chill until ready to serve.

TO PREPARE THE VINAIGRETTE DRESSING

In a small bowl, combine the olive oil, red wine vinegar, finely chopped garlic and herbs and mix well. Season with salt, freshly ground black pepper and Worcestershire sauce, to taste. Reserve.

WHEN READY TO SERVE

Sauté the chicken or duck livers in olive oil until they just begin to stiffen. Season with salt and freshly ground black pepper. With a slotted spoon, remove the livers from the pan. Cut into thick slices and place with the juices in a small bowl.

Add the sliced wild mushrooms to the pan and sauté for a minute or two, stirring, until the mushroom slices begin to brown. Add to the chicken livers.

TO ASSEMBLE THE SALAD

Pour half the vinaigrette dressing over the salad leaves and very carefully mix the salad. Pour the remaining dressing over the warm sliced livers and mushrooms, spoon over the salad and serve immediately.

Salade de mesclun, served in Provençal style with gizzards (*gésiers*) instead of the more readily available duck or chicken livers.

Potato salad niçoise

SERVES 4–6

2 lb long thin salad potatoes

6–8 tbsps olive oil

6–8 tbsps dry white wine or beef consommé

2–3 tbsps wine vinegar

4 tbsps finely chopped shallots

2 tbsps finely chopped parsley

salt and ground black pepper

anchovy fillets

black olives

tomato slices

Boil the potatoes in their skins until cooked. Peel and cut into thick slices. While still hot, pour over the marinade of olive oil, dry white wine (or beef consommé) and wine vinegar. Add the finely chopped shallots and parsley; season to taste with salt and freshly ground black pepper.

Arrange the anchovies in a lattice on top, and place a black olive in the center of each square. Garnish the salad with a ring of tomato slices.

Salade frisée 'aux frottés d'ail'

Curly endive (chicory) salad with garlic croûtons

SERVES 4–6

1/2 loaf French bread

2–4 cloves garlic

coarse salt

8–12 anchovy fillets, in oil

extra-virgin olive oil

2 tbsps red wine vinegar

½ tsp Dijon mustard

salt and ground black pepper

1–1½ heads curly endive (chicory), small inside leaves only, washed and dried

4 hard-boiled eggs, cut in half lengthwise

small black olives, in oil

Slice the French bread into 8–12 thin rounds. Dry them in a hot oven and then rub them on both sides with a cut clove of garlic; sprinkle with a little olive oil and coarse salt (moist sea salt from Guérandes is best for this). Place 1 anchovy fillet on each round.

In a large salad bowl, prepare a well-flavored French dressing with 6–8 tablespoons extra-virgin olive oil, 2 tablespoons red wine vinegar, ½ teaspoon Dijon mustard, finely chopped garlic, salt and freshly ground black pepper to taste.

Add the washed and dried curly endive leaves and toss until each leaf glistens with dressing. Garnish with the garlic-rubbed *frottés d'ail* and halved hard-boiled eggs. Sprinkle with black olives.

Salade de pommes de terre à la provençale

Provençal anchovy and potato salad

SERVES 4–6

1 lb tiny new potatoes,
  scrubbed

salt

8 tbsps dry white wine

ground black pepper

1 small green pepper,
  seeded, cored and sliced

3 tomatoes, peeled, seeded
  and quartered

3 tbsps black olives,
  pitted

2 tbsps wine vinegar

2 shallots, finely chopped

1 tsp chopped chives

2 cloves garlic, finely
  chopped

2 oz can anchovy fillets,
  drained

In a saucepan of boiling salted water, cook the new potatoes in their skins for 10 minutes or until tender but still firm. Drain quickly; holding each one in a cloth, peel and place them in a bowl.

In a clean saucepan bring the wine to a boil and pour over the potatoes. Season generously with salt and freshly ground black pepper to taste and leave to cool, tossing occasionally.

Add the sliced pepper, peeled, seeded and quartered tomatoes, pitted black olives, wine vinegar, finely chopped shallots, chives and garlic. Toss to mix and season with salt and freshly ground black pepper to taste. Transfer to a shallow serving dish and level off the top as much as possible.

Cut each anchovy fillet into 3 fine slices and arrange them in a lattice over the top.

Les petites salades de tomates à la provençale

Little tomato appetizer salads

This attractive group of quickly-made Provençal appetizers is based on a series of star or flower shapes made by cutting tomatoes into 6–8 wedges and opening them up. These are then used as bases for a variety of salads made from leftover cooked rice, lentils, tuna fish or black olives and diced orange, moistened with a garlic and herb dressing.

LA SALADE DE TOMATES AU RIZ DE CAMARGUE
For each serving, cut 1 large ripe chilled tomato into thin wedges to form a 'star' or 'flower', being careful not to cut all the way through the tomato.

Place the tomato 'stars' on chilled salad plates. Garnish each dish with 5 small lettuce leaves and sprinkle each serving with 3–4 tablespoons of day-old

cooked rice tossed in a little garlic and herb dresssing. Garnish with black olives.

LA SALADE DE TOMATES AUX MIETTES DE THON

Prepare the tomato 'stars' as above. Garnish each dish with small lettuce leaves, as above, and sprinkle with crumbled canned tuna fish and rice moistened with Provençal herb dressing.

LA SALADE DE TOMATES AUX OLIVES

Prepare the tomato 'stars' as above. Garnish each dish with lettuce leaves, as above. Sprinkle with chopped black olives and diced orange segments. Moisten with Provençal herb dressing.

Salade de berger

—

Shepherd's salad

—

SERVES 4

This salad is memorable when cooked in the embers of a brushwood fire in the open air (or even on a backyard barbecue) with herbs.

If you are preparing the salad on a gas or electric broiler, slice the vegetables before cooking; brush them with olive oil and cook on both sides until the vegetable slices are tender and well colored.

2 long thin eggplants	slices fresh *country*
4 long green peppers	*bread*
4 large tomatoes	olive oil
4 large yellow onions	salt and black pepper
dry white wine (or water)	leaves of fresh basil

In a barbecue or outdoor fireplace make a fire of dry brushwood; when the fire has died down, sprinkle it with sprigs of dried summer savory, rosemary and wild thyme. Put the vegetables, unpeeled, directly in the glowing embers. Turn them from time to time with a stick until all the skins are black. Take the vegetables from the embers as they become charred and cooked. Put them into a plastic bag to steam, and – through the plastic – rub off the charred skins.

Rinse any remaining black bits from the vegetables with a little dry white wine (it adds to the flavor) or water; cut the vegetables into strips and layer them on slices of fresh country bread which you have toasted over the embers. Sprinkle with a little olive oil and salt and ground black pepper. Leaves of fresh basil make a colorful garnish.

Olive oil and salt are enough to season a simple tomato salad.

107

Artichauts à la barigoule

SERVES 2

Barigoule is the Provençal name for a type of edible mushroom. It is probably the similarity between the upturned cap of the *barigoule* and a scooped-out artichoke waiting to be filled with its garnish that has given this famous artichoke dish its name, or could it mean artichokes cooked like mushrooms in the Provençal manner?

salt	1 medium-sized onion,
2 large artichokes	finely chopped
4 tbsps olive oil	1 carrot, finely chopped
2 thin bacon slices,	*bouquet garni* (1 sprig
finely chopped	parsley, 1 sprig thyme, 1
2 thin slices lean ham,	small bay leaf)
finely chopped	3 tbsps dry white wine
2 level tbsps finely	6–8 tbsps chicken stock
chopped parsley	
ground black pepper	

Select a pan large enough to hold the artichokes side by side; half-fill it with salted water and heat it gently while you prepare the artichokes.

Trim off the stalks of artichokes and cut ½ inch from the tips of the outer leaves with a pair of scissors. Pull out the inedible mauve leaves from the center and, using a table knife or a sharp-pointed spoon, scoop out the chokes, taking great care not to leave any of the hairlike fibers. Rinse well under cold running water.

When the water comes to a boil, plunge the artichokes in it stems downwards. Bring back to a boil and simmer for 15–20 minutes (depending on size and quantity), or until they feel tender when a knife is pushed through the base. Remove from the pan and leave upside-down to drain in a colander.

Heat half the olive oil in a heavy skillet and sauté the finely chopped bacon and ham until lightly golden. Stir in the parsley and season to taste with salt and freshly ground black pepper.

Heat the remaining oil in a heavy oven-proof casserole just large enough to hold the artichokes side by side, and simmer the finely chopped onion and carrot until soft and golden. Add the *bouquet garni* and salt and pepper to taste, and moisten with dry white wine. Simmer for 5 minutes longer.

Pre-heat the oven to moderate (350°F).

Fill the center of the artichokes with the chopped bacon and ham mixture (*duxelles*) and lay them in the casserole on the bed of vegetables. Simmer, uncovered, for 10–15 minutes, until the liquid is almost completely reduced.

Add 4 tablespoons chicken stock to the casserole; cover tightly and transfer to the oven. Bake for 30 minutes, basting frequently.

Lift the artichokes out carefully with a slotted spoon and transfer to a heated serving dish. Pour over the pan juices and chopped vegetables.

Artichauts à la nîmoise

SERVES 4

8 small tender artichokes or 4 Breton artichokes
2 large Spanish onions, finely chopped
2 cloves garlic, finely chopped
4 tbsps olive oil
4 tbsps butter
1¼ cups fresh spinach leaves, finely chopped
1¼ cups fresh sorrel leaves, finely chopped
4 tbsps finely chopped parsley
2 tbsps finely chopped tarragon

Prepare the artichokes as for the previous recipe. Cook the artichokes in boiling salted water for 20 minutes until just tender. Drain.

In the meantime, sauté the finely chopped onion and garlic in olive oil until transparent. Add the butter and finely chopped spinach and sorrel leaves and continue to cook, stirring, until the sauce is green.

Cut the artichokes in half lengthwise and put them to warm through in the sauce, spooning the sauce over them. Sprinkle with the finely chopped parsley and tarragon and serve immediately.

Halved Provençal artichokes cooked

F E A S T

Chez Bruno

La Campagne Mariette, Lorgues

Travelers in Provence who confine themselves to eating in the much-publicized starred restaurants along the coast are certain to miss out on some spectacularly creative food. For it is doubtful whether they would be tempted to stop, as I did with a friend, at a simple oval sign bearing the words 'Chez Bruno' on the road from Les Arcs to Lorgues. The way to the restaurant led, via a little unpaved track through some farm buildings, to a house perched halfway up the hillside. This first impromptu visit proved to be a gamble that paid off: one of those unexpected gastronomic treats to be savored for years afterwards. For this is one of the best restaurants in the entire region, well worth a trip from St Tropez, or even Cannes, Nice or Monte Carlo for that matter.

Among the locals, Bruno Clément is earning quite a reputation for food. His restaurant, created in his grandmother's house, is a stone's throw from where he was born. It is a simple Provençal farmhouse, arranged with consummate taste in tones of off-white, honey and stone, and furnished with the Provençal antiques that Bruno and his wife Nicole love. The floor-to-ceiling French windows of the dining room lead out to an open terrace in front of the house, used in the summer months for additional seating under a large natural-colored awning.

Bruno's kitchen is the dream kitchen of a man who knows exactly what he likes: antique wooden cabinets, cool marble-topped work surfaces and practical overhead lighting. But not content with this perfection, he is already digging up the adjoining garden in the back to create a perfect pastry kitchen.

Bruno works alone in his spacious kitchen with one or two young student chefs and a pale young Moroccan girl who looks like a saint. In a three-star restaurant in France there would be a master chef

BELOW Game and preserves, Chez Bruno. His forte is the use of the wild harvest of the countryside: truffles, asparagus, mushrooms and game.
BELOW RIGHT A young assistant prepares *cèpes (porcini)* for one of Bruno's specialities.

presiding over a brigade of cooks and any number of young *commis*. Bruno is practically a one-man band, and that is how he likes it. It is his nature to work more or less alone, with only two or three serious-minded assistants. Nicole serves as hostess and *maître d'hôtel*, and a young girl helps at table.

Bruno will never expand; he is a born perfectionist, and no chef could ever meet his exacting standards. He could raise his prices but he doesn't. And when

you consider that Bruno's forte is the use of the fresh black truffles and wild mushrooms of the countryside to accompany wild game and wild asparagus, you have an idea of the gift that this jovial giant has on offer. There is no written menu *chez* Bruno. No wine list. Just what Bruno chooses to serve you that day:

OVERLEAF The dining room of Chez Bruno is decorated in soft tones of off-white, honey and stone: the antique furniture and primitive Provençal paintings provide an elegant setting for Bruno Clément's eclectic cuisine.

three superb courses, plus a dessert that seems to come right out of the pages of a nineteenth-century family album of *cuisine bourgeoise*.

Sometimes at the height of an evening at Bruno's there are only eleven customers in his dining room. His capacity is forty, with a private dining room next door which can seat twenty more. In the summer the open terrace in front of the house can handle a few more bookings. He manages that number from time to time, but more often he will cook for fewer than thirty or forty.

Dinner is a ritual *chez* Bruno. First he appears at your table to recite the menu for that evening. Then he comes out after you have had a few moments to savor the food and asks you (tells you, rather) how good it is before disappearing into the kitchen again to prepare the next dish.

Ask Bruno what his favorite dish of the moment is and he will probably tell you it is a dish of green lentils simmered with baby carrots and minute pearl onions, topped just before serving with a typically Bruno-esque flourish of a fat slice of fresh goose liver, sautéed for seconds in foaming butter so that it is served gently crisped and colored by the pan juices on the outside, and pink and moistly tender within.

Bruno served this dish to a sortie of famous chefs of the coast at the Château de Vignelaure in Rians. Alain Ducasse, master chef of the Louis xv restaurant in the Hôtel de Paris in Monte Carlo and one of the best chefs in France, tasted it and declared Bruno an 'alchemist' of flavors. This signature dish, destined to become a classic, combining as it does the elegance of fresh *foie gras* with the earthiness of lentils, exemplifies his happy flirtation with contrasts of flavor and texture – and his entire approach to cooking.

Bruno does most of his preparation in the middle of the kitchen at a long working table, at least 20 feet long, which runs down the entire length of the room. It is wonderfully constructed, with deep drawers for knives, whisks, strainers, pastry tins, so right that it is obviously his own design.

Along one wall of the kitchen is a spacious Provençal dresser on which he displays his chef's elements of flavor: preserved lemons and tiny mandarins; earthy black truffles and spices; hazelnuts and filberts; his specially-cured olives.

With Bruno in the kitchen, we are taking photographs of the colossus at work: in a skillet he tosses tiny segments of the local wild asparagus in foaming butter; then he adds salt and white pepper, liquid cream from the carton, and shakes it over a high heat until the sauce emulsifies. He spoons this onto a heated plate; tops it with five fat poached asparagus; heats butter until it is frothing in another pan; slides in a generous slice of fresh *foie gras*, cooks it for what seems a second; turns it over, and while it is still cooking in the foaming butter, walks over to the central table and places it on top of the asparagus. Simple in execution; intriguing in its remarkable levels of taste and texture: a culinary masterpiece.

Les asperges vertes de pays à la mousseline d'asperges sauvages des oliviers et aux morilles sauvages

Green asparagus with a mousseline of wild asparagus and morels

SERVES 4

1 lb green asparagus	1 cup heavy cream
12 spears wild asparagus	6 small morels, cut in half
1 tbsp olive oil	(use soaked dried ones if
4 tbsps butter	fresh not available)

Trim the green asparagus and cut them in two. Poach the top halves in boiling salted water for 6–8 minutes, or until just tender. Remove from the heat, drain, and place in a bowl of iced water. Drain again.

The dream kitchen of a man who knows exactly what he wants.

Chop the wild asparagus finely and sauté them in olive oil and 2 tablespoons butter until tender. Reserve.

Add the remaining butter to the pan; when it froths, add the heavy cream and cook over high heat, stirring constantly, until it is thick and smooth. Add the chopped sautéed wild asparagus and halved morels and continue to cook until heated through.

TO SERVE

Arrange the asparagus spears (5–6 spears per serving) on heated plates. Spoon over the mousseline of wild asparagus and mushrooms. Serve immediately.

115

Lapin, ou râble de lièvre, sauce poivrade, Chez Bruno

Bruno's rabbit – or hare – poivrade sauce

SERVES 4

1½ rabbits, cut into
serving pieces, or 1
saddle of hare (boned by
the butcher from the
stomach, without
perforating the skin)

salt and ground black
pepper
dried *herbes de Provence*

The highly flavored pepper-based sauce called *poivrade* (see page 26) is one of the great standbys of Provençal cuisine where game is concerned, or when a gamey flavor is sought to give more emphasis to roast lamb or beef. This wine-based marinade for hare, rabbit, partridge, pheasant or venison is part of the classic Provençal repertoire. I give you Bruno's flamboyant version based on two bottles of Cabernet Sauvignon red for the marinade, which is then reduced to one-quarter of the original quantity for a deliciously rich and highly colored sauce.

Râble de lièvre, sauce poivrade, Chez Bruno.

Bruno's stuffing for hare or rabbit

Bruno makes an elegant but, I am afraid, prohibitively expensive stuffing for his hare using ground veal and belly of pork, diced black truffles and *foie gras*, seasoning it with dried *herbes de Provence* or a *poudre aromatique* such as one of the ones on page 18. A simpler version would be to stuff the hare with just the ground veal and breast of pork, seasoned with salt, freshly ground black pepper and dried *herbes de Provence* and let the intense and wondrous flavor of Bruno's *poivrade sauce* carry the day.

1 lb ground veal
12 oz ground belly of pork
8–10 tbsps diced black
truffles (optional)
7 oz diced *foie gras*
(optional)

dried *herbes de Provence*
(or *poudre aromatique*,
page 18)
veal stock

TO PREPARE THE RABBIT (OR HARE)

Place the rabbit pieces (or boned saddle of hare) on a sheet of plastic wrap. Season generously with salt, ground black pepper and dried *herbes de Provence*.

Note: If you plan to use hare and wish to stuff it with Bruno's special stuffing, prepare the stuffing by mixing the ground veal and belly of pork with diced black truffles and *foie gras*. Season with salt, freshly ground black pepper and dried *herbes de Provence* (or *poudre aromatique*) and spread the hare (which you have laid out on its sheet of plastic wrap, cavity side up) with this savory mixture.

Bring the sides of the hare up over the stuffing, folding the edges over to form a shape like a roast. Close it up like a 'roast' with the plastic wrap; then tie into a perfect roast shape with pieces of string.

TO COOK THE STUFFED SADDLE OF HARE

Place the hare in a large casserole; add veal stock to cover and bring gently to a boil. Cover the casserole and poach the hare for 1½ hours.

TO COOK THE RABBIT OR HARE (WITHOUT STUFFING)

Season rabbit pieces (or saddle of hare) generously with salt, freshly ground black pepper and dried *herbes de Provence*; wrap in plastic wrap; tie securely and poach in veal stock for 1½ hours.

TO SERVE THE RABBIT OR HARE

Remove the rabbit (or hare) from the casserole; untie the string and remove. Cut the hare into slices or arrange the rabbit pieces on a heated serving dish. Spoon the hot sauce (see opposite) over the rabbit or hare and serve immediately.

Sauce poivrade au Cabernet Sauvignon

Poivrade sauce with Cabernet Sauvignon

bones and trimmings of rabbit, hare or venison	1 *bouquet garni* (parsley, thyme, bay leaf, green of leek)
4 tbsps peanut oil	
4 cloves garlic, chopped	24 juniper berries
1 tsp dried thyme	4 cloves
2 bay leaves	2 bottles Cabernet Sauvignon, or a full-bodied red wine of Provence
4 carrots	
2 onions	
10 shallots	
3 ribs celery	veal or beef stock
1 leek	4 tbsps diced butter
24 black peppercorns	

Chop the bones and trimmings coarsely with a cleaver. In a large heat-proof casserole, sauté the chopped bones in peanut oil with the garlic, thyme and bay leaves. Add the carrots, onions, shallots, celery, leek, *bouquet garni* and spices and cook over medium heat, stirring from time to time, for 20 minutes.

Add the red wine; bring to a boil; skim off impurities and cook over high heat until the sauce is reduced to a quarter of the original quantity, about 30 minutes.

Add enough veal or beef stock to cover the bones and aromatics. Cook for 2 minutes to amalgamate the flavors. Then strain the sauce through a fine sieve into a clean saucepan; return to the heat and reduce to the desired consistency. Reserve until ready to serve.

When ready to serve, bring the sauce back to a boil; remove from the heat and add the diced butter, piece by piece, whisking it in with a balloon whisk.

La gourmandise de Mémé Mariette au caramel chaud et à la glace minute

Granny Mariette's apple tart with hot caramel and vanilla ice cream

SERVES 4

4 rolled-out squares of puff pastry, 4½ inches square	2 Granny Smith apples, peeled, cored and diced
4 tsps melted butter	2 tsps granulated sugar
FOR THE *CARAMEL CHAUD*	
½ cup unsalted butter	2 cups heavy cream
⅔ cup granulated sugar	

Pre-heat the oven to 375°F.

TO PREPARE THE APPLE SQUARES

Place the pastry squares on a baking sheet: prick each square with the tines of a fork and bake in a pre-heated oven for 5 minutes. Remove from the oven and, if the pastry has puffed up too much during baking, press down gently with a spatula. Allow pastry to cool but keep oven hot.

TO PREPARE THE APPLE MIXTURE

Sauté the finely diced apples in butter and sugar until the apple begins to take on a little color. Remove from the heat and allow to cool.

TO BAKE THE APPLE SQUARES

Top each cooled pastry square with a layer of sautéed diced apple; return to the pre-heated oven and bake for 20 minutes, or until the apples are crisp and golden.

TO PREPARE THE *CARAMEL CHAUD*

In the meantime, in a small saucepan melt the butter over low heat, stirring constantly with a wooden spoon. When the butter has melted (and before it changes color) stir in the sugar, continuing to stir over low heat until the caramel is a rich caramel color.

Remove the saucepan from the heat and carefully stir in the heavy cream, being sure to stir the mixture constantly until the caramel sauce is well mixed. Return to cook over low heat, still stirring constantly, for 5 more minutes.

TO SERVE

Place each apple square on a heated dessert plate, cover with the hot caramel sauce, top with a ball of vanilla ice cream and serve immediately.

Glace minute

Vanilla ice cream

MAKES APPROXIMATELY 1 PINT

1 scant cup milk	6 tbsps granulated sugar
1¼ cups heavy cream	1 vanilla pod, split
	4 egg yolks

Bring the milk, heavy cream and sugar to a boil with the vanilla pod, stirring continuously. Remove from the heat and beat in the egg yolks, one by one. Strain the mixture into an ice cream machine and freeze according to the manufacturer's instructions.

5 Villages in

MAIN DISHES: MEATS, POULTRY AND GAME

If you look closely at the map of southern France, focusing in on the mountain ranges behind St Tropez and Fréjus, you will discover clusters of little hilltop villages rising out of the soft-shouldered mountains of inland Provence: Callian, Fayence and Seillans are hidden away in the hills between Draguignan and Grasse; just a little further to the east, behind Cannes, you will find Mougins, and then Peillon. Now look west to the hills of the Lubéron, and you will come across the most magical hill towns of them all: Bonnieux, Lacoste, Ménerbes and Oppède-le-Vieux, each set like a jewel on its peak. Here in the high-thrown mountain villages you will find a Provence that might have existed hundreds of years ago; where silver olive trees dot the arid hills and green and purple grapes and orchards of plum, apricot and almond cover the lower slopes. Today it is a land of plenty, of carefree living and hedonistic pleasures, based around a glass of chilled rosé wine and a plate of delicious little crinkled black olives, bathed in chopped herbs and a caressing glaze of the extra-virgin olive oil that is the pride of Provence. You do not have to be rich to get the best out of Provence . . .

Let us say that you have a little village house among the vines on the outskirts of one of the delightful small villages behind the coast, like Cotignac or Sillans-la-Cascade. It must have a terrace of course, with one section of it shaded by a vine for long, lazy lunches in the great outdoors. It would help

the sky

if it had a view, too – to the sea, perhaps, or to the citadel of a neighboring hilltop village. On my last visit to Haute Provence I fell in love with the view from the plain below Lacoste to the sheer gray forms of the brooding eleventh-century castle at the top of the village. Here I knew I would have time to make a five-hour daube of beef, cooked in the ashes of the chimney as they did in the old days in the Camargue, its rich, dark sauce redolent of the red wine of Lirac, full of the flavors of herbs from the neighboring *garrigue*, of garlic, and of the sudden Arabian perfume of dried orange peel, and its meat so meltingly tender that you could cut it with a spoon. Or the seven-hour *gigot* of the famous doctor from Marseilles, or the magical twelve-hour *marinade de train de lièvre rôti, sauce piquante* (marinade of loin and saddle of hare, served with a piquant red wine sauce) to be found in the nineteenth-century cookbook of Marius Morard, master chef at the Palace Hôtel de la Réserve (named after his own crawfish reserve) near Marseilles.

As I traveled so happily through the rain and mist-shrouded countryside, I remembered other tastes that I would be able to celebrate here: *lous crous*, the Provençal ravioli (inherited from the ancient Romans) that traditionally accompanies the daube – a great shallow earthenware casserole of ravioli, stuffed with *blettes* (Swiss chard), spinach, sorrel, basil and chervil and layered with the freshly grated trio of cheeses that spells Provence for me, even if they are all imported: Gruyère, Hollande and Parmesan. And I longed, too, for the sharp, bitter taste of *mesclun*, the shepherd's salad gathered from the hillsides. Just as the Arab shepherd today might carry with him little rumpled papers of salt and cumin and green tea and cracked lumps of sugar, the Provençal shepherd in the old days would keep in his knapsack a tomato, a small piece of *chèvre* and a small corked bottle of his own olive oil, along with a round, crusty loaf of freshly baked bread. This is the direct ancestor of the perfect Provençal lunch today: a sliced tomato still warm from the vine, an oil-drenched salad of gathered herbs, a piece of *chèvre* cheese and a crusty piece of home-baked bread, all washed down with a glass or two of well-cooled wine.

Such food hungers are age-old. A Greek caique owner might have shared them, or a Roman legionary, or a nineteenth-century Italian worker from the potteries at Salernes. And this kind of food, simple and joyous, is as evident in Provence today as it was in the era before Christ was born.

In the hills behind the coast you will find a Provence that might have existed hundreds of years ago. In those days the Provençal shepherd would keep in his knapsack a tomato, a small piece of *chèvre* cheese, a corked bottle of his own olive oil and a crusty loaf of freshly baked bread: the perfect Provençal lunch.

Food from the barnyard and the forests

Until fairly recently, except for the weekly visits of the meat or fish vans, the little villages of inland Provence were not particularly favored with fish or meats. It was the barnyard and the hunt that provided the extras for the meager diet of the region. Provence was a poor country in those days, burned by an ardent sun in the summer months and assailed by the cold winds of the Mistral in the winter.

The diet of its people – except for the produce from the surrounding smallholdings – was unvaried for those who were unable or unwilling to gather the fresh herbs from the surrounding hills and to search out the wild mushrooms and black truffles in the neighboring forests of scrub and oak.

The men in the family would take time out from working the farms or from their village shops and offices to hunt for wild rabbits and hare, for the occasional game bird, or for those tiny wild birds called *grives* now protected by law – although one still comes across the occasional delectable pâté of the little birds flavored with bay leaves, wild thyme and juniper berries.

The little café-restaurants in hill villages like Grimaud and Ramatuelle still boast homemade terrines made of wild rabbit or hare, or perhaps a *civet*

The little café-restaurants in the hill villages of Provence often still boast home-made terrines or *civets* of rabbit or hare, or sometimes wild boar.

(an old-fashioned ragout of rabbit or hare, or sometimes of suckling pig, its long-simmered sauce thickened at the last minute with the blood of the beast kept liquid with a little wine vinegar). Wild boar can still be found in the oak forests, and occasionally a lucky hunter will serve succulent racks of young wild pig, called *marcassin*, or a tasty saddle of wild boar cooked with black truffles from the forest.

Provençal cooks are expert in the art of changing organ meats into delicious meals – *pieds et paquets*, for instance, tender little parcels made of sheep's innards wrapped in tripe, cooked with lambs' feet in a sauce of white wine and aromatics; or *la caille* (quail) a sort of free-form pâté made of chopped liver and innards, spiced to resemble game, and wrapped in caul before being boiled in a light stock. Served hot, *la caille* makes a lovely country supper dish; and sometimes it is served cold as a delicious hors d'oeuvre at elegant Provençal restaurants like La Bonne Auberge at Antibes. *Fressure* is a similar dish (Arab in inspiration, it is still found in Morocco today) consisting of a ragout of lamb's liver, heart, lungs and tripe in a sharp, peppery sauce flavored with plenty of herbs and spices.

Recently I traveled for weeks with photographer friends, feasting in the little villages behind the coast; stopping off at the region's great hotels, from La Bonne Etape in Château Arnoux in Haute Provence to the lovely Hôtel-Restaurant de la Valmoraine just outside Les Baux, and staying for one glorious month in a little stone bastide overlooking a magic valley just behind St Antonin-de-Var, a tiny village hidden away in the mountains of the upper Var.

When we weren't tucking into great dishes of Mediterranean fish simmered in saffron- and herb-tinted broths, we were enjoying succulent daubes of beef, slow-cooked to fork-tenderness in rich brown sauces redolent of orange and the red wine of the Camargue; creamy scrambles of new-laid eggs studded with fresh black truffles; and braces of pheasant, woodcock and wild duck roasted to perfection over open wood fires.

For two delicious weeks we feasted in this manner, from the Michelin-starred restaurants along the coast to the little restaurants tucked away among the lavender hills of Haute Provence. Between meals, when we were not eating or photographing, we

strolled through the tiny, crooked streets of the ancient villages, visiting the churches and the little museums of Provençal painting, or poetry, or even truffles.

Perhaps the most fun was shopping at the weekly markets in the villages, with their forthright displays of fresh produce, clothing and even antiques. I must confess, too, that a great deal of our time was spent in sun-dappled cafés in the village squares, tossing down glasses of chilled Pastis and fresh-tasting rosés from Bellet, Bandol and Taradeau. It was here that we learned that people-watching in Provence from a tranquil café terrace could be one of the great pleasures in life.

And we took time, too, to fall in love successively with Arles and Aix-en-Provence and finally, most of all, with that seedy, run-down, sometimes dangerous melting pot of East and West called Marseilles, where we walked at night under the stars, wondering at the closeness of the Greek and Roman and Arab warriors who had preceded us, caught up themselves, perhaps, in the magic of the warm perfumed winds from the sea or the hills.

Les côtelettes d'agneau grillées au feu de braise

Lamb chops grilled over an open fire

SERVES 4

FOR THE LAMB CHOPS	salt and ground black
12 small loin lamb chops	pepper
olive oil	dried thyme or rosemary
FOR THE BRUSHWOOD FIRE	
wood from the hills	3 or 4 pine cones
branches of thyme and	1 handful black
rosemary from the hills	peppercorns

Brush the lamb chops on both sides with olive oil and season with salt and freshly ground black pepper.

Light a fire with the wood in an indoor fireplace or outdoor grill. Let the wood burn until there is a flat layer of ashes; then add pine cones and dried rosemary and thyme branches. When the flames from these have died down, place the lamb chops on the grill and scatter a handful of black peppercorns under the chops.

Cook the lamb chops for 3 minutes on each side until tender, sprinkling a little dried thyme or rosemary over them as you turn them.

Gigot à la provençale

Roast leg of lamb Provençal

1 leg of lamb (about 6 lb)	salt and ground black
1 tbsp butter	pepper
6 cloves garlic	4–6 tbsps finely chopped
1 lb 8 oz potatoes, peeled	parsley
and sliced	1¼ cups rich chicken stock

Ask the butcher to trim and tie a leg of lamb. Pre-heat the oven to slow (300°F). Butter a shallow oven-proof casserole or gratin dish just large enough to hold the leg of lamb comfortably and rub it lightly with a cut clove of garlic. Peel the potatoes, cut them into thick slices and arrange them in the bottom of the dish in overlapping rows. Salt and pepper the potatoes generously. Chop the remaining garlic finely and sprinkle it over the potatoes with the finely chopped parsley. Place the raw lamb on the potatoes and moisten with rich chicken stock.

Roast in the pre-heated oven for 1¼–1½ hours, or until the lamb is pink and tender. If you prefer lamb less pink, increase the cooking time. Serve.

Epaule d'agneau farcie

Roast stuffed shoulder of lamb

1 shoulder of lamb	lemon juice
olive oil	all-purpose flour
salt and ground black	2 tbsps butter
pepper	2 tbsps olive oil
FOR THE STUFFING	
8 oz sausage meat	2½ cups spinach, chopped
½ large yellow onion,	and sautéed in butter
chopped and sautéed in	salt and ground black
2 tbsps butter	pepper
1 tbsp finely chopped	juniper berries
parsley	black peppercorns
1 egg, beaten	

Ask the butcher to bone and trim a shoulder of lamb ready for rolling, but not to roll it.

Pre-heat the oven to slow (300°F).

Brush the lamb with olive oil and sprinkle with salt and pepper to taste. Sprinkle with lemon juice.

TO PREPARE THE STUFFING

In a large mixing bowl, combine the sausage meat, finely chopped onion which you have sautéed in butter until transparent, finely chopped parsley, beaten egg and sautéed spinach, seasoning to taste with salt, freshly ground black pepper and spices. Mix well. Lay this stuffing on the meat; roll and sew it up with fine string.

Dust the lamb roll with flour; place it in a roasting pan with 2 tablespoons each of butter and olive oil, and roast it in the pre-heated oven for about $1\frac{1}{2}$–2 hours, basting frequently with the fat.

Selle d'agneau à l'arlésienne

Roast saddle of lamb

1 saddle of lamb	6 medium-sized zucchini
softened butter	6 tomatoes, thinly sliced
salt and ground black pepper	1 large yellow onion, finely chopped
crushed rosemary	sprigs of thyme
2 cups hot beef stock	6–8 cloves garlic, unpeeled
1 tbsp butter	olive oil
1 tbsp all-purpose flour	

FOR THE GARNISH

6 tbsps chopped mushrooms and 2 tbsps each chopped parsley and truffles, sautéed in butter

24 new potatoes, boiled and sautéed in butter
watercress

Pre-heat the oven to moderately hot ($375°$F).

Spread the lamb with softened butter and sprinkle to taste with salt, pepper and rosemary.

Place the saddle in a roasting pan, pour $\frac{1}{2}$–$\frac{2}{3}$ cup water around it, place it in the pre-heated oven and roast it for 1 hour, basting frequently.

Remove the roast from the oven; skim off the fat from the pan; add the beef stock and a *beurre manié* made from 1 tablespoon of butter kneaded to a smooth paste with 1 tablespoon of flour, and cook over a high flame, stirring in all the crusty bits from the sides of the pan, until the sauce is smooth and thick. Strain and keep warm.

Slice each zucchini lengthwise into 4 or 5 slices, without cutting all the way through, to make a fan shape. Place a thin slice of tomato in each opening. Place the partially roasted saddle of lamb in an oiled roasting pan in which you have scattered finely chopped onion, sprigs of thyme, garlic cloves and salt and pepper to taste. Surround with the stuffed zucchini; sprinkle with a little olive oil and roast for

Selle d'agneau à l'arlésienne.

about another 45 minutes, or until tender (allow about 15 minutes per lb in all).

TO SERVE

Place the lamb on a large heated serving dish; place the stuffed zucchini at one end of the dish and the sautéed potatoes at the other. Sprinkle the vegetables with finely chopped mushrooms, parsley and truffles, which you have sautéed in butter. Garnish with watercress. Serve the sauce separately.

Gigot d'agneau piqué d'ail, d'anchois et de romarin, uncooked (left) and cooked (opposite). Ratatouille makes a deliciously fresh accompaniment to the richness of the meat.

Gigot d'agneau piqué d'ail, d'anchois et de romarin

Roast leg of lamb armored with garlic, anchovies and rosemary

1 leg of lamb (about 6 lb)
4 fat cloves garlic, cut into 24–32 slivers
6–8 anchovy fillets, cut into 24–32 small pieces
24–32 small sprigs rosemary
FOR THE GARNISH
sprigs of rosemary (optional)

4 tbsps olive oil
salt and ground black pepper
cayenne pepper
6–8 tbsps red wine
4–6 tbsps diced butter

Pre-heat the oven to moderately hot (400°F).

With the point of a sharp kitchen knife (or the tip of a metal skewer) cut slits 1 inch apart down the leg of lamb in 4 evenly spaced rows, making between 6 and 8 slits per row.

Insert 1 sliver of garlic into each hole, leaving a third of the length of each sliver sticking out of the lamb. With the point of a knife (or skewer) insert 1 small piece of anchovy into each hole with the garlic; finally, insert 1 small sprig of rosemary into each hole with the garlic and anchovy.

Place the leg of lamb in a well-buttered heat-proof oval gratin dish (or roasting pan); spoon over the olive oil; season generously with salt, freshly ground black pepper and cayenne pepper and roast in the pre-heated oven for 1¼–1½ hours, basting with the pan juices occasionally, not frequently. If you prefer lamb less pink, increase the cooking time. Ten to fifteen minutes before the end of the cooking time, if desired, surround the roast with rosemary sprigs. Continue cooking until the meat is tender.

When the roast is cooked to your liking, transfer it to a hot serving platter and leave it to 'set' for 10–15 minutes at the open door of the oven before carving into evenly-sized slices.

Skim the fat from the pan juices; stir in the red wine, scraping in all the crusty bits from the bottom and sides of the pan; whisk the diced butter into the sauce; correct the seasoning, adding a little more salt, freshly ground black pepper and cayenne pepper to taste, and serve immediately with the roast.

Daube de mouton

Daube of lamb with red wine marinade

SERVES 4–6

3 lb boned shoulder of lamb	thin strips pork fat
	thin strips bacon
FOR THE MARINADE	
2 onions, sliced	1 large yellow onion, sliced
4 carrots, sliced	1 clove garlic, finely
1 *bouquet garni* (thyme, parsley and bay leaf)	chopped
	2½ cups hot beef stock
salt and ground black pepper	2–4 tbsps tomato paste
2½ cups red wine	2 tbsps finely chopped parsley
4 tbsps olive oil	
4 oz bacon (in one piece), diced	

Cut the lamb into large, even-sized cubes; lard each piece with thin strips of pork fat and bacon and place in a large bowl or earthenware casserole with sliced onions and carrots, a *bouquet garni*, salt, pepper and red wine. Marinate overnight.

Pre-heat the oven to slow (300°F).

Remove the lamb from the marinade and drain. Heat the olive oil in a skillet or heat-proof casserole; sauté the diced bacon and sliced onion until the onion is transparent. Add the lamb and sauté it with bacon and onion until browned, shaking the pan from time to time. Add the chopped garlic; moisten with the marinade which has been reduced to half the original quantity. Pour over 2½ cups hot beef stock mixed with the tomato paste.

Cover the skillet or casserole with greaseproof paper and the lid, and cook in the pre-heated oven for 3–4 hours. Remove, skim the fat from the surface, sprinkle with parsley and serve in the casserole.

Daube de mouton à l'avignonnaise

Daube of lamb with white wine

SERVES 4–6

3 lb leg of lamb	2 cloves garlic, chopped
all-purpose flour	1 strip dried orange peel
salt and black pepper	2 bay leaves
8 oz bacon (in one piece), uncut	2 cloves
	2 sprigs thyme
6 tbsps olive oil	2½ cups dry white wine
4 yellow onions, chopped	

Cut the lamb into large even-sized cubes. Dust the pieces with flour and season generously with salt and freshly ground black pepper.

Slice the bacon thickly (¼ inch) and then cut the slices into ¼-inch-thick 'fingers'. Sauté the bacon pieces in olive oil until golden. Remove and reserve. Sauté the lamb cubes a few at a time in the remaining fat until they are browned on all sides. Remove and reserve.

Sauté the chopped onions and garlic in the remaining oil, adding a little more oil if necessary, until the vegetables are transparent. Then return the bacon pieces and lamb to the casserole and add the dried orange peel, bay leaves, cloves, thyme and dry white wine. Season to taste with salt and freshly ground black pepper and simmer, covered, for 1–1½ hours or until tender. Correct the seasoning and serve.

Grillade des mariniers du Rhône

Boatmen's braised beef from the Rhône delta

SERVES 4

This recipe for a *grillade* of beef in the manner of the fishermen from the Rhône delta sweats the beef in a blanket of sliced onions before adding red wine and aromatics, in which the meat is simmered to melting tenderness. It is not really a *grillade* at all, of course, but a 'boatmen's braise' of beef and onions in red wine. Anchovies are sometimes added to the dish to give it emphasis, as in this recipe, much in the way that the ancient Romans used to add *garum salarum* (a distilled essence of sun-dried fish) to their stews of beef and veal.

coarse salt and ground black pepper	3 tbsps butter
1 slice rump steak, about 2½ inches thick	3 tbsps olive oil

FOR THE *MARINADE COURTE*

6 tbsps olive oil	4 tbsps chopped Italian (flat-leaf) parsley
2 tbsps red wine vinegar	½ tsp dried thyme
4 tbsps cognac	½ tsp dried rosemary
coarse salt	1 *bouquet garni* (1 bay leaf,
3 tbsps butter	1 sprig thyme, 1 sprig
3 tbsps olive oil	parsley, 4-inch sections
3 large yellow onions, thinly sliced	celery)
3 cloves garlic, crushed	½ bottle red wine
cracked peppercorns	6 anchovy fillets, chopped

FOR THE GARNISH

4 tbsps diced butter rolled in chopped parsley

Rub the meat on both sides with the coarse salt and freshly ground black pepper. Leave to absorb the flavors for 1 hour.

In the meantime, in a large flat gratin dish or roasting pan large enough to hold the rump steak, combine the marinade ingredients.

Place the meat in this marinade, turning it once or twice. Leave it in the marinade for 1–2 days in the refrigerator, turning it several times to ensure that it is well impregnated with all the flavors.

WHEN READY TO COOK

Heat the butter and olive oil in a large skillet or shallow casserole; place half the sliced onions in the pan or casserole and toss once. Place the meat on the bed of onions; pour over the marinade juices, add the garlic and *bouquet garni* and cover with the remaining onions. Cover the pan and cook over very low heat for 45 minutes.

Towards the end of this cooking time, in a medium-sized saucepan, heat the red wine to boiling. Remove the wine from the heat and pour enough into the skillet or casserole to just cover meat and onions. Add the chopped anchovies and continue to simmer over low heat for 1 hour more, or until the meat is meltingly tender.

TO SERVE

Transfer the meat to a heated serving dish and reduce the sauce over a high heat to a quarter of its original quantity. Slice the meat diagonally into slices ⅓ inch thick. Spoon over the hot reduced sauce and dot with diced butter which you have rolled in chopped parsley. Serve immediately.

Boeuf en daube à l'ancienne

Slow-cooked daube of beef

SERVES 6

This is an unusual daube in that the meat is cooked – like a pot roast – in one rolled piece. It is then sliced just before serving.

3 lb 8 oz lean top rump of beef, rolled	4 shallots, finely chopped
3 cloves garlic, halved	2 cloves garlic, finely chopped
4 oz fat salt pork	12 button onions
3 tbsps olive oil	1½ cups mushrooms, quartered
salt and ground black pepper	4 sprigs parsley
4 tomatoes, peeled, seeded and diced	1¼ cups beef stock

FOR THE MARINADE

3 lemon slices	3 tsps finely chopped herbs (chives, tarragon, parsley)
1 bay leaf	
1 pinch thyme	3 tsps olive oil
⅔ cup dry white wine	ground black pepper

Make 6 small incisions in the top of the beef with a sharp knife and bury half a clove of garlic in each.

In a deep long dish, large enough to hold the rolled beef, make the marinade. Combine the lemon slices, bay leaf, thyme, finely chopped herbs, wine and olive oil, and season with freshly ground black pepper to taste. Stir to blend. Add the rolled beef to the marinade, cover and refrigerate for 12 hours, turning occasionally.

Pre-heat the oven to 250°F.

Remove the rind from the fat salt pork and dice the pork; reserve the rind. In a heat-proof casserole large enough to hold the rolled beef, heat the olive oil, add the diced pork and sauté for 5 minutes, or until golden brown, turning the cubes with a spatula. Remove with a slotted spoon and keep warm.

Drain the beef and pat it dry with absorbent paper. Reserve the marinade. Season the beef generously with salt and freshly ground black pepper. Add it to the fat remaining in the casserole and brown it all over. Remove the beef from the casserole and keep warm.

Put the reserved rind in the bottom of the casserole. Place the beef on top and surround it with the diced, sautéed pork, finely chopped shallots, peeled, seeded and diced tomatoes, finely chopped garlic, button onions, quartered mushrooms and parsley sprigs. Strain the reserved marinade over the rolled beef and pour in the beef stock. Season with salt and freshly ground black pepper to taste.

Cover the casserole and cook in the pre-heated oven for 6 hours.

Remove the beef to a board and carve in thick slices. Arrange the slices on a heated serving dish and spoon round the vegetables and cooking juices.

Boeuf en daube à la provençale.

Boeuf en daube à la provençale

Provençal daube of beef

SERVES 6–8

4–5 lb lean beef	4 tbsps olive oil
2 onions, sliced	8 lean bacon slices, diced
2 carrots, sliced	1 large yellow onion, cut in
1 *bouquet garni* (2–3 sprigs thyme and parsley and 1 bay leaf)	quarters
	4 cloves garlic
	1 piece orange peel
salt and freshly ground black pepper	1¼ cups or more hot beef stock or water
1¼ cups red wine	½ cup pitted ripe olives
4 tbsps cognac	

Cut the meat in 1-inch cubes and place in a large bowl or earthenware casserole with the sliced onions and carrots, *bouquet garni*, salt, freshly ground black pepper, red wine and cognac, and marinate in this mixture for 5–6 hours, stirring occasionally.

Heat the oil in a large skillet or heat-proof casserole; melt the diced bacon in it and brown the onion quarters in the fat. Drain the meat, reserving the juices of the marinade, and sauté the meat with the bacon and onion until browned, shaking the pan from time to time. Add the garlic cloves and orange peel; then moisten with the marinade which has been reduced to half the original quantity. Pour over hot beef stock or, failing this, hot water. Cover the pot with a tight-fitting lid, and cook in a very slow oven (250–275°F) for 3–4 hours. Remove from the oven; skim the fat from the surface; add the olives and correct the seasoning. Cook for another 30 minutes. Serve in the casserole.

Daube de boeuf 'à la feignasse'

Lazy man's daube of beef

SERVES 4–6

This recipe for lazy man's daube of beef contains, surprisingly enough, no liquids. You will find that the meat alone (with the juices from the large onions) provides more than enough sauce for this easily made dish. Originally, the daube was cooked in the ashes of an open fire, with the hot embers being swept up around the casserole of gently simmering meats. I still cook it in this age-old way. But for those of you who prefer a more modern method of cooking, I suggest a very low oven heat to achieve the same results.

3 lb shin of beef, cut into 2-inch cubes	coarse salt and ground black pepper
1 lb bacon, in a single piece	1–2 cloves garlic
3 large yellow onions, sliced	1 strip dried orange peel
3 tbsps olive oil	2 cloves
3 tbsps butter	*bouquet garni* (2 sprigs thyme, 4 sprigs parsley,
all-purpose flour	2 bay leaves)

Cut the bacon into large cubes; combine with the sliced onions, olive oil and butter, and sauté in a heat-proof casserole until the onions are transparent. Sprinkle the beef, cut into 2-inch cubes, with flour; add to the casserole and continue to cook, stirring constantly, until the beef browns. Then add the coarse salt and freshly ground black pepper, garlic, dried orange peel, cloves and *bouquet garni*. Place a thick shallow serving dish filled with cold water on top of the casserole to close it hermetically and place the casserole in the center of hot ashes (bringing the ashes up around the casserole) for 2½–3 hours, replacing the water in the soup plate as necessary.

Alternatively, place the casserole in a pre-heated, very slow oven (250–275°F) for 2½–3 hours.

Daube de boeuf à la feignasse.

Pieds et paquets marseillais

*P*ieds et paquets – literally 'feet and packets' – is one of the great specialities of Marseilles. The 'feet' are carefully cleaned lambs' feet and the 'packets' are attractive little bundles of lemon-rubbed tripe filled with a well-seasoned mixture of chopped lean bacon, salt pork, tripe, parsley, garlic and onion. As made by Suzon Hézard, the delightful chef-patronne of the Relais des Templiers restaurant in Montfort, just behind Carces, this is a real country dish designed for big appetites. Her little corner restaurant, the first floor of a narrow village house that once belonged to the Knights Templar, is the secret dream of every Provençal cook. Its one room contains only five or six close-set tables seating 18 diners, and the front door and windows open straight on to the little narrow street in the town center. There is a tiny bar (two could stand at it almost comfortably) and a small

Suzon's little corner restaurant is the secret dream of every Provençal cook, a single room containing five or six tables and opening straight on to the street. Behind the tiny bar is a small open-fronted kitchen containing a vast eleventh-century chimney and a modest 1930s stove. From here Suzon presides as mistress of the revelries.

Pieds et paquets, Relais des Templiers.

open-fronted kitchen which, apart from an enormous eleventh-century chimney where Suzon cooks her long-simmered casseroles and grills her meats and game, boasts only a small 1930s stove, a sink and a rather narrow work surface hidden behind a counter opening to the dining area. This ensures that guests are part of the festivities and that Suzon is mistress of the revelries. Just as it must have been in the time of the Knights Templar.

Le Relais des Templiers is one of those old-fashioned country restaurants where you take pot-luck when you come in. There is no menu, just three courses of whatever Suzon happens to want to serve you that day. On my last visit (at two-thirty in the afternoon) a delicious *terrine de lièvre* was plonked down with a pot of little homemade gherkins and

pickled onions, a basket of freshly cut bread, a huge block of farm butter and a bottle of Cuvée de Papé (*sic*) de Ste Croix from Montfort. The main course, a *steak au poivre à la provençale*, the peppered steak fried over the open fire and accompanied by melting golden-fried potatoes, was served with a generous sprinkling of finely chopped garlic and Italian (flat-leaf) parsley.

A delicious country salad of lettuce leaves and pine nuts came next ... and for dessert, a *crème caramel* (served in a homely earthenware crock) followed by a *crêpe à l'orange*: two fat folded pancakes, sprinkled with sugar and orange liqueur, and topped with a slice of unpeeled orange. The price for all this munificence? A little less than thirty dollars for two. Suzon is famous in the region for providing feasts *sur commande*

at extremely reasonable prices: you can choose your own menu by telephone from the following: *brouillade aux truffes du pays*, *fricassée de volaille aux cèpes*, *pot-au-feu à la provençale*, *pieds et paquets marseillais*, a superb *gratin de langoustines*, and a much-praised *soufflé aux trois fromages*.

It is interesting to note, too, that the Relais des Templiers is more than a restaurant: it is a little inn with three lovely, high-ceilinged Provençal rooms, each with its own tiled bathroom. The one I have bagged for my next visit to Provence has a wood-burning fireplace, a great brass bed which fills the center of the room, some comfortable nineteenth-century furniture, and a wide, low window cut into the ancient, meter-thick walls. All this at around thirty-five dollars a night. How can one resist?

Pieds et paquets, Relais des Templiers

—

To make your own version of *pieds et paquets*, you will have to order a fresh lamb's tripe and 12 lambs' feet from your butcher. Most butchers will provide them for you, cleaned and ready for cooking, if you give them two or three days' notice.

1 fresh lamb's tripe	2 sprigs parsley
12 lambs' feet	2 bay leaves
½ lemon	2 cloves
6 bacon slices	¼-inch slice cooked ham, finely chopped
1 large yellow onion, finely chopped	salt and ground black pepper
2 whites of leek, finely chopped	1¼ cups well-flavored lamb or beef stock
4 tomatoes, peeled, seeded and chopped	1¼ cups dry white wine
1 large yellow onion, cut into quarters	cognac (optional)
4 cloves garlic	
2 sprigs thyme	

FOR THE STUFFING

5–6 oz fat salt pork (soaked for 2 hours in cold water to remove excess salt), finely chopped	1 bunch parsley, finely chopped
	2 cloves garlic, finely chopped
trimmings from the tripe (see below)	salt and ground black pepper

TO MAKE THE *PAQUETS*

Rub the cleaned tripe with the cut side of the lemon on both sides. Rinse well. Put the tripe in a saucepan; cover with cold water and, over medium heat, bring the water gently to a boil. Skim the impurities from the surface of the water; remove the pan from heat; drain the tripe and allow to cool enough to handle. Cut it into pieces about 4 inches square.

In a medium-sized bowl, combine the finely chopped fat salt pork with the trimmings from the tripe (cut into thin strips) and the finely chopped parsley and garlic. Season with salt and freshly ground black pepper, to taste, and mix well, adding a little more chopped parsley if the stuffing does not look 'green' enough.

Lay the tripe squares out on a clean working surface; divide the stuffing mixture between the squares and then roll up each square around its stuffing, tying each herb and tripe 'olive' securely with 2 pieces of string. Reserve.

TO COOK THE *PIEDS ET PAQUETS*

Pre-heat the oven to very cool (225°F). Arrange the bacon slices to cover the bottom of a large heat-proof casserole. In a skillet, sauté the finely chopped onion and whites of leek in olive oil until the vegetables have changed color. Pour the sautéed vegetables over the bacon slices and put the casserole over medium heat to allow the fat to sizzle gently from the bacon.

When the bacon slices have given up their fat, add the peeled, seeded and chopped tomatoes, garlic,

quartered onion, thyme, parsley, bay leaves and cloves. Place the cleaned lambs' feet and pre-prepared tripe and herb packets alternately on this bed of aromatics; sprinkle with the chopped cooked ham; season generously with salt and freshly ground black pepper; moisten with stock, 1¼ cups water and white wine and, if desired, a little cognac.

Over medium heat, bring the pan juices to the boil; cover the casserole, transfer to the pre-heated oven and cook for 3–4 hours, or until the lambs' feet and little packets of tripe and herbs are meltingly tender.

Le Relais des Templiers, located on the first floor of an ancient village house that once belonged to the Knights Templar, is one of those old-fashioned country restaurants where you take pot luck. There is no menu, just three courses of whatever Suzon happens to want to serve you that day.

Rôti de porc et ses légumes farcis

Roast loin of pork with stuffed vegetables

SERVES 6–8

1 loin of pork (6–8 cutlets)	½ tsp dried *herbes de*
6 dried mushroms	*Provence*
2 large cloves garlic	
salt and ground black	
pepper	

FOR THE STUFFED VEGETABLES

1 tbsp butter	½ tsp each finely chopped
3 tbsps finely chopped	fresh tarragon and
onion	chives
8 oz pork sausage meat	salt and ground black
6 tbsps grated Parmesan	pepper
cheese	6 large ripe tomatoes
1 tbsp finely chopped	4 large mushrooms
parsley	

Ask the butcher to skin and chine the loin of pork so that it will be easier to carve when roasted.

Soak the dried mushrooms in warm water for about 30 minutes. Pour the mushrooms and their soaking water into a small pan and simmer gently until the mushrooms are soft and swollen, and the water has almost evaporated. Cut off any hard ends of the mushrooms stalks.

Reserve 3 of the mushrooms. Cut each remaining mushroom into 4 strips, making 12 strips in all. Cut 1 of the garlic cloves into 12 slivers. Reserve the remaining clove for the stuffing.

Weigh the loin of pork and calculate the cooking time, allowing 35–40 minutes per lb. Make 12 deep slits in the pork fat with the point of a sharp knife and push a strip of mushroom and a sliver of garlic well down into each slit. Season the pork all over with freshly ground black pepper. Sprinkle the fat only with salt and dried *herbes de Provence*. Leave the pork to stand at room temperature for 2 hours, so that it absorbs the flavors and loses its chill. Towards the end of the time, heat the oven to 450°F.

Transfer the pork to a roasting pan and roast for 20 minutes, then reduce the oven temperature to 300°F and roast the pork for the calculated cooking time, basting it occasionally with the juices. It may be necessary to add a spoonful or two of water from time to time to prevent the juices in the pan from drying up and burning.

Meanwhile, prepare the stuffed vegetables. Finely chop the remaining garlic clove. Melt the butter in a small pan and sauté the finely chopped onion and garlic for 3–4 minutes until soft. Leave to cool. Finely chop the reserved mushrooms and place them in a bowl with the cooled onion mixture, sausage meat, Parmesan cheese, parsley, tarragon and chives. Mix well and season to taste with salt and pepper.

Slice the tops off the tomatoes and scoop out the seeds, taking care not to break the shells. Lightly sprinkle the insides of the tomatoes with salt, then leave them upside down on a rack for a few minutes to drain. Wipe the mushrooms clean and carefully remove the stems. Stuff the tomatoes and mushrooms with the sausage meat mixture, smoothing the top surfaces neatly.

About 45 minutes before the end of the cooking time for the pork, place the stuffed tomatoes around the pork; 15 minutes later, place the stuffed mushrooms around the pork. Complete the cooking time.

Transfer the roast pork to a heated serving platter and surround it with the stuffed tomatoes and mushrooms. Pour off the excess fat from the roasting pan, then moisten the pork and stuffed vegetables with the remaining juices. Serve immediately.

Carré de porc à la provençale

Loin of pork Provençal

SERVES 6–8

1 loin of pork (6–8 cutlets)	olive oil
8–12 sage leaves	6 tbsps dry white wine
salt and ground black	6 tbsps olive oil
pepper	2–3 cloves garlic
thyme and bay leaf	

Ask the butcher to bone and tie the loin of pork. Pierce it with the point of a sharp knife to insert the sage leaves into the meat. Season to taste with salt, freshly ground black pepper, crumbled thyme and bay leaf. Sprinkle with a little olive oil and allow to stand for at least 12 hours to absorb the flavors.

When ready to cook, pre-heat the oven to moderate (350°F). Place the pork in a heat-proof casserole; add the water, dry white wine and olive oil; crush the garlic cloves with the flat of your hand and add them to the cooking liquid. Roast the pork in the pre-heated oven until tender, about 35–40 minutes per lb.

Côtes de veau à la niçoise

Veal chops Niçoise

SERVES 4

4 veal chops	16 black olives, pitted
seasoned all-purpose flour	4 tbsps shredded fresh
olive oil	basil

FOR THE *SAUCE NIÇOISE*

2 tbsps olive oil	2 tbsps tomato paste
1 large yellow onion, finely	6 fresh basil leaves, finely
chopped	chopped
4 cloves garlic	salt and ground black
4 cups canned chopped	pepper
tomatoes with juice	

Lightly dust the veal chops with seasoned flour and sauté them in olive oil for about 5 minutes, turning once, until they are lightly browned on both sides.

TO MAKE THE *SAUCE NIÇOISE*

Heat the olive oil in a medium-sized pan and cook the finely chopped onion and garlic for 10 minutes, or until the onion is soft and transparent

Add the canned tomatoes and juice, tomato paste, finely chopped basil and salt and freshly ground black pepper to taste. Bring to a boil, reduce the heat and simmer, uncovered, for about 1 hour, or until the sauce is reduced to about $2\frac{1}{2}$ cups, stirring occasionally with a wooden spoon. Taste and add more salt and pepper if necessary.

Pour the *sauce niçoise* over the chops in the pan. Cover with a lid and simmer for about 15 minutes, until the chops are tender. Transfer to a heated serving dish and sprinkle with the pitted black olives and shredded fresh basil. Serve immediately.

Aillade de veau

Sauté of veal with sweet garlic

SERVES 4

2 lb 4 oz lean veal,	12 fat cloves fresh garlic,
cut from the leg	peeled and blanched in
lard	boiling water to cover
olive oil	for 2 minutes
4 tbsps fresh white	salt and ground black
breadcrumbs	pepper
4 tbsps tomato paste	cayenne pepper
	$\frac{1}{2}$ cup dry white wine

Cut the veal into pieces 1 inch square. In a large shallow skillet, sauté a third of the veal cubes in 1 tablespoon each of lard and olive oil until the veal is golden brown on all sides. Remove the veal cubes from the pan with a slotted spoon and reserve.

Add half the remaining veal cubes to the pan and proceed as above, adding a little more lard and oil as necessary. Remove the veal from the pan with a slotted spoon and reserve. Sauté the remaining veal.

In a clean heat-proof casserole, heat 1 tablespoon each of lard and olive oil. Add the browned veal cubes, fresh breadcrumbs, blanched garlic and tomato paste. Cook over gentle heat, stirring continuously, for 5–7 minutes.

Season with salt, freshly ground black pepper and cayenne pepper, to taste. Moisten with dry white wine and $\frac{1}{4}$ cup water and simmer over the lowest of heats, covered, for 1 hour, adding a tablespoon or two more water if necessary. The sauce – just enough comfortably to coat the veal and garlic – should be quite thick. Serve with boiled rice.

Poulet aux olives

Chicken with black olives

SERVES 4

1 chicken, 3 lb	salt and black pepper
2 tbsps olive oil	sprigs of fresh watercress

FOR THE *TAPENADE* GARNISH

4 lean bacon slices, finely chopped	2 tbsps chopped Italian (flat-leaf) parsley
2 tbsps olive oil	1–2 tbsps chopped fresh thyme
½ large yellow onion, finely chopped	2 tbsps small capers, drained
2 cloves garlic	salt and black pepper
36 black olives, chopped	crushed red pepper flakes
½ red pepper, cut into tiny dice	
4 anchovy fillets, chopped	

TO MAKE THE *TAPENADE* GARNISH

In a large skillet, sauté the chopped bacon in olive oil, stirring, until it begins to crisp; add the chopped onion and garlic and continue to cook, stirring constantly, until vegetables are transparent.

Add the chopped olives and diced red pepper to the pan with the chopped anchovy fillets and parsley, fresh thyme and drained capers and continue to cook, stirring constantly, for 3–4 minutes, or until all the flavors of the *tapenade* mixture amalgamate. Season generously with salt, freshly ground black pepper and crushed red pepper flakes and, with a slotted spoon, transfer the mixture to a medium-sized bowl.

TO ROAST THE BIRD

Pre-heat the oven to hot (425°F). Brush the bird with olive oil and season with salt and pepper to taste. Place on a rack and roast in the pre-heated oven, basting occasionally with the pan juices, until cooked through, about 1 hour.

Remove the chicken from the oven. Remove the strings and leave to rest for 10 minutes. In the meantime, re-heat the *tapenade* mixture. Keep warm. Carve the bird into serving pieces and arrange on a heated serving platter. Garnish with the sprigs of watercress and mounds of *tapenade*.

Poulet sauté Pont du Gard

Provençal sautéed chicken

SERVES 4–5

3 lb 8 oz chicken, cut into serving pieces	3 large tomatoes, blanched, skinned, seeded and chopped
6–8 sprigs fresh thyme, or 1½–2 tsps dried	1½ cups dry white wine
6–8 slices lean bacon, one for each chicken portion	salt and ground black pepper
1 large onion, roughly chopped	7 tbsps black olives, pitted and halved
2 cloves garlic, chopped	4 tbsps parsley, chopped

Wrap each chicken portion with a sprig of fresh thyme, or a pinch of dried thyme, in a slice of bacon. Secure the bacon with a cocktail stick, 'stitching' it so that the stick lies along the side of the packet.

Put the olive oil in a wide heat-proof casserole over medium heat and fry the portions on both sides until lightly cooked.

Add the onions, garlic and tomatoes, and pour in the white wine. Simmer the mixture, covered, for about 25 minutes.

Remove the lid from the pan, season with salt and freshly ground black pepper, and cook for 8–10 minutes longer over a slightly higher heat to let the sauce reduce. Add the black olives, sprinkle with the parsley and serve.

The barnyards of inland Provence have always provided welcome extras for a meager diet. Traditional recipes for chicken, including *poulet aux olives* (opposite), can equally well be adapted to suit other poultry such as pigeon or guinea fowl.

Pigeons aux petits pois à la provençale

Pigeons with peas Provençal

SERVES 4

4 plump pigeons, oven-
  ready
4 thick slices fat bacon
3 tbsps butter
3 tbsps olive oil
2 large yellow onions,
  chopped
1¼ cups chicken stock
salt and black pepper

bouquet garni (2 sprigs
  thyme, 2 sprigs parsley,
  1 piece celery)
2 tbsps fat salt pork, finely
  diced
1–2 carrots, peeled and cut
  into chunks
1½ cups shelled peas
¼ tsp dried thyme
½ bay leaf

Pre-heat the oven to 325°F.

Wipe the pigeons with a damp cloth inside and out. Wrap each with one slice of fat bacon and push a small skewer through one wing and out through the other, securing the bacon.

In a heavy, heat-proof casserole, heat 2 tablespoons each butter and olive oil, and sauté the pigeons until well browned all over, about 10 minutes. Remove to a plate. In the fat in the pan, cook half the onions for 10 minutes or until golden.

Return the pigeons to the casserole. Add the stock and *bouquet garni* and season with salt and ground pepper to taste. Cover, transfer to the oven and bake for 1 hour, or until cooked but still firm.

In a heavy saucepan, melt the remaining butter and olive oil, and sauté the remaining chopped onion gently for 5 minutes. Add the diced salt pork and diced carrot, and continue to sauté gently for 10 minutes or until the onions are rich golden brown. Stir in the shelled peas and cook over low heat for a further 5 minutes, stirring frequently. Add 1¼ cups water to the pea mixture, with the thyme, bay leaf and freshly ground black pepper, to taste. Bring to a boil and lower the heat to simmering point. Cover and cook for 20 minutes. Remove the pan from the heat.

When the pigeons are cooked, remove them from the casserole. Discard the skewers, slice the pigeons in half lengthwise. Cut the bacon slices into thin strips.

Combine the pea mixture with the juices remaining in the casserole. Bury the pigeon halves in the peas and add the bacon strips. Return the casserole to the oven and continue to cook until the pigeons are heated through and very tender. Serve immediately.

Provençal cooks have always known how to turn simple ingredients into dishes that are both delicious and nourishing. *Pigeons aux petits pois à la provençale* (left) and *lapin 'à la sauvage'* both take the hunter's catch of the day and combine it with vegetables and herbs from the *potager* and hillsides to make a satisfying main course.

Pigeons aux petits pois à la provençale.

Lapin 'à la sauvage'

Wild-flavored rabbit with roasted garlic

SERVES 4

1 young rabbit
4 tbsps olive oil
4 tbsps *marc de Provence*
8–12 fat cloves garlic
2 tbsps butter

well-flavored stock, made with the bones and trimmings of the rabbit (including the head, if you have it) and a chicken stock cube

FOR THE WILD-FLAVORED MARINADE

4 tbsps olive oil
4 tbsps red wine vinegar
1 tsp each chopped fresh thyme, rosemary and summer savory

2 strips dried orange peel
2 bay leaves
$\frac{1}{4}$ tsp freshly grated nutmeg
coarse salt and ground black pepper

TO PREPARE THE RABBIT

Forty-eight hours before you wish to serve the rabbit, cut it into serving pieces. In a large shallow gratin dish or roasting pan combine the olive oil, red wine vinegar, chopped fresh herbs, dried orange peel, bay leaves and freshly grated nutmeg. Season the mixture generously with coarse salt and ground pepper.

Place the rabbit pieces in this marinade; mix well and place in the refrigerator for 48 hours, stirring from time to time.

TO COOK THE RABBIT

Pre-heat the oven to fairly hot (375°F). Heat the olive oil in a large heat-proof casserole; add the rabbit pieces and brown thoroughly on all sides. Heat the *marc de Provence* in a metal ladle until it begins to bubble; pour it over the rabbit pieces and flame. When the flames die down, pour in enough well-flavored stock (or stock and water) to come halfway up the rabbit pieces, and continue to cook until the liquids just come to a boil; then cover the gratin dish or roasting pan with aluminum foil and put it in the pre-heated oven for 30 minutes, or until tender.

TO ROAST THE GARLIC CLOVES

In the meantime, blanch the garlic cloves in two changes of boiling water. Drain.

In a medium-sized skillet melt the butter; add the blanched garlic cloves and sauté in the hot butter, shaking the pan from time to time, until the garlic cloves begin to change color. Then, with a slotted spoon, add them to the rabbit and continue to cook until the rabbit is tender.

141

La soupe de lapin

Old-fashioned rabbit in bouillon

SERVES 4–6

1 to 1½ young rabbit(s), cut into serving pieces	coarse salt and ground black pepper
dried *herbes de Provence*	

FOR THE BOUILLON

2 bacon slices	2 fat cloves garlic, in their skins
1 slice fat salt pork	1¼ cups dry white wine
1 slice raw ham	1 large onion, stuck with 2 cloves
1 *bouquet garni* (thyme, rosemary, parsley)	
2 bay leaves	

FOR THE GARNISH

½ small Savoy cabbage	4 new potatoes, 3–4 inches long
½ small celeriac	
4 ribs celery	2 tbsps coarsely chopped Italian (flat-leaf) parsley
4 small carrots	
4 tomatoes	

Cut the rabbit into serving pieces. Rub the pieces well with coarse salt, freshly ground black pepper and dried *herbes de Provence* and leave for 1 hour to absorb the flavors.

Make a bouillon by combining the chopped bacon, salt pork and raw ham in a stockpot with the *bouquet garni*, bay leaves and garlic. Add 4¼ cups water and the dry white wine; bring to a boil. Skim and add the pieces of young rabbit and the Spanish onion (stuck with cloves) and cook over low heat, covered, until the rabbit is cooked through but still firm.

TO PREPARE THE GARNISH

Remove the outer leaves from the cabbage. Shred the inner leaves; wash well and drain dry. Cut them across the grain into ¼-inch strips.

Peel the celeriac, carrots and potatoes and wash the celery. Cut all the vegetables into strips 3 inches long and ¼ inch square. Peel the tomatoes, press out the seeds and dice the flesh.

Cook all the vegetable strips in a little bouillon until *al dente*, about 10 minutes. Keep warm.

TO SERVE

Heat the rabbit pieces in a little of the bouillon until hot. Transfer the pieces to a heated shallow soup bowl. Garnish with hot vegetables, add the tomatoes and parsley and serve immediately.

Le cul de lapin au basilic

Rabbit in basil sauce

SERVES 4

2 lb rabbit, dressed weight	2 medium-sized onions, sliced
2–3 tsps finely chopped fresh basil	4 medium-sized tomatoes, sliced
2 tbsps Dijon mustard	2 cloves garlic, chopped
softened butter	¼ tsp dried thyme
salt and ground black pepper	1 bay leaf, crumbled
2–3 thin slices fat salt pork	⅔ cup dry white wine
	2–3 tsps cornstarch

Cut the rabbit into 8 serving pieces.

Pre-heat the oven to 450°F.

Mix the fresh basil with 2 tablespoons each of mustard and softened butter.

Season each piece of rabbit with salt and freshly ground black pepper, and spread lightly with the basil mustard. Wrap each piece of rabbit in fat salt pork, securing it with string.

Select a casserole that will hold the rabbit pieces in a single layer. Grease it with butter and cover the base with a layer of sliced onions and tomatoes. Sprinkle with chopped garlic, thyme, crumbled bay leaf and a little salt and freshly ground black pepper. Lay the rabbit pieces on the bed of vegetables.

Bake, uncovered, for 10 minutes, or until the rabbit pieces are lightly colored. Remove from the oven and lower the heat to 325°F.

Moisten the casserole with the dry white wine, cover tightly and return to the oven for a further 40–45 minutes, or until the rabbit is tender. Untie the rabbit pieces and discard the pork fat. Arrange the joints in a shallow oven-proof serving dish and return them to the oven while you finish the sauce.

Strain the contents of the casserole through a fine sieve into a saucepan, pressing the vegetables against the sides of the sieve with the back of a spoon to extract their juices without rubbing them through.

Mix the cornstarch to a smooth paste with 2 tablespoons cold water, then blend in 2–3 tablespoons of the sauce. Stir into the remaining sauce; bring to a boil and simmer, stirring, for 2–3 minutes or until the sauce has thickened and no longer tastes of raw cornstarch. Spoon over the rabbit and serve.

La soupe de lapin.

FEAST

Roger Vergé
Le Moulin de Mougins

Going to a great restaurant is a great experience – Bocuse in Lyons, Senderens and Robuchon in Paris, Girardet in Chrissier, Roger Vergé in the south of France. Can the restaurant live up to its lofty reputation? Will the service and the welcome complement the cuisine? Will the food be worthy of the setting? Will we?

And, perhaps for me the most important of all: will I discover a combination of flavors that will remain long in my memory, sing in my senses, 'explode' in my mouth so that years from now I will be able to bring the dish back into sharp focus to set against other great dishes I have tasted?

Roger Vergé's Moulin de Mougins scored high on every one of these points on my first visit. And the risks were great: first of all it was lunchtime on Easter Sunday, one of the great public holidays in the south of France, when everyone beetles off to the restaurant of his or her choice with a group of old friends. Whole families arrive, complete with granny and *les enfants*. As a result the restaurants are apt to be overcrowded, the kitchens overextended and the staff rushed off their feet.

The Moulin was no exception: French families were there *au complet*; visiting tourists seemed to have arrived from all over the world and groups of businessmen were there taking a well-deserved weekend break from their conferences in Nice or Cannes. But it was a total success, from the moment we entered the door until we left, four blissful hours later.

The Moulin stands in a tree-shaded garden under the old village of Mougins, at the bottom of the hill as you go up the road from the *autoroute*, and far from the noise and bustle of the coast. It also stands apart from the crowded little streets of the old town which has now become a tourist spot, one of the over-restored hill villages that are almost required viewing if you are traveling in the south of France. Roger Vergé's

restaurant might well have fallen into the same trap. Miraculously, it hasn't.

There is a family feeling about the mill house. One senses, even if one does not know, that Denise Vergé does the flowers and has arranged the decor; that Vergé himself is on the premises making sure that everything goes well in the kitchen, coming out to oversee the dining room, greeting his many friends and the regulars, making sure he meets the newcomers, smiling, and putting his guests at their ease like a good host at a private party. His son-in-law Serge Chollet heads the busy kitchens under the master's sure direction. It is a family business. It is quite obvious that everyone cares.

Roger Vergé is one of the most imaginative and inventive cooks on the coast, making the most delicious and unexpected dishes out of the best that the nearby Nice and Menton markets have to offer. Lunching or dining at the Moulin de Mougins is an experience. Even on Easter Sunday. The dining room was comfortable and casually beautiful. The service was impeccable. The wines suggested by the *sommelier* were perfect. The whole meal was evidence of a carefully defined cooking style – Vergé's own – that does away with disguises, complex sauces and elaborate combinations of ingredients to let the essential quality and flavor of the food shine through.

When the culinary guides declared that *nouvelle*

cuisine was finished and that cooks and restaurateurs should now return to the country cooking of their ancestors, Roger Vergé seemed surprised. 'I had no problem,' he said softly with a smile. 'I had never changed: *je reste dans le vrai.*'

His polenta is the best I have ever tasted. The secret? It starts off with shallots cooked in butter, then the polenta is dribbled into the butter and shallot mixture and stirred until the savory fat has impregnated the cornmeal; much like a risotto, in fact. This simple touch makes all the difference.

And all his cooking is like that, whether it is the secret of his sauce '*insolite*' for oysters (a hint of lemon, orange and dill) or the magic ingredients of his salmis of pigeons (bitter chocolate and cinnamon). The main problem when making a sauce is not to make it heavy with fats, he says, but to use a combination of a little walnut oil and olive oil, with just a touch of butter to 'soften' the dish. With fish he likes to add a splash of vermouth, or equal quantities (minute) of Noilly Prat and cassis; with lobster, a little Sauternes at the end of the cooking time to accentuate the sweetness of the lobster.

According to Vergé, today's cooks are excitedly returning to the use of chocolate and almonds, to reductions of fruit and vegetable juices to thicken and flavor their sauces, and to ancient Arabian spices like cinnamon, pepper, turmeric, cumin and saffron, as if these sensual flavors from the Middle Ages were absolutely new. The result is a subtle layering of warm scents and hidden flavors that gives a whole new personality to today's cooking.

Vergé's sauces are suave: there is no other word for them. There is a gentle buildup, with each subtle gradation and hidden flavor more intriguing and elusive than the last. Sauces like these can be achieved only by blending careful reductions of special ingredients and flavors. The sauce for the restaurant's key dish, for instance – a fragile golden zucchini blossom stuffed with a mousse of *foie gras* and earthy chopped black Provençal truffles – is a case in point. A rich ivory color, shiny and full-flavored, it is slightly thickened with a reduction of vegetable juices and wine, with butter beaten in at the last moment to give it a final richness and added lightness. It had a honeyed flavor which lingered on the tongue: a blend of wild mushroom, white wine, butter and the

Salade de noix de St Jacques.

reduced essences of young vegetables. It was indescribably good.

And the next course, a salad of thin petals of fresh scallops, cooked on one side only to preserve their natural tenderness and flavor, was served with thin slices of fresh artichoke and a buttery dressing flavored with a reduction of fresh orange juice.

We chose two main courses. The first was a piquant *cassolette* of breast and thighs of young pigeon, tossed in butter and oil and then simmered in a salmis sauce of red wine, cognac and aromatics. A hint of bitter chocolate and cinnamon lent a certain Arabic darkness and richness to the wine-red sauce. The other dish, *aumonières de volaille*, was simpler but no less delicious. The *aumonières* (beggars' purses) of breast of chicken were flattened out and stuffed with a delicate quenelle of ground breast of raw chicken, heavy cream, egg white, truffle juice and chopped black truffles, poached in chicken stock and served with a rich port and red wine-flavored velouté sauce.

TO BOIL THE ARTICHOKES

To a large pan of salted water add a little lemon juice or a squeezed-out lemon half. Bring to a boil. Immerse the trimmed artichokes and simmer for 30 minutes, or until just tender. Drain.

Remove the choke of each artichoke with the edge of a sharp teaspoon (or a small kitchen knife). Slice thinly and reserve.

TO PREPARE THE SPINACH OR LAMB'S LETTUCE LEAVES FOR THE GARNISH

Wash the leaves in several changes of water. Remove the tough stems and any damaged or yellowed leaves. Drain well and dry in a clean kitchen towel.

Skin and seed the tomatoes and cut into a fine julienne. Peel the oranges, making certain that you remove all the white pith. Then, over a bowl and using a sharp kitchen knife, cut each orange segment from its fibrous membrane, catching all the juices.

In a small saucepan, over high heat, reduce the orange juice to half of its original quantity; then remove the pan from the heat and whisk in 10 tablespoons diced butter. Season with salt and white pepper and keep warm.

In a non-stick skillet, heat the olive oil and add the drained spinach or lamb's lettuce; season with salt and freshly ground black pepper and sauté the spinach or lamb's lettuce for one or two minutes. Strain off the juices through a sieve and reserve.

Cut each scallop into 4 thin rounds. Arrange them on a baking sheet and season with salt and white pepper.

TO COOK THE SCALLOPS

Add the remaining butter to a large non-stick pan (or 2 pans); add the scallop slices in one layer and allow them to cook for 30–40 seconds over high heat. Do not turn them. Drain them immediately, adding the cooking juices to the orange butter with a little heavy cream to thicken and lighten the sauce.

TO ARRANGE THE SALAD

Place the spinach or lamb's lettuce leaves to make a circular base on each heated salad plate; arrange a ring of sliced artichokes around the outside edge of the leaves. Place a rosette of overlapping slices of scallop in the center (pan-browned sides up), spoon over a little sauce and top with a garnish of orange segments and a sprig of fresh chervil or dill. Serve immediately.

Salade de noix de St Jacques

Scallop salad with orange dressing

SERVES 4

12 fresh scallops	2 oranges
4 artichokes	²⁄₃ cup orange juice
juice and rind of ½ lemon	12 tbsps butter
salt	white pepper
2 cups fresh young spinach leaves (or large lamb's lettuce leaves)	2 tbsps olive oil
	heavy cream
	4 sprigs chervil or dill
3–4 medium tomatoes	

TO PREPARE THE ARTICHOKES

With a strong sharp knife, slice all the leaves off level with the tips of the shortest ones. Strip away all the outer leaves, one by one; then slice around to remove those closest to the heart. Trim the base and stem.

Note: While you are working on each artichoke, keep dipping it into a bowl of water acidulated with the rind and juice of half a lemon to prevent it from turning brown.

Malfatis au fromage de St Moret, sauce à la crème de basilic

Cheese-filled malfatis with basil cream sauce

SERVES 4

1½ cups St Moret cream cheese, or Philadelphia Lite	1 egg
	salt and white pepper
½ cup all-purpose flour	oil

FOR THE BASIL CREAM SAUCE

6 tbsps water	4 tbsps chopped fresh basil leaves
6 tbsps heavy cream	
½ cup diced butter	salt and white pepper

TO MAKE THE *MALFATIS*

In a large mixing bowl, combine the cream cheese, flour and egg. Season generously with salt and white pepper and beat until the mixture is well blended.

Pipe a long sausage of mixture on to a piece of oiled saran wrap. Roll up the saran wrap, patting the 'sausage' into an even shape, and freeze. When ready to poach the *malfatis*, remove the cheese sausage from the freezer and bring it to room temperature; strip off the saran wrap and cut the cheese sausage into slices ¾ inch thick.

Poach in boiling salted water for 10 minutes or until tender. Remove with a slotted spoon and keep warm.

TO MAKE THE BASIL CREAM SAUCE

Combine the water and heavy cream in a saucepan and bring to a boil; whisk in the diced butter until the sauce is smooth and thick.

Stir in the chopped basil and season to taste with salt and white pepper. Keep warm.

TO SERVE

Toss the *malfatis* in basil cream sauce until well covered. Serve immediately, garnished with peeled, seeded and diced tomato and black olives.

Malfatis au fromage de St Moret, sauce à la crème de basilic.

Aumonières de volaille, Moulin de Mougins

Beggars' purses of stuffed chicken

SERVES 4

4 chicken breasts

FOR THE CHICKEN STOCK

1 chicken carcass, coarsely chopped
1 tbsp olive oil
1 tbsp butter
6 tbsps chopped shallots

1 clove garlic, chopped
1 pinch rubbed thyme
1 bay leaf
1 chicken stock cube

FOR THE CREAMED CHICKEN STUFFING

¾ cup raw chicken breast (or trimmings from raw chicken breasts)
1 scant cup heavy cream
2 egg whites
salt and black pepper

2 tbsps finely chopped black truffle (or substitute dried black mushrooms, soaked in a little port until soft, squeezed dry and finely chopped)

FOR THE CHICKEN VELOUTÉ SAUCE WITH PORT

½ recipe chicken stock
⅔ cup red wine

6 tbsps port
2–4 tbsps butter

TO MAKE THE CHICKEN STOCK

Sauté the chopped chicken carcass and trimmings in olive oil and butter until well browned. Add the chopped shallots and garlic to the pan with the thyme and bay leaf and sauté until the vegetables are transparent. Add the chicken stock cube and 7–8 cups water and continue to cook over medium heat, skimming from time to time, for 45 minutes. Remove from the heat and strain into a clean saucepan. Reserve.

TO MAKE THE CREAMED CHICKEN STUFFING

In a food processor, process the raw chicken breast with the heavy cream until smooth. Add the egg whites and process again until doubled in bulk. Season generously with salt and pepper. Stir in the chopped black truffles (or black mushrooms).

TO MAKE THE *AUMONIÈRES*

Cut the chicken breasts open on each side to make a large flat piece. Beat each opened breast lightly between two pieces of plastic wrap. Lay the flattened chicken breasts out on a work surface and fill the center of each with creamed chicken stuffing. Form each stuffed breast into a wrap round and then wrap with plastic wrap to make a perfect ball.

TO COOK THE *AUMONIÈRES*

Pre-heat the oven to moderate (350°F). Place the *aumonières* in a large heat-proof porcelain or earthen-

Aumonières de volaille, Moulin de Mougins.

ware casserole (attractive enough to bring to the table); add half the chicken stock. Cover the casserole, sealing the lid hermetically with a paste made of flour and water. Place the casserole in the pre-heated oven and cook for 45 minutes.

TO MAKE THE CHICKEN VELOUTÉ SAUCE WITH PORT

Add the red wine and port to ½ cup of the remaining half of the chicken stock and reduce, stirring constantly, until the liquids have almost evaporated, leaving only their flavors. Moisten with the remaining chicken stock; lower the heat and simmer until reduced to half the original quantity. Remove from the heat and beat in the diced butter until the sauce is smooth and thick. Keep warm.

TO SERVE THE *AUMONIÈRES*

For full effect, bring the sealed casserole to the table and open the seal before your guests. Serve 1 *aumonière* for each person; spoon a little of the chicken velouté sauce with port around each *aumonière* and garnish with vegetables of your choice. At the Moulin de Mougins, this recipe is served with diced cooked artichoke hearts and ravioli stuffed with ricotta.

Les pêches et les poires au vin de poivre et de miel de lavande

Peaches and pears in wine flavored

with peppercorns and lavender

SERVES 6

2 cups ruby port

thinly pared peel of 1 lemon
and 1 orange

1 vanilla pod

2 tbsps black peppercorns
(tied up in a little muslin
bag)

1 bottle red wine of a good
dark red color

5 tbsps lavender (or
acacia) honey

6 bay leaves

6 yellow peaches

6 large Williams dessert
pears

1 cinnamon stick

TO MAKE THE WINE AND PEPPERCORN SYRUP

In a large saucepan, combine the port, citrus peel, vanilla pod, black peppercorns and red wine and bring gently to a boil; skim and stir the honey into the hot liquid. Remove the saucepan from the heat; add the bay leaves and allow the flavors to amalgamate while you prepare the fruits.

TO PREPARE THE FRUITS

In another saucepan bring 5 cups water to a boil; place the peaches in the water and bring the water to a boil again; cook the peaches for 2 minutes over moderate heat, then remove from the water and gently peel the skins from the peaches. With a vegetable peeler, peel the pears, being careful to remove as little of their flesh as possible.

TO COOK THE PEACHES AND PEARS

Put the peaches in the hot liquid; bring gently to a boil; boil for 10 minutes, or until the peaches test tender with the point of a skewer or sharp kitchen knife. Carefully remove the peaches from the pan with a slotted spoon and place in a shallow bowl to cool. Refrigerate until ready to serve.

Place the peeled pears in the hot liquid, bring to a boil again and boil for 10 minutes, or until the pears test tender with the point of a skewer or sharp knife. Remove from the pan with a slotted spoon. Place the pears in a shallow bowl to cool and then refrigerate with the peaches.

Remove the peppercorns, bay leaves and vanilla pod from the syrup. Reserve. Reduce the syrup over high heat to the desired consistency. Cool to room temperature and then place in the refrigerator with the peaches and pears.

TO SERVE

Decorate each pear with 1 bay leaf (to resemble pear leaves). Cut the cinnamon stick into 6 equal segments and decorate each peach with a piece of cinnamon (to resemble peach stalks). Pour a little of the reduced syrup over the poached peaches and pears. If desired, sprinkle a few peppercorns over the peaches and pears. Serve immediately.

*Les pêches
et les poires au vin
de poivre
et de
miel de lavande.*

6 Markets of

VEGETABLE MAIN COURSES AND ACCOMPANIMENTS

Provençal cooking, with its accent on fresh fruits and vegetables (home-grown or bought daily in the market) and lightly broiled meats, poultry or fish, its use of highly flavored first-pressing olive oil, and its reliance on fresh and dried herbs, ties in closely with our newfound interest in healthy eating.

During the past decade grilling has become one of the most popular ways of cooking in Britain and America, where trendy new restaurants often cook over open fires of esoteric woods such as apple or mesquite. Provençal cooks have been doing this for centuries, using olive branches, uprooted vine stumps and prunings and trimmings from the abundant fruit orchards to cook exciting and healthy meals in a matter of minutes. The rapidly grilled meats, poultry or fish, brushed with a little olive oil, sprinkled with a hint of crumbled wild thyme, rosemary, sage or summer savory, with the addition of a little chopped garlic and cracked black pepper, make for excellent eating. Sometimes a branch or two of dried bay leaves, a few fennel stalks, a clove or two of fresh garlic or a strip of dried orange peel is thrown on the fire to give added flavor.

A five-minute walk through any of the bustling street markets of Provence will provide ample proof – if proof were needed – that Provençal cooking is healthy cooking. Brilliant red, irregularly shaped tomatoes and pale green asparagus with violet-colored tips vie for attention with purple-tipped tiny dark green artichokes. Pointed green peppers and glossy dark eggplants jostle with round zucchini-like squash, large red-fleshed pumpkins and shiny pink sweet onions. Green *cébettes* (halfway between a scallion and an onion) and *mesclun*, that delicious mix of young salad shoots, all underline the possibilities for a healthy way of eating.

Provence

Provençal cooking is so rich and so varied – and so exactly right for today's desire for healthy eating. Witness the way Provençal cooks quick-grill sliced and whole vegetables – dressed only with a splash of extra-virgin olive oil and a pinch of dried *herbes de Provence* – to serve as a robust vegetable accompaniment or as a sparkling fresh course on their own.

Until fairly recently the cooking of Provence was still family cooking, not restaurant cooking. But now a new group of dedicated professionals and gourmet chefs is taking over Provençal kitchens and creating new traditions of cooking throughout the region. Many of these newcomers, not content with adapting the old recipes of Provence, are looking closely at the beautiful vegetables, fruits, fish and game of the region to create exciting new dishes that will be the patrimony of the future. It is this combination of old culinary masterpieces and the new creations of young talents that now makes the cooking of this whole area one of the most exciting gastronomic experiences in the world.

In the weekly market there is usually a pasta stall where you can choose from the many varieties of fresh ravioli and thin strands of eggy noodles, and an herb and spice stall where the huge sacks of colorful culinary herbs and spices provide a favorite backdrop for the tourist photographers. But perhaps my most frequent stop at the market in Lorgues is at the stall of the dark-eyed southern lady, with her Arabian *harissa* and pickled vegetables and every kind of olive one can think of.

Fresh fish and salt cod are always available at the weekly market, as is a vast variety of dried herbs and spices at the spice stall. And the jam man is a must, with his brilliantly colored, fabulously flavored jars of fresh fruit jams and marmalades. All homemade, they are the best in the region, as are his baskets of hand-gathered wild strawberries and his wild asparagus when in season. Italian olive oil is on sale now in the market along with bottles of local provenance: one particular brand with a gold oil wrapping is much in evidence (even on the tables of the renowned Chantecler restaurant at the Negresco in Nice and at Franck Cerutti's Don Camillo restaurant nearby). And Italy – thanks to the opening of borders in the EEC – is also sending delicious little tomatoes on the vine, and green globes of round zucchini to hollow out and fill with rice and seafood before baking them in the oven.

Ratatouille

More than forty years ago, when I first visited Provence, I was introduced to a wonderfully colorful and savory melange of oil-infused vegetables – eggplants, zucchini, tomatoes, onions and garlic – called ratatouille. From that very first taste (I believe it was at lunch in one of the little café-restaurants on the Port of St Tropez) ratatouille became for me the true taste of Provence.

Today, I can't exist without it: served hot as a first course, with a lightly fried egg atop the glistening chunks of Mediterranean vegetables bathed in fragrant olive oil, with just that hint of fresh garlic, sweet onion and Provençal herbs in its preparation that spells Provence. Or cold in a saffron-flavored *gelée* the vegetables softly glowing in their transparent amber glaze and the hesitant saffron making the perfect accompaniment to their robust heartiness.

A simpler version of cold ratatouille tosses the cooked vegetables in a light herb and garlic-flavored vinaigrette, and twins it with chilled saffron rice salad. Or try it as a spicy filling for tomato cases or crisp green peppers.

Served hot straight from the pan, it is delicious folded into a creamy omelet or a soft scramble of beaten eggs (a sort of Provençal *piperade*) to make an intriguing first course or light lunch dish. I also like to serve ratatouille, cut smaller this time, as a savory accompaniment to grilled lamb chops cooked over the open fire; to steamed sea bass or red snapper stuffed with saffron-tinted couscous; or as a delicious bed for vine-grilled fish.

Believe it or not I once traveled a thousand miles to satisfy my craving for this homely vegetable dish. And even now, whenever I head for France's southern coast, I make a devout pilgrimage to Provence for my ratatouille 'fix'.

Today my way of preparing ratatouille is not exactly that of Provençal tradition, which stews the vegetables together in oil. I prefer to simmer the onion, garlic, eggplants, peppers and zucchini separately, in the best olive oil I can find, until the vegetables wilt without taking on color. I then combine them, add chunky tomato wedges while they are still in the pan and sprinkle them with chopped herbs. Perfection.

Ratatouille

SERVES 4

8 tbsps olive oil	salt and ground black
2 large onions, sliced	pepper
2 green peppers, diced	1 tbsp chopped parsley
2 eggplants, diced	1 pinch marjoram or
2 zucchini, cut in	oregano
½ inch slices	1 pinch basil
4–6 ripe tomatoes, peeled,	1 large clove garlic,
seeded and cut in	crushed
wedges	

Heat the olive oil in a large skillet, add the onion slices and sauté until they are transparent. Add the diced green pepper and eggplants and, 5 minutes later, the zucchini and tomatoes. The vegetables should not be fried but stewed in the oil, so simmer gently in a covered pan for 30 minutes. Add salt and freshly

ground black pepper to taste, with the chopped parsley, marjoram or oregano, basil and crushed garlic. Cook, uncovered, for about 10–15 minutes, or until the ratatouille is well mixed and has the appearance of a ragout of vegetables – which it is. Serve hot from the casserole, or cold as a delicious beginning to a summer meal.

My ratatouille

SERVES 4

My ratatouille – a lighter, crisper version – uses the same ingredients as above but simmers the vegetables separately for minutes only.

Heat 2 tablespoons olive oil in a skillet; add the onions and green peppers and sauté until the onions are transparent. Lower the heat and continue to cook the vegetables for 5 more minutes, stirring from time to time. Transfer the vegetables to a large bowl.

Heat 2 more tablespoons olive oil in the pan; add the garlic cloves and eggplants and sauté, stirring from time to time, until the eggplants are lightly browned. Lower the heat and continue to cook for 5 minutes. Season as above. Transfer to the bowl.

Heat 2 more tablespoons of olive oil in the pan; add the zucchini and cook, stirring from time to time, for 5 minutes; add the tomato wedges and cook for 3 more minutes or until the vegetables begin to soften. Season as above and add to the bowl.

WHEN READY TO SERVE

Combine the vegetables in a heat-proof casserole and heat through. Correct the seasoning. Sprinkle with chopped parsley and basil and serve immediately.

More than forty years ago, when I first visited Provence, I was introduced to a wonderfully colorful and savory melange of oil-infused vagetables – eggplants, zucchini, tomatoes, onions and garlic – called ratatouille. From that very first taste, ratatouille became for me the true taste of Provence.

155

Ratatouille in tomato cases
SERVES 6

½ quantities of recipe for ratatouille (see page 154)	salt and ground black pepper
6–8 tbsps olive oil	dry mustard
2–3 tbsps wine vinegar	6 large ripe tomatoes
	finely chopped parsley

Prepare the ratatouille as in the recipe on page 154, then chill it.

Combine the olive oil and wine vinegar, and season to taste with salt, freshly ground black pepper and dry mustard. Toss the ratatouille in this dressing.

Plunge the tomatoes into boiling water, one by one, and remove their skins. Slice the cap off each tomato and carefully scoop out all the pulp and seeds. Cover loosely with foil and chill in the refrigerator until ready to use.

Just before serving, fill the tomato cases with the ratatouille mixture and sprinkle with parsley.

Provençal stuffed vegetables

If any method of cooking symbolizes Provence, it has to be *les farcis*, little stuffed vegetables which are probably a culinary leftover from the long years of Saracen domination, for they are found today in every Moroccan city, from Fez to Agadir.

Provençal cooks stuff vegetables – small eggplants, zucchini, tomatoes, onions and saffron-tinted potatoes – with a mixture of the chopped interiors of the hollowed-out vegetables, finely chopped cooked veal, grated cheese and herbs and spices. At other times, they stuff halved eggplants with onion, garlic and tomato, in the Eastern fashion; large Spanish onions with garlic, onion and herbed breadcrumbs; and cabbage leaves with chopped cooked meats and rice flavored with sage, onion, garlic and parsley.

The *farcis* can be served either hot or cold as a first course, as a main course, or even as a vegetable accompaniment for a roast of lamb (see page 195). Jean-Claude Guillon serves diminutive *farcis* with his roast *carré d'agneau* at the Hôtel Bel Air at St Jean-Cap-Ferrat: his *farcis* are stuffed with a saffron-flavored mixture of finely chopped ham and ratatouille flavored with chopped basil and garlic, olive oil and freshly grated Parmesan cheese.

Now a new group of
dedicated professionals
and gourmet chefs
is taking over Provençal
kitchens and creating
new traditions of cooking
throughout the region.
Many of these
newcomers are looking

closely at the beautiful
vegetables, fruits, fish
and game of the region
to create exciting dishes
which will be the
patrimony of the future.

Over the years I have tasted many variations on the *farcis* theme: artichokes stuffed with a tomato *coulis* to which ground meats have been added (much like a super-rich Bolognese sauce); onions stuffed with chopped cooked Swiss chard flavored with onion, garlic and herbs; lettuce hearts stuffed with herb and anchovy-flavored fresh breadcrumbs; potatoes stuffed with diced *petit salé* (salt pork) and Provençal *persillade* (a rather dry mix of finely chopped onion, garlic, Italian (flat-leaf) parsley and basil, combined with fresh breadcrumbs moistened with a little olive oil); and round, zucchinilike squash stuffed with diced pumpkin, aromatics and rice in a cheese sauce.

Les farcis
—
Provençal stuffed vegetables
—
SERVES 6
—

FOR THE VEGETABLE CASES

6 zucchini	olive oil
6 small eggplants	salt
6 medium onions	butter
6 small tomatoes	

FOR THE PROVENÇAL STUFFING

8 oz ground veal	1 egg, beaten
2 tbsps diced fat salt pork	2 tbsps grated Parmesan
1 onion, chopped	cheese
olive oil	6 tbsps boiled rice
1–2 cloves garlic, crushed	tomato and eggplant pulp
finely chopped fresh	salt and black pepper
tarragon and parsley	

Poach the zucchini and onions whole for 1 minute in boiling salted water. Cut the tops off the tomatoes, eggplants and onions. Scoop out the interiors of the vegetables and keep the pulp of the eggplants and tomatoes for the stuffing.

TO MAKE THE STUFFING

Pre-heat the oven to moderate (375°F). Sauté the meats and onion in olive oil. Mix the other ingredients in a bowl and add them to the meat and onion mixture, seasoning to taste with salt and freshly ground black pepper. Sauté for a few minutes, stirring continuously, and then stuff the scooped-out vegetables with the mixture.

Place the stuffed vegetables in a heat-proof baking dish to which you have added a little olive oil; place a pat of butter on each vegetable and bake in the pre-heated oven for 30 minutes.

157

Chou farci (lou fassoum)

Provençal stuffed cabbage

SERVES 6–8

In the old farm kitchens around Grasse there was always a special string net for making *lou fassoum*, the delicious stuffed cabbage of Provence and one of the triumphs of *la cuisine grassoise*. Substitute a clean tea towel which has been well rinsed to remove any possible traces of detergent.

leaves of 1 Savoy cabbage, blanched	2 cloves garlic, chopped
1 large yellow onion, chopped	1 small package frozen peas
olive oil	4 oz sausage meat
1¼ cups Swiss chard or spinach, green parts only, chopped	8 oz fat salt pork, finely chopped
2 large ripe tomatoes, peeled, seeded and chopped	2 eggs, beaten
	salt and black pepper
	crushed red pepper flakes
	9 cups *pot-au-feu* bouillon (or rich beef stock)

Lay out the string net (or damp towel) on your working surface. Arrange a bed of several thicknesses of blanched cabbage leaves on this net (or towel), layering the leaves to form a large circle.

TO MAKE THE STUFFING

Chop the remaining blanched cabbage leaves finely and place them in a large bowl. Sauté the chopped onion in 2 tablespoons olive oil, stirring constantly until the onion is transparent; add the chopped Swiss chard (or spinach) and continue to cook, stirring, for 1–2 minutes more. Add to the chopped blanched cabbage. Then add the chopped tomatoes and garlic, peas, sausage meat, chopped fat salt pork and beaten eggs. Season generously with salt, ground black pepper and crushed red pepper flakes. Mix well.

TO FORM THE STUFFED CABBAGE

Place the stuffing in the center of the layered cabbage leaves. Bring the outer leaves up around the stuffing and bring the string net (or damp towel) up around them to form a ball. Tie loosely.

TO COOK THE STUFFED CABBAGE

Bring the *pot-au-feu* bouillon to a boil; add the stuffed cabbage to the bouillon and simmer gently over low heat for 2 hours, adding a little more bouillon, or water, as necessary.

TO SERVE

Drain the stuffed cabbage, reserving the bouillon for another use; remove the net or towel; cut the stuffed cabbage into thick slices and arrange on a heated serving dish. Serve – as in Grasse – with a richly flavored sauce from a *daube de boeuf* or, more simply, with a light tomato sauce.

Capounets

Little parcels of stuffed cabbage

SERVES 4–6

This way of dealing with stuffed cabbage is essentially Niçoise.

1 medium-sized Savoy cabbage	2 eggs, beaten
1 lb roast beef, lamb or pork	salt and ground black pepper
1 large yellow onion, chopped	crushed red pepper flakes
olive oil	2–4 tbsps freshly grated Gruyère cheese
leaves from 3–4 sprigs of parsley, chopped	⅔ cup (or more) well-flavored bouillon
1 clove garlic, chopped	½ cup well-flavored tomato sauce

TO PREPARE THE CABBAGE

Discard any damaged outer leaves. Then remove 10–12 large leaves and blanch them in lightly salted water. Remove with a slotted spoon and drain.

Blanch the remaining cabbage in the cabbage water until tender. Remove and drain.

TO MAKE THE STUFFING

Chop the whole blanched cabbage coarsely and combine it with the chopped roast beef, lamb or pork. Sauté the chopped onion in 2 tablespoons olive oil until transparent. Add the chopped parsley and garlic and the beaten eggs, and season to taste with salt, black pepper and crushed red pepper flakes. The mixture should be highly flavored. Transfer it to a bowl and add the Gruyère cheese. Mix again.

TO MAKE THE *CAPOUNETS*

Place 4 tablespoonsful of stuffing in each cabbage leaf. Roll up to form a little 'parcel' and tie securely with a piece of string. Repeat with all the leaves.

In a large thick-bottomed skillet, sauté the little cabbage parcels in olive oil until lightly colored on all sides. Add the well-flavored bouillon and simmer for 10 minutes. Then add the tomato sauce and continue to simmer until the cabbage leaves are tender. Serve immediately.

Les tians

Another typical Provençal dish is the *tian*, or gratin of layered vegetables, sprinkled with olive oil and dried *herbes de Provence* and baked in the oval or round glazed earthenware dish (*tian*) from which the recipe gets its name. Practically any sliced combination of vegetables can be used for a Provençal *tian*: eggplants, tomatoes and zucchini; tomatoes, onions and potatoes; or combinations of green vegetables – spinach, Swiss chard and sorrel – or of diced pumpkin and marrow, *haricots blancs* and lentils. And *tians* of leeks, Swiss chard and cardoons are a regular at Christmas, when they are often dressed with diced croûtons and an anchovy-flavored cream.

Today these comforting gratins of vegetables are cooked at home in the oven, but in the old days most cooks would have prepared their *tians* at home and then taken them to the village baker to be cooked, along with the roasts of lamb or pork *à la boulangère*, after he had finished baking the day's breads.

Tian à la provençale

Provençal vegetable gratin

SERVES 4–6

4 small eggplants	4 tbsps finely chopped
4 small zucchini	parsley
olive oil	thyme and marjoram
2 green peppers	8 tomatoes
2 red peppers	butter
2 yellow peppers	4 tbsps fresh
4 cloves garlic, finely	breadcrumbs
chopped	

Cut the eggplants and zucchini in thin strips and sauté them separately in olive oil. Cut the peppers (green, red and yellow) in rings and sauté them. A few minutes before the end of cooking, sprinkle the eggplants and zucchini with 2 cloves garlic, finely

Tian à la provençale, a gratin of layered eggplants, zucchini, tomatoes and peppers.

chopped, 2 tablespoons parsley, and thyme and marjoram to taste.

Cut the tomatoes into thick rounds; place them in a buttered gratin dish, and cook *à la provençale*, sprinkled with the remaining garlic and parsley and the breadcrumbs.

Arrange the cooked vegetables in a large ovenproof gratin dish, with the tomatoes in the center, the eggplants on one side, and the zucchini on the other. Then place the red, yellow and green pepper rings in a lattice over the vegetables. Brown under the broiler and serve immediately. This dish is also good served cold.

Potatoes

Even potatoes seem different in Provence. Full-flavored *bintje* or *belle de Fontenay* potatoes make delicious *estouffades* or gratins of potatoes and cream beautifully to accompany roasts of beef or lamb; or, when teamed with sliced black truffles and morels *à la crème*, wonderfully earthy first courses on their own. Try them too as a layered *tarte fine* or *galette* (a delicately thin potato cake) to top or support pan-fries of prawns, fresh anchovies or wild mushrooms (see pages 83 and 194).

Provençal potato gratins are different too – thinly sliced new potatoes layered with the trio of imported cheeses that has been customary in Provence since the seventeenth century (Gruyère, Hollande and Parmesan), anointed with golden *crème fraîche* and sprinkled with dried *herbes de Provence* before being baked in a 325°F oven.

Then, when the sweet-tasting potatoes are taken from the oven, a final dousing with olive oil makes the dish the perfect accompaniment to a roast loin of pork *à la provençale*, or rose-pink lamb chops grilled over the embers with the faintest hint of chopped fresh garlic and Italian (flat-leaf) parsley to give them flavor and color. And a generous sprinkling of finely chopped garlic and Italian (flat-leaf) parsley, or an aromatic mixture of dried *herbes de Provence* will always enhance the flavor of all these rustic potato dishes.

Pommes de terre sautées à l'ail

Pan-fried garlic potatoes

SERVES 4–6

2 lb small new potatoes
2 tbsps butter
4 large cloves garlic,
  coarsely chopped
4 tbsps olive oil

2 tbsps chopped Italian
  (flat-leaf) parsley
salt and ground black
  pepper

Wash the potatoes well but do not peel them.

In a large saucepan of boiling salted water, cook the potatoes until just tender, about 15 minutes. Drain and cool. Quarter the potatoes and set them aside.

When ready to cook the potatoes, melt the butter and olive oil in a large skillet; add the quartered potatoes and cook over medium heat for 5 minutes, stirring frequently. Then increase the heat to high and cook the potatoes, turning frequently, until deep golden brown on all sides. Add the chopped garlic and parsley, salt and freshly ground black pepper, to taste, and sauté for 3 minutes more. Transfer to a heated serving dish and serve immediately.

Pommes de terre au four à la provençale

Provençal baked potatoes

SERVES 6

12 medium-sized baking
  potatoes
olive oil

salt and ground black
  pepper
dried *herbes de Provence*

Wash the potatoes well but do not peel them. Pre-heat to the oven to 425°F.

Cut the potatoes in half lengthwise. With a sharp kitchen knife, score the cut sides of the potatoes in a latticework pattern (as you would an eggplant), down to but not through the skin.

Arrange the prepared potatoes on a baking tray, cut sides up. Sprinkle each half-potato with a little olive oil; season generously with salt, freshly ground black pepper and dried *herbes de Provence*.

Cook in the pre-heated oven for 30–40 minutes, or until the potatoes are golden brown on the cut sides and tender.

Any Provençal market will offer an abundance of superbly fresh fruit and vegetables.

Aubergines en barbouillade

Provençal eggplant casserole

SERVES 6

4–6 eggplants, peeled and
    thinly sliced into rounds
4–6 tbsps olive oil
4–6 ripe tomatoes, peeled,
    seeded and diced
1 large yellow onion, thinly
    sliced

2 cloves garlic
salt and ground black
    pepper
4–6 tbsps finely chopped
    parsley

In a large thick-bottomed skillet or heat-proof casserole, sauté enough eggplant slices to make a single
layer on the bottom of the pan. When they are golden
on both sides, remove them and allow them to drain
on absorbent paper. Repeat with the other slices.

Add the remaining olive oil to a clean pan or
casserole. Return the sautéed eggplant slices to the
pan (or casserole); add the peeled, seeded and diced
tomatoes, thinly sliced onion and garlic cloves
and simmer over low heat until the vegetables are
tender.

Season to taste with salt and freshly ground black
pepper; sprinkle with finely chopped parsley and
serve immediately.

Papeton d'aubergines

SERVES 4

3 medium-sized long
    eggplants, about 1 lb
    altogether
salt
olive oil

FOR THE FILLING

1 tbsp butter
1 tbsp olive oil
1 medium-sized onion,
    finely chopped
1 clove garlic, crushed
½ cup cooked pork, finely
    chopped
⅓ cup cooked ham, finely
    chopped

tomato *coulis* (see page 24)
sprigs of watercress, to
    garnish

2 large tomatoes,
    blanched, skinned,
    seeded and chopped
1 tbsp finely chopped
    parsley
salt and ground black
    pepper
1 large egg, lightly beaten

Wipe the eggplants with a damp cloth. Slice them
thinly without peeling them. Sprinkle with salt and
leave in a colander for 30 minutes to allow the bitter
juices to drain away.

Green peppers, tomatoes and eggplants: the 'holy trinity' which forms
the basis of so many delicious Provençal vegetable dishes.

TO PREPARE THE FILLING

In a small saucepan, heat the butter and olive oil.
When the butter has melted, sauté the finely chopped
onion for 5 minutes, stirring occasionally with a
wooden spoon. Stir in the garlic, finely chopped pork
and ham, tomatoes and parsley. Season to taste with
salt and freshly ground black pepper and sauté for 5
minutes.

Remove the pan from the heat. Leave to cool a
little and stir in the beaten egg. Rinse the eggplant

slices thoroughly in cold water and pat them dry firmly with absorbent paper to remove excess moisture.

TO COOK THE EGGPLANT

In a large skillet, heat 4 tablespoons of olive oil and sauté $\frac{1}{3}$ of the eggplant slices for 2 minutes each side, or until golden, turning them over with a spatula. Remove and drain on absorbent paper. Repeat with the remaining 2 batches, using 2–4 tablespoons of the olive oil for each batch.

Pre-heat the oven to 350°F.

Oil a medium-sized oven-proof bowl and line the bowl with even-sized sautéed eggplant slices,

---

Just say the word Provence to

any food-loving traveler and they will

probably respond with dreamy

evocations of the first bouillabaisse,

aïoli, ratatouille, or even *salade niçoise*

they ever tasted. Say Provence and

eyes begin to glisten and talk

immediately turns to food: dishes

made from local produce cooked

in the age-old country way.

---

reserving the rest for the filling. Cover the eggplant at the bottom with a layer of meat mixture. Top this with a layer of eggplant and continue untill all the ingredients are used up, ending with an eggplant layer.

Cover the bowl with a plate or piece of aluminum foil. Place the bowl in a roasting pan and pour in enough hot water to come halfway up the sides of the bowl. Bake for 1 hour.

Turn the eggplant mold out carefully onto a large flat heated serving dish. Pour over the hot tomato *coulis*. Garnish with sprigs of watercress and serve immediately.

Les pommes d'amour à la marseillaise

Tomatoes à la marseillaise

SERVES 4–6

4 large ripe tomatoes, cut in half crosswise	4 tbsps finely chopped garlic
4 tbsps olive oil	4 tsps sugar
4 tbsps finely chopped parsley	salt and ground black pepper

Heat the olive oil in a large thick-bottomed skillet. Place the tomato halves, cut sides down, in the pan; cover the pan and cook over medium heat for 30 minutes. Remove from the heat; turn the tomatoes cut sides up; sprinkle each with a mixture of finely chopped parsley and garlic; then a little sugar and salt, and continue to cook, covered, for 20 minutes more.

Just before serving, sprinkle with freshly ground black pepper. Serve immediately.

Les pommes d'amour à la provençale

Provençal tomatoes

SERVES 4

The traditional recipe for tomatoes cooked *à la provençale* is different from the recipe from Marseilles in that the tomatoes – smaller ones, cut in half as before – are cooked over high heat so that they caramelize a little and have a more 'fried' taste. But the main difference is that the finely chopped parsley and garlic are added right at the end of the cooking time, so that their rustic flavor comes through a touch more emphatically.

12 small ripe tomatoes, cut in half crosswise	3 tbsps finely chopped garlic
6 tbsps olive oil	salt and freshly ground black pepper
3 tbsps finely chopped parsley	

Heat the olive oil in a large thick-bottomed skillet; arrange the tomato halves, cut sides up, in the pan and cook over high heat for 20 minutes. Turn the tomato halves over and cook for 20 minutes more. Then turn the tomatoes cut sides up again, and sprinkle with finely chopped parsley and garlic, salt and freshly ground black pepper to taste; cover the pan and cook for 2 minutes more. Serve immediately.

165

FEAST

Famille Gleize

La Bonne Etape
Château Arnoux

It is a wise traveler who breaks his journey at La Bonne Etape in Château Arnoux, on the Route Napoléon, halfway between Grenoble and Nice: in fact it is worth making a detour in order to stay a night or two at this charming hostelry run by Pierre and Arlette Gleize and their son Jany. The former Hôtel de la Gare of this town just below Sisteron in the Haute Provence has been transformed by the Gleize family into what is to all intents and purposes a little French château, with beautifully arranged bedrooms, an elegant dining room and a comfortable bar. One senses immediately upon arriving that it is a family-run business, comfortable and unpretentious.

The area around Château Arnoux, arid and beautiful, is a land of honey, olive oil and almonds. The only factories make nougat and *calissons* or distill lavender. And the only busy day in town is when the weekly market sets up its stalls in the Place de la République, and the farmers come in from the hills to bring honey for the *calissons* and lavender for the distillery, or little goat cheeses called Banons or *picadons* to sell.

The weather is changeable, and in winter the cold winds of the Mistral scourge the valleys. 'It is a crossroads of the four winds,' according to Pierre Gleize. 'When you feel the Mistral from the northeast you really know you are in Provence.'

Château Arnoux is surrounded by little villages which produce the excellent raw products of the region. Banon, population 850, seems straight out of a fairy tale with its narrow stone houses, fountains and blue-shuttered shops. In the small open-air weekly market old farm ladies offer creamy rounds of fresh Banon cheese, just two or three days old and decorated with sprigs of fresh herbs.

The food at La Bonne Etape is not *nouvelle cuisine*, but the glorious and sensible fare that French country people have always loved to eat. Food cultists elsewhere might regale themselves with breasts of undercooked duck fanned out in a puddle of raspberry purée, or gorge themselves on a taster's platter of unidentifiable sweets, but the Gleizes, father and son, have gone about the serious business of glorifying the products of their region.

You can't fail to be carried away by the rustic simplicity of their light, clear sauces, thickened not with butter or cream or flour, but with simple reductions of pan juices, with vegetables such as leeks, onions or fennel. Their sauces do not stay too long on the tongue: their savors are lively, piquant reminders of a cuisine which sings of the herbs of the *garrigue* and of the fruits of the vineyards and olive groves that surround the town.

It would be difficult to find two chefs who are simpler, more joyous, more pleasant than the Gleizes, father and son. They live for their *métier*, without excess, without pretension. Their cooking is close to the land; the southern sun touches everything that goes into their saucepans. Under their management the restaurant has become a repository of the unique savors of this part of the world, though not in any way fixed in the past. They are both classicists, and their cuisine is imbued with a vivacity and a sensitivity that is very much in the rhythm of today.

Provençal food has always been healthy food, and the menu at La Bonne Etape bears witness to this, whether in the spiraled salad of raw *cèpes* on a bed of *mesclun* picked from the garden minutes before being brought to the table, or in the *consommé à l'ail, à la sauge et à l'oeuf poché* (garlic and sage consommé with poached egg), with its intriguing threads of saffron and slivers of red rose petals (see page 95). I like, too,

Salade de cèpes au mesclun.

their wonderful country-style winter soups – *soupe de potiron* (pumpkin soup served in its shell) and *soupe d'épeautre* (see pages 98 and 97).

Other delicious specialities to look out for are their *roulade de lapereau à l'hysope* (ballotine of young rabbit flavored with hyssop); *les totènes farcies aux herbes vertes et aux pignons de pin* (baby squid stuffed with green herbs and pine nuts, served with a sublime sauce); and the fabulous house dessert, *crème glacée au miel de lavande* (a super-rich honey and lavender ice cream).

Salade de cèpes au mesclun

Wild mushroom salad with mesclun

SERVES I

1 medium-sized fresh *cèpe*	salt and ground black
1 handful of *mesclun*	pepper
salad, with the greatest	juice of $\frac{1}{8}$ lemon
variety of leaves	2 tbsps extra-virgin
possible, seasoned with	olive oil
a well-flavored	
vinaigrette dressing	

It is important that *cèpes* for a salad should be as fresh and firm as possible, not soaked in water.

Clean the *cèpe* with a kitchen towel, brushing off any impurities.

Toss the salad leaves in a well-flavored vinaigrette. Arrange them in the center of a salad plate. Then,

with the sharpest knife you have, cut thin slices of *cèpe*; arrange these in an attractive domed spiral on the salad greens.

Season with salt and freshly ground black pepper and a squeeze of lemon juice, and then moisten with enough olive oil (approximately 2 tablespoons) to cover all the slices of *cèpe*.

Raviolis aux herbes et aux cèpes

Ravioli filled with herbs and cèpes

SERVES 8

FOR THE PASTA DOUGH

3½ cups all-purpose flour	3 tbsps olive oil
2 eggs	1 glass water
1 tbsp salt	

FOR THE FILLING

2½ cups Swiss chard	8 tbsps freshly grated
2½ cups spinach	Parmesan cheese
8 tbsps parsley, chopped	2 tbsps fresh basil leaves,
2½ cups *cèpes*, chopped	finely chopped
4 tbsps olive oil	salt and freshly ground
2 cloves garlic, chopped	black pepper

FOR THE GARNISH

1 small *cèpe*	2 tbsps clarified butter
lemon juice	

TO PREPARE THE PASTA DOUGH

Sift the flour in a ring on a pastry board or working surface. Combine the other ingredients in the center

Jany Gleize gathers the mixture of delicate young salad leaves (left) that go to make up traditional mesclun (right).

of this ring and gradually work in the flour with your fingertips to make a smooth floppy dough. Wrap the dough in plastic wrap or aluminum foil and put it in the refrigerator to rest for 1 hour.

TO PREPARE THE FILLING

Place the trimmed and washed Swiss chard, spinach and parsley in a saucepan; add just enough water to cover and bring to a boil. Transfer the blanched greens to a large sieve or colander and pour cold water over. Drain them well and then squeeze them dry, being careful to remove all excess moisture.

In a large frying pan, sauté the mushrooms in 2 tablepoons olive oil until they begin to change color; add the prepared greens and finely chopped garlic. Mix well. Then add the finely chopped basil, grated Parmesan and remaining olive oil. Mix well; remove from the heat and transfer the mixture to a chopping board. Chop the mixture of greens and aromatics until very fine.

Season generously with salt and freshly ground black pepper.

TO PREPARE THE RAVIOLI

Divide the pasta dough into two equal parts. Roll each part out on a floured surface until it is as thin as a sheet of paper. This is important, otherwise your ravioli will be clumsy.

Cut the dough into strips 2 inches wide, and place

Raviolis aux herbes et aux cèpes.

teaspoonfuls of filling at 2-inch intervals. Moisten the pastry left showing between the filling with water (using your finger); cover with another strip of dough. Then, with your finger, press the dough down around the filling, and separate the ravioli into neat squares with a pastry wheel.

TO COOK THE RAVIOLI

In a large saucepan, combine water, 2 tablespoons olive oil and $\frac{1}{2}$ teaspoon salt and bring to a rolling boil. Add the ravioli and poach gently. If your ravioli are very fine, 5 minutes should be enough cooking time. If they are thicker, add a few minutes more. When they rise to the surface, they are cooked.

Drain the ravioli well and then let them finish draining on a clean folded kitchen towel. Serve the ravioli in a ring on a hot plate; place a small *cèpe* which you have sautéed in clarified butter in the middle of the plate and spoon over a little of the hot butter in which you have squeezed a little lemon juice.

Loup poêlé sauce aux fruits de Provence, selon 'Denostitin'

Pan-fried sea bass with a special fruits of Provence sauce

SERVES 4–6

This elegant recipe for pan-fried sea bass with *tapenade* borrows a relatively simple cooking method from classic Provençal cuisine, and gives it *haute cuisine* stature with a subtle, multiflavored sauce. At La Bonne Etape (opposite) they add a witty garnish of a *trompe l'oeil* 'chestnut', of mashed potato, black truffle and fried spaghetti.

4–6 sea bass fillets (5–6 oz each)	1 egg, beaten
2–3 tbsps *tapenade* (home-made or bought)	1½ tbsps fine cornmeal

FOR THE *SAUCE AUX FRUITS DE PROVENCE*

¼ clove garlic, finely chopped	2 tbsps freshly grated almonds
4 tbsps finely grated carrot	⅔ cup eating apple, peeled, cored and finely grated
½ tsp finely grated lemon zest	1 small piece dried orange peel (thumbnail-sized)
2 tbsps olive oil	4 tbsps milk
4 tbsps dry white wine	pinch saffron
4 tbsps fish *fumet*	salt and ground black pepper
⅔ cup tomato *coulis* (see page 24)	
2 tbsps melted bitter chocolate	

TO PREPARE THE SAUCE

In a saucepan, sauté the finely chopped garlic, grated carrot and lemon zest in olive oil until the vegetables are soft. Add the dry white wine and fish *fumet* and bring to a boil, scraping in the aromatics from the bottom of the saucepan. Add the tomato *coulis*, melted chocolate, grated almonds, grated apple, orange peel and milk. Season with saffron, salt and freshly ground black pepper to taste. Bring the mixture to a boil; skim; cover the pan and cook over low heat for 30 minutes, or until the sauce has reduced to half its original quantity, adding a little more liquid (dry white wine and/or milk) if the sauce becomes too thick.

Loup poêlé sauce aux fruits de Provence, selon 'Denostitin' in the kitchen at La Bonne Etape.

Transfer the sauce to the bowl of a food processor and process until the sauce is smooth; then pass it through a fine sieve into a small clean saucepan. Cover and keep warm until ready to use.

TO COOK THE FISH (I)

Spread the fish fillets with the *tapenade* mixture. Then cook in a non-stick pan, over high heat, for 3 minutes on each side.

TO COOK THE FISH (II)

Brush the fish with beaten egg on both sides; dredge in cornmeal and sauté in a non-stick pan, over high heat, for 3 minutes on each side. Spread the top of each fillet with the *tapenade* mixture.

TO SERVE

Cover the bottom of heated dinner plates with hot sauce (3–4 tablespoons for each serving); place one fillet of sea bass in the center of each plate and arrange sliced potatoes, cooked in a little saffron-flavored tomato *coulis*, and some green beans on each side of the fish.

TO MAKE THE SPECIAL 'CHESTNUT' GARNISH

An attractive garnish of a golden, truffle-centered 'chestnut' is served with this glamorous dish at La Bonne Etape. If you wish to make these 'chestnut' garnishes for a special occasion, Jany's directions are as follows: for each 'chestnut', roll 1 table-spoon mashed potato into a small ball; cut a slit in each ball and insert a small black truffle (see above) to resemble a chestnut in its shell; then stick the potato ball 'shell' with even-sized spikes of raw spaghetti. Just before serving, deep-fry the 'chestnuts' until the spikes are crisp and golden.

Note: For a less opulent garnish, I suggest stuffing shiny black pitted olives with *tapenade* and then inserting them in place of the black truffles. Equally charming and a tenth of the cost.

Crème glacée au miel de lavande

Honey and lavender ice cream

MAKES 1 ½ PINTS

8 tbsps lavender honey	2½ cups light cream
4 egg yolks	1 vanilla pod
1¼ cups milk	

Heat the lavender honey until it just melts. Remove from the heat.

Beat the egg yolks briskly until they are light-colored and foamy. Then, at a lower speed, gradually add the hot melted honey.

In a medium-sized saucepan, bring the milk and cream to a boil with the vanilla pod; remove the pod and add the hot milk and cream gradually to the beaten egg yolks and honey, beating all the while.

Pour the mixture into a clean saucepan and cook over medium heat until the mixture thickens slightly and coats the back of a spoon, about 8 minutes. Be sure not to let it boil or it will curdle. Strain into a clean bowl and allow to cool.

TO FREEZE

Strain the cooled mixture into the bowl of an ice cream maker and freeze for 20–25 minutes, according to the manufacturer's instructions.

In the kitchen at La Bonne Etape Pierre and Jany Gleize produce glorious and sensible fare, exulting in the fine products of their region. One of their delicious specialities is *crème glacée au miel de lavande*, the super-rich house dessert.

7 Chefs on the

A FEW SWEETS, DESSERTS AND PUDDINGS

The Côte d'Azur – that fabled stretch of coast which runs from Menton near the Italian border to St Tropez – boasts more millionaires and would-be millionaires per square meter than any similar vacation spot in France, with the exception perhaps of aristocratic Deauville. Blessed with a seductive climate, a history full of princes, famous artists, infamous courtesans and the legendary 'breakers' of the bank of Monte Carlo, this area has been almost exclusively British since the eighteenth century, when Tobias Smollett arrived in Nice with his family. The year was 1763. A little under a century later, Lord Brougham was to set his social imprimatur on the Riviera when he settled in Cannes; and within a few years more than thirty imposing English-owned villas had been built around the little fishing port. The English had already invaded Nice: there were 100 families living there at the time of Lord Brougham's visit, and the Promenade des Anglais, built in 1822, was one of the wonders of the coast.

In 1856 the famous casino of Monte Carlo opened its doors, bringing to the little municipality an influx of titled visitors, moneymen, courtesans, mountebanks and others who came from far and near to gamble at its tables. But the Côte d'Azur remained a winter resort until the jazz age, when the young American writers Ernest Hemingway, Scott Fitzgerald and their friends the Murphys came to make it fashionable during the hitherto empty months of summer.

Then finally the French, realizing what had been lying under their noses all this time, moved in: Jean Cocteau, André Fraigneau, Boris Kochno and the dancers from the Ballets Russes de Monte Carlo made their headquarters at the Hôtel Splendide in Villefranche-sur-Mer; Suzy Solidor opened a nightclub in Vieux Cagnes; the music-hall star Mistinguette and the writer Colette called St Tropez

174

Water

their own, and the stage was set. The Riviera, with its beautiful villas, its sleek yachts and fast motor cars, its glorious climate, tropical trees and great hotels – veritable palaces along the Littoral – became a living legend that continues to draw crowds to this day. Among the palaces on the coast my favorite is the Hôtel Bel Air, on the tip of the promontory of Cap Ferrat and one of the loveliest and most luxurious hotels on the coast with acres of superb gardens, and a vast swimming pool that seems to be suspended over the sea, its waters blending into the blue Mediterranean sky. There is, moreover, a private funicular to carry you effortlessly to and from the swimming pool with its own terrace restaurant, thus saving you a walk through the beautifully tended exotic gardens. I like the hotel's cool, shaded terraces, its great marble halls filled with beautiful furniture and astounding dried-flower pieces, its comfortable suites, and its aura of unruffled calm and beauty on a strident coast.

The spacious terraces shaded by big parasol pines make a wonderful setting for leisurely breakfasts, informal lunches that stretch on into the afternoon, or romantic candle-lit dinners with a view of the night sea and sky from Monte Carlo to Antibes. Presiding over all this is master chef Jean-Claude Guillon, who has been in charge of the hotel's spacious kitchens since 1976.

The whole coast is truffled with great chefs today, just as it was in the fabulous days of the Belle Epoque: among the most distinguished are Guy Cibois at the Gray Albion in Cannes, Alain Ducasse in the Hôtel de Paris in Monte Carlo, Dominique le Stanc at the Chantecler restaurant in the Hôtel Negresco in Nice, Jacques Maximin at the Diamant Rose restaurant in La Colle-sur-Loup, and Jean-Jacques Jouteux in his own Le Provençal restaurant in the little resort of St-Jean-Cap-Ferrat. Every one of this handful of starred chefs on the water is unmatched; in their restaurants you will discover some of the most exciting dishes in the world. Their cuisine, influenced by the products of the sea and the sun and graced by the healthy simplicity of the traditions of Provence, is sophisticated but unpretentious cooking at its very best.

The sweets of Provence

Perhaps the best way of ending a meal in Provence is with the excellent fresh fruits of the region – cherries from Lauris and Lourmarin, table grapes from Le Thor near Carpentras, fine figs from Marseilles and the best plums from Brignoles – and a bit of cheese, one of those delicious little *chèvres*, Banons or *picadons*, dressed with chopped or rubbed herbs and a little olive oil. Or try a cooling fresh fruit sorbet or ice cream accompanied by sliced fresh peaches from the Gard or summer berries. Roasted purple figs caramelized with a little burnt sugar are delicious when served hot with a vanilla or cinnamon-flavored ice cream. Or little hot tarts of glazed sliced figs or peaches baked on thin rounds of pastry; or, more traditionally, an open tart of thinly sliced lemons or oranges, the thin pastry made with olive oil, or a combination of oil and butter, the fruit left unpeeled so that the bitter taste of the oven-browned peels adds its special tang and chewy texture to the baked lemons or oranges. This is the country, too, of the famed Cavaillon melon. Each musky globe is served whole, iced and with the top taken off. This melon alone is enough to be the making of every meal throughout the long hot summer: its dense flesh is so aromatic. It should never be too ripe and must have plenty of weight.

Old-fashioned sweets and pastries from the nineteenth century are much in evidence today in the country cooking of Provence. *Tarte au potiron* (a sweet pumpkin tart); *tourte de blettes*, or *torta de blea* in old Provençal (a flat tart made of Swiss chard, *crème patissière*, pine nuts and sometimes glacéed orange peel), and *frangipane* (an almond-flavored covered tart, its creamy filling thickened with ground almonds) are all direct throwbacks to the Middle Ages. *Bugnes* – deep-fried airy puffs of parchment-crisp pastry, dusted with confectioners' sugar and piled high in a basket under a white cloth, are popular, as are *oreillettes*, diminutive 'little ears' or 'pillows' of paper-thin pastry flavored with orange

flower water and served hot dusted with confectioners' sugar and, sometimes, crisp pine nuts.

And don't forget the orange flower-flavored *tian au lait d'Avignon*, a creamy flan or gratin of milk and eggs (*tian* being the name of the earthenware gratin dish used to make this delicately flavored sweet).

Poumpo (or *pompe à l'huile*) is the most traditional of the sweets of Provence. It is often served as the centerpiece of the thirteen desserts which traditionally end each Provençal Christmas feast. The oil of the olive (which gives the cake its name) replaces butter in the rich sweetened dough studded with diced glacéed fruits.

Tarte tropézienne is a soft, bunlike sponge, cut horizontally and filled with a thick vanilla custard cream, the top covered with a crisp almond crumb topping more characteristic of Alsace-Lorraine than of Provence. Indeed it was reputedly created by an Alsace-born cook who worked in the region (but try telling that to a Tropézien).

Calissons d'Aix – almond-shaped lozenges fashioned from ground almonds and candied melon and topped with vanilla royal icing – make wonderful little *petits fours*, as do squares of creamy *nougat blanc* (tasting of lavender honey and chopped pistachio nuts and almonds) and *nougat noir* (cooked at a higher temperature to produce its dark caramel flavor and traditional crunch).

Clafoutis aux raisins

White grape clafoutis

SERVES 4

20–24 white seedless grapes	4 eggs
	¾ cup granulated sugar
1 cup milk	½ cup all-purpose flour
½ cup heavy cream	butter
¼ vanilla pod	

Pre-heat the oven to 500°F.

In a medium-sized saucepan, bring the milk, cream and vanilla pod to a boil; remove from the heat and allow to cool. Remove the vanilla pod.

In a medium-sized bowl, beat the eggs and sugar until light and creamy. Then beat in the flour, little by little.

Butter 4 individual tart molds or shallow ramekins

PREVIOUS PAGES A sumptuous spread of Jean-Jacques Jouteux's desserts at Le Provençal restaurant (clockwise from left): *clafoutis aux raisins, melon glacé, soufflé au citron, crêpes dentelles, macaronnade de chocolat, crème brûlée* and *assiette glacée de fruits frais*.

and put 5–6 buttered white seedless grapes in each.

Gradually beat the vanilla cream mixture into the egg, sugar and flour mixture. When well mixed, spoon into the tart molds or ramekins. Bake in the pre-heated oven for 10–12 minutes, or until the clafoutis tests done.

Soufflé au citron

Lemon soufflé

SERVES 4

4 egg yolks	3 tbsps all-purpose flour
8 tbsps granulated sugar	4 egg whites
grated zest and juice of 1 large lemon	softened butter

Pre-heat the oven to 400°F.

In a medium-sized bowl, beat the egg yolks and sugar until pale and creamy.

Add the finely grated zest and juice of 1 lemon. Then gradually whisk in the flour.

In another bowl, whisk the egg whites until stiff.

TO PREPARE THE SOUFFLÉ MOLDS

Butter 4 individual soufflé molds. Make 4 'collars' for the soufflé dishes out of folded pieces of aluminum foil. Butter 1 side of the folded foil and, with the buttered side on the inside, wrap the strips of foil around the tops of the soufflé dishes. Fasten the ends of each 'collar' with a paper clip.

Gradually fold the beaten egg whites into the soufflé mixture, spoon the mixture into the soufflé dishes and place the soufflé dishes in the oven. Reduce the heat to 375°F and bake for 20–25 minutes, or until the soufflés test done. Serve immediately.

Assiette glacée de fruits frais

Fresh fruits with raspberry sorbet

MAKES 1 ¾ PINTS

raspberries, strawberries, blueberries, cherries, and slices of melon, apricot, plum or nectarine

FOR THE RASPBERRY SORBET

2 cups raspberry pulp	2 cups granulated sugar
2 cups water	juice of 1–1½ lemons

TO MAKE THE RASPBERRY SORBET

In a medium-sized saucepan, combine the water and sugar and bring to a boil. Cook, stirring from time to time, until the sugar has dissolved completely. Remove from the heat and allow to cool.

In a medium-sized bowl, combine the strained raspberry pulp and syrup; add lemon juice to taste. Mix well; pour into a sorbet-maker and make sorbet according to the manufacturer's instructions.

TO ASSEMBLE THE DESSERT

Arrange the sliced fruit (melon, apricot, plum or nectarine) in a fan shape on one side of each dessert plate. Then spoon summer fruits (raspberries, strawberries, blueberries, cherries) in separate clusters on to the plate. Top just before serving with a small ball of sorbet, and serve immediately.

Crêpes dentelles

Lace pancakes

SERVES 4

⅔ **cup all-purpose flour**	**butter**
2 small eggs	**4–6 tbsps *crème patissière***
1 cup milk	**(see below)**
½ **tsp vanilla extract**	

In a mixing bowl, beat the flour and eggs together until well blended. In another bowl combine the milk and vanilla extract.

In a small skillet, heat 2 tablespoons of butter until it begins to change color (*beurre noisette*). Add to the milk; then stir in the *crème patissière* and fold into the flour and egg mixture.

TO COOK THE PANCAKES

Melt half a teaspoon of butter in a non-stick skillet. Pour in 1 small ladle of batter and tilt the pan so that the batter covers the bottom of the pan completely. Cook the pancake on one side until the top begins to bubble and the underside is a rich brown (the pan must be very hot to create the 'lace' effect). Turn the pancake and cook until the other side is brown. Then remove from the pan, fold in four and keep warm. Cook the other pancakes in the same manner.

Crème patissière

1 egg yolk	**4 tbsps granulated sugar**
⅔ **cup milk**	
1 tsp cornstarch, mixed to	
a smooth paste with 1	
tbsp water	

In the top of a double boiler, whisk the egg yolk into the milk. Add the cornstarch mixed with water and sugar and cook over lightly simmering water, stirring continually with a wooden spoon, until the sauce is thick enough to coat the back of the spoon. Do not let the mixture come to a boil. Remove from the heat; cool and use as directed above.

Macaronnade de chocolat

Dark chocolate pudding

SERVES 4

4 oz bitter chocolate	**4 egg yolks**
4 tbsps butter	½ **cup granulated sugar**
1 tsp coffee crystals	**4 egg whites**

Pre-heat the oven to 300°F.

In the top of a double boiler, melt the butter and chocolate over simmering water. Beat in the coffee crystals. Remove from the heat.

In a mixing bowl, beat the egg yolks and sugar until light-colored and a ribbon forms when you lift the spoon.

In another bowl, with a clean whisk, beat the egg whites until stiff.

Gradually beat the melted butter and chocolate into the beaten egg yolks and sugar. Then fold this mixture into the beaten egg whites.

Pour the mixture into 4 individual soufflé dishes and bake in the pre-heated oven for 30 minutes.

Provençal fruit tarts

Provençal fruit tarts are usually flat discs of flaky or olive oil-based pastry pre-baked for minutes only on a baking tray – to prevent the pastry from becoming soggy – before being topped with thinly sliced fresh fruits of the season: apricots, peaches, figs, apples, pears, plums and even lemons and oranges. The citrus tarts are a little more complicated to produce than the others, as it is necessary to simmer the thinly sliced lemons and oranges in syrup over very low heat for 40–50 minutes before arranging them in overlapping circles on the pastry bases and then baking them. This processs both tenderizes the peels and sweetens the citrus fruits to create a bitter-sweet tart that is quite delicious.

Pastry bases for Provençal fruit tarts

1 (14 oz) package puff pastry, brought to room temperature

TO PREPARE THE PASTRY BASES

Roll the puff pastry out to ¼ inch thick and cut it into 4 squares (or circles) approximately 4–5 inches in diameter. Place the pastry on a baking sheet; prick with the tines of a fork (to prevent puffing up during pre-baking) and leave to rest for 30 minutes in the refrigerator.

TO PRE-BAKE THE PASTRY BASES

Pre-heat the oven to 400°F. Remove the pastry from the refrigerator and bake in the pre-heated oven for 5–7 minutes. If the pastry puffs up during the cooking time, press it down gently with a spatula or the back of a wooden spoon. Remove from the oven and allow to cool.

Tartes au citron ou à l'orange

Lemon or orange tarts

SERVES 4

4 pre-baked pastry bases, as above
3–4 lemons or small oranges
¾ cup granulated sugar
1 cup water
apricot jam, diluted with a little water or *marc de Provence*
confectioners' sugar
soft whipped cream, or *crème fraîche* (optional)

TO PREPARE THE LEMON OR ORANGE SLICES

Scrub the lemons (or small oranges) with a stiff brush, and cut into thin slices.

In a medium-sized enameled iron or stainless-steel skillet or shallow saucepan, combine the sugar and water and cook over medium heat, stirring constantly, until the sugar has melted and a syrup has formed. Place the lemon or orange slices in the syrup and simmer over the lowest of heats for 40–50 minutes, or until the peel is tender and the liquids are reduced to a syrup with an intense citrus flavor.

TO PREPARE THE TARTS FOR BAKING

Pre-heat the oven to 400°F. Place the overlapping lemon (or orange) slices on the pastry bases, leaving a ¼-inch border all around, and bake in the pre-heated oven for 15 minutes. Remove from the oven and brush with apricot jam. Sift a layer of confectioners' sugar to coat. Serve immediately.

Tarte aux figues fraîches, Hôtel Bel Air

Fresh fig tart, Hôtel Bel Air

SERVES 4

4 pre-baked pastry bases (see page 181)
12–16 ripe figs
½ cup granulated sugar
confectioners' sugar

Pre-heat the oven to 425°F.

With a sharp kitchen knife, peel the figs and cut them into thin slices. Arrange the fig slices on pre-baked rounds of pastry, mounding them up rather high. Sprinkle each with granulated sugar and bake in the pre-heated oven for 20 minutes, or until the figs are lightly caramelized. Sift with confectioners' sugar just before serving. Place the tarts on warmed dessert plates and serve immediately.

Tatin de pêches jaunes avec son coulis de framboises, Hôtel Bel Air

Peach upside-down tart with raspberry coulis, Hôtel Bel Air

SERVES 4

4 raw puff pastry circles cut to fit the tops of 4 individual tart pans (with removable bottoms for easy handling)	4 yellow peaches 2 tbsps softened butter 4 tbsps granulated sugar

FOR THE VANILLA SYRUP

¾ cup granulated sugar (plus 4 tablespoonsful)	1 cup water

FOR THE RASBERRY *COULIS*

1 cup puréed raspberries 4 tbsps granulated sugar	*crème fraîche* or yogurt (optional)

On the evening before you plan to serve the tarts, poach the peaches in the vanilla syrup until tender (10–20 minutes). Allow the peaches to cool in the syrup; then remove the peel. Return the peeled peaches to the syrup and reserve.

When ready to bake, heat the oven to 425°F. Spread the inside of the tart pans generously with softened butter and sprinkle with granulated sugar. Slice the peaches and arrange the slices in overlapping circles in the bottom of the pans. Cover with the raw pastry circles.

Bake the tarts in the pre-heated oven for 20 minutes; then open the oven door and place the tart pans on the bottom of the oven to caramelize the peach juices (about 5 minutes). Then unmold the tarts rapidly, turning them over so that the caramelized peaches are on top.

Note: If the peaches are not caramelized, sprinkle with a very little sugar and place under the broiler for a few seconds until the edges go brown.

TO MAKE THE RASPBERRY *COULIS*

While the peach tarts are baking, prepare a raspberry *coulis* by making a pale caramel with 4 tablespoons sugar. Stir in the puréed raspberries and bring to a boil. Process the sauce in a food processor; strain into a small bowl and chill.

TO SERVE

Place the peach upside-down tarts on 4 dessert plates; spoon a little raspberry *coulis* on one side of the plate. Decorate the sauce, if desired, by tracing a few lines with a little *crème fraîche* or yogurt.

Tartes aux pommes, aux poires ou aux prunes

Apple, pear or plum tarts

SERVES 4

4 pre-baked pastry bases (see page 181) 3–4 apples, pears or plums	confectioners' sugar soft whipped cream, or *crème fraîche* (optional)

Pre-heat the oven to 400°F. Cut the fruit into four. Do not peel. Core the apples or pears or pit the plums and cut into thin slices.

Place overlapping slices of the fruit on the pastry squares (or circles), leaving a ¼-inch border.

Bake the fruit tarts in the pre-heated oven for 15 minutes. Remove from the oven and sift a layer of confectioners' sugar to coat. Serve immediately, with whipped cream or *crème fraîche* if desired.

Tarte tropézienne

SERVES 4

FOR THE CAKE

4 eggs	½ cup butter
½ cup granulated sugar	¾ cup all-purpose flour
grated rind of ½ lemon	4 tbsps cornstarch

FOR THE *CRÈME PATISSIÈRE*

2 cups milk	2 tbsps all-purpose flour
1 2-inch piece of vanilla pod, split	1 tbsp cornstarch
5 egg yolks	1 tbsp butter
½ cup granulated sugar	Kirsch

FOR THE ALMOND CRUMB TOPPING

2 tbsps softened butter	½ tsp ground cinnamon
4 tbsps all-purpose flour	½ cup chopped almonds
4 tbsps granulated sugar	

FOR THE DECORATION

confectioners' sugar

Pre-heat the oven to 350°F.

TO MAKE THE *CRÈME PATISSIÈRE*

Pour the milk into a medium-sized pan and add the vanilla pod. Bring to a boil over low heat. Cover the pan and set aside to infuse until needed.

In a bowl, whisk the egg yolks with the sugar until thick and light. Gradually whisk in the flour and cornstarch.

Fish out the vanilla pod. Gradually pour the milk into the egg yolk mixture, beating with the whisk until well blended.

Pour the mixture back into the pan. Bring to a boil over a moderate heat, stirring constantly. Then simmer for 3 minutes longer, beating vigorously with a wooden spoon to disperse lumps. (These lumps invariably form, but they are easy to beat out.)

Remove the pan from the heat. Beat in the butter and continue to beat for a minute or two longer to cool the cream slightly before adding the Kirsch.

Pass the cream through a sieve if necessary. Put it in a bowl and cover with a sheet of lightly buttered plastic wrap to prevent a skin from forming.

When quite cold, chill until required.

TO MAKE THE CAKE

Combine the eggs, granulated sugar and grated lemon rind in a bowl and whisk until well blended. Set the bowl over a pan of simmering water and whisk the mixture until it is light and thick and lukewarm, about 10–15 minutes. Remove the bowl from the pan and beat at high speed with an electric mixer for 3–5 minutes, or until the mixture is cool and holds its shape.

Melt the butter in the top of a double boiler, taking care that it does not bubble or separate. Cool.

Sift the flour and cornstarch and fold them carefully into the mixture, a little at a time, until thoroughly blended. Add the melted butter to the mixture and pour into a buttered and floured loose-bottomed (8 inch diameter by $1\frac{1}{2}$ inches deep) cake pan. Bake for 20 minutes in the pre-heated oven.

TO PREPARE THE ALMOND CRUMB TOPPING

Combine the softened butter, flour, sugar, ground cinnamon and chopped almonds in a bowl and work together with your fingers to a crumbly mixture.

Remove the cake from the oven and sprinkle with the almond crumb topping, and continue to bake for a further 25 minutes.

Allow the cake to cool, and remove from tin. Slice into two layers. Place the bottom layer, cut side up, on a flat cake plate and spread with a thick layer of chilled *crème patissière*. Top with the other layer and chill until ready to serve. Sprinkle the top with a little sifted confectioners' sugar just before serving.

185

Frangipane aux fraises

Frangipane with strawberries

FOR THE PASTRY

14 oz frozen puff pastry, at room temperature
butter

1 egg yolk, blended with 1 tbsp milk

FOR THE ORANGE ALMOND CREAM

6 tbsps granulated sugar
3 eggs
1 cup milk

6 tbsps all-purpose flour
1–2 strips orange peel

FOR THE *FRANGIPANE* BLEND

⅔ cup ground almonds
4 tbsps granulated sugar

2 tbsps orange flower water

FOR THE DECORATION

apricot preserve
orange flower water
confectioners' sugar

fresh strawberries
chilled whipped cream

TO MAKE THE ORANGE ALMOND CREAM

In a medium-sized stainless-steel bowl, beat the sugar with the eggs until smooth and light-colored. In another bowl, mix the milk into the flour, whisking all the time, to make a smooth batter. Pour this into a saucepan; add the orange peel, and cook over low heat until the mixture thickens like a sauce and no longer tastes of raw flour. Remove the pan from the heat and pour the sauce into the egg and sugar mixture, whisking all the time until well blended.

Place the stainless-steel bowl over simmering water and continue to cook, whisking continuously, until the mixture thickens again. Pour it into a clean bowl; remove the orange peel and allow the sauce to cool, stirring occasionally to prevent a skin from forming.

In the meantime, mix the ground almonds with the sugar and the orange flower water. Stir into the sauce and chill for at least 2 hours.

TO ASSEMBLE THE *FRANGIPANE*

Pre-heat the oven to 375°F.

Butter and lightly flour a baking sheet. Cut the puff pastry into 2 even-sized pieces. Roll out one piece of dough to a sheet a little over 12 inches square; then cut a circle 10–12 inches in diameter. Place the round of dough on the prepared baking sheet. Spoon the cold cream into the center of the pastry, leaving a border of 1⅔ inches. Smooth the top with a butter knife. Wet a pastry brush and moisten all exposed surfaces of the pastry. Roll out the remaining pastry to a circle the same size as the first. Place this top layer carefully over the cream-filled pastry round and press the edges together without flattening the dough too much. With a sharp knife, trim the edges into a perfect circle and mark them decoratively with the tines of a fork.

With a small sharp kitchen knife, cut 4–6 small leaf-shaped openings in the top crust to allow the steam to escape; brush the pastry with the beaten egg and milk; then mark the top crust with decorative lines with the tines of a fork. Bake in the pre-heated oven for 30 minutes, or until the pastry is golden brown. Cool the *frangipane* on a wire cake rack; brush the pastry and visible almond filling with apricot preserve diluted with a little water or orange flower water, and sprinkle if desired with sifted confectioners' sugar. Serve with strawberries and cream.

Sweet local strawberries make a delicious addition to the traditional recipe for *frangipane*.

Cheeses of Provence

As far back as I can remember, the beautiful meals I have most enjoyed in Provence have ended not with a superb sweet, but with a simple platter of local cheeses, a bowl of glistening fresh fruit and perhaps a glass of velvety *vin cuit*.

The cheeses have usually been *chèvre*, served fresh or matured or often a combination of the two; for in Provence the major cheeses are made from goat's milk or sheep's milk, both of which get firmer and sharper in flavor as they age. Every cheese fancier has his or her preferences, and a perfect cheese platter always includes cheeses of different ages and densities.

An authentic cheese platter in a Provençal restaurant is likely to consist almost entirely of small rounds of goat cheese flavored with a little garlic, thyme or bay leaf. And even though cheeses are not really a *richesse du pays*, there are a fair number of delightful little goat's cheeses which, especially in season, are dressed with chopped or rubbed herbs to bring out their full flavor, or sometimes with olive oil. I love the names of the different varieties – *picadons, bossons, cachats* (mixed with wine, oil and aromatics to make the strong cheese from the Ventoux), *tomes fraîches à l'huile*, and, more difficult to find, *tomes arlésiennes*.

Brousse is another goat's milk cheese served in country districts. Made by heating and curdling freshly drawn goat's milk, draining off the whey and treating it – often with sugar, like *fromage blanc* – the same day, this light cheese makes an excellent sweet when served with toasted almonds, crystallized sugar and an accompaniment of tart-flavored fruit conserve. Jean-Marc Banzo, chef-proprietor of the Clos de la Violette restaurant in Aix-en-Provence, serves Brousse as a savory first course, the creamy white cheese layered with three colorful fillings, black *tapenade*, chopped green herbs and bright red peppers, and accompanied by crusty olive-flecked bread.

The cheese course – especially when the cheeses are of local production – is an important matter in Provence, where the platter of cheeses is often decorated with fresh fig leaves or the glossy green leaves of lemon or orange. Sometimes fresh pears or apples are added; or a few ribs of celery and a cluster of walnuts to add moist freshness or crunch to the cheese.

Another type of cheese dessert often served in the hinterlands of Provence is *fromage frais*, a very light creamy cheese, served with black pepper and just a sprinkling of olive oil, or as a fresh-tasting pudding accompanied by lavender or acacia honey and preserved cherries.

Banon

The king of cheeses of Haute Provence is without doubt the Banon. Named after the little village of Banon, it is made according to the classic local method. The cheese is put into little baskets to dry, after which it is brushed with water, dipped into an aromatic bath of *marc de Provence*, enveloped in oak leaves from the nearby forests and tied up with a strip of raffia. After these traditional preliminaries it is set to mature in a cool cellar until it acquires the hardy savors of a Maroilles or a Pont-l'Evêque. The oak leaves are not merely decorative, but also function as excellent conserving agents, and are essential to the flavor of the matured Banons because of their rich tannins. I like Banons, too, in their fresh state, when the creamy-white discs are moist and gentle in flavor. To know Banons as they are traditionally served in Provence it is best to sample these little cheeses in varying states of maturity. In this way, you will be able to judge just how different the freshly made creamy rounds are from the mature Banons, each neatly wrapped in its casing of oak leaves.

LEFT AND OVERLEAF In Provence nearly all cheese is made from the milk of goats or sheep: most characteristic are small rounds of *chèvre* flavored with garlic, thyme or bay.

Fresh Banon cheeses are tied in oak leaves and set to mature in cool cellars.

FEAST

Jean-Claude Guillon

Hôtel Bel Air,
St Jean-Cap-Ferrat

There has been what seems like a whirlwind change in the great hotels along the coast. Now – as in the good old days of Escoffier and Diat – the great chefs are returning. No longer is it necessarily true that hotel food is boring food and that hotel decor is just hotel decor.

With the advent of Alain Ducasse at the completely refurbished Hôtel de Paris in Monte Carlo, Dominique le Stanc at the Chantecler restaurant in the Hôtel Negresco in Nice and Guy Cibois at the Hôtel Gray Albion in Cannes the scene has been transformed, and once again the gilded clientele of the casinos and the yachts are heading towards the great hotels of the coast for evenings where cuisine reigns supreme.

A fine example of the new genre is the elegant Hôtel Bel Air, hidden away in its spacious gardens at the very tip of Cap Ferrat, with one of the most impressive coastal views of the south of France. The hotel, originally baptized the Grand Hôtel Cap Ferrat, was built in 1912, at the same time as the Negresco in Nice. From the beginning it attracted the international élite who wintered on the Riviera, becoming the winter stopping-off place of Russian grand dukes, members of the British royal family, and great entrepreneurs of finance and industry.

After the First World War the procession of the rich, the great and the famous continued, but this time in the summer months, when American visitors began coming to the coast to enjoy the sun and the bathing – and even the French began to discover the pleasures of the summer season.

Today the hotel – recently renamed Hôtel Bel Air – is open all year long for both summer and winter visitors. With its rooms and suites decorated with antique paintings and furniture, its rare marble bathrooms and beautiful views, it is unquestionably

The great chefs are returning to the Riviera; and now the sumptuous finesse of Hôtel Bel Air is complemented by the elegant, Michelin-starred cuisine of Jean-Claude Guillon, sophisticated in its presentation and meticulous in its attention to flavor and detail.

one of the most luxurious and enjoyable places to stay on this opulent coast.

And not least among the Bel Air's many attractions is the restaurant where chef Jean-Claude Guillon, Michelin-starred, brings his own personal touch to the wonderful fresh produce of the markets of Nice and Menton.

Although not native born (he comes from the north), Guillon loves working and living on the coast,

for it gives him unmatched opportunities for dealing with only the freshest and best-quality raw ingredients, just hours from the depths, or minutes from the garden.

So at home at the Bel Air – he has been at the helm of the hotel's kitchens since 1976 – he seems to play the part of the quintessentially gracious host, serving as a diplomatic buffer between the old guard at the hotel and the new owners; as concerned with the splendid new decorations to the hotel and the restaurant as he is with the installation of his new kitchens, and with the food he produces there for the hotel restaurant and the open-air Dauphin restaurant at the swimming pool below.

Guillon's menus for both restaurants are well in keeping with the carefully tended hotel, featuring smooth sauces, sophisticated presentation and careful attention to flavor and detail: take, for example, his *galette* of shrimp, a delicate dish of pan-fried large shrimp and sliced wild mushrooms in a lemon-flavored butter, peeking out from under a golden rosette of crisp fried potato slices.

I like, too, his miniature stuffed vegetables filled with an herb- and garlic-flavored mousse of ground ham and breadcrumbs, with which he accompanies his roast rack of lamb *à la provençale*. I have recently taken a leaf out of the great chef's book and served these same little stuffed vegetables as an unusual garnish for square-cut fillets of John Dory, cooked for 3 minutes only in a hot oven. They would also be good served on their own as an attractive first course for a light evening meal.

Guillon is one of those super-generous chefs who like to surprise with subtle gradations on a flavor theme: one evening he produced a surprise menu made up of six different seafood dishes, each more inventive and exciting than the last, and at another meal – lunch this time – he served five different individual sweets, ranging from sugar-roasted fresh figs to a deceptively simple *tarte Tatin* made with sliced yellow peaches. I give you some of his special recipes below.

The 'grand hotel' decor of the Bel Air dining room, in soft gray and whites and muted pinks, provides the perfect foil for the controlled lightness of Jean-Claude Guillon's cuisine.

Galette de pommes de terre aux scampis

Potato galette with shrimp

SERVES 4

1 potato, about 2 oz
2 tbsps clarified butter
1 large *cèpe* (porcini) or
    other wild mushroom,
    about 3 oz
extra-virgin olive oil
salt and ground black
    pepper
6 large shrimp
crushed red pepper flakes

2 tbsps butter to which
    you have added an equal
    amount of lemon juice
tender mixed salad leaves,
    tossed with vinaigrette
    dressing
4 chives, finely chopped
1–2 sprigs chervil, finely
    chopped

TO PREPARE THE POTATO *GALETTE*

Peel the potato and cut it into a 'cork' shape ($^3/_4$ inch in diameter). Slice thinly crosswise and arrange the potato slices in an overlapping circle in a non-stick skillet which you have brushed with clarified butter. Cook the galette until golden brown on both sides.

In another pan, sauté the sliced mushroom in 1–2 tablespoons olive oil. Season to taste with salt and freshly ground black pepper.

In another pan, sauté the shrimp in a little olive oil until heated through. Season with crushed red pepper flakes and salt to taste.

TO MAKE THE CITRON BUTTER

Heat the butter with the lemon juice in a pan, and whisk until an emulsion forms.

TO ASSEMBLE THE DISH

Arrange the mixed salad leaves on one side of the dish. Place the potato *galette* in the center of the dish; top with mushrooms and arrange the shrimp to one side. Sprinkle with chives; moisten the shrimp with citron butter and decorate with sprigs of chervil.

Carré d'agneau provençal

Roast lamb with Provençal stuffed vegetables

This delicious rare-roasted *carré d'agneau* is cooked in two stages: first it is roasted for just 20 minutes, then it is spread with a Provençal paste of finely chopped garlic and parsley, fresh breadcrumbs and olive oil, and then it is put under the broiler until the coating is golden brown. The roast is served surrounded by a host of miniature vegetables – zucchini, tomatoes, zucchini flowers and saffron-tinted potatoes – stuffed with a ratatouille and ham mixture.

1 *carré d'agneau* (**rack of lamb**), **trimmed (about 1 lb
    4 oz)**

FOR THE MARINADE

2 sprigs thyme
2 sprigs basil
2 sprigs rosemary
$^2/_3$ cup olive oil
salt and black pepper
$^2/_3$ cup lamb stock (made
    with bones and
    trimmings from *carré*)

$^1/_2$ cup butter, diced
2 tbsps finely chopped
    Italian (flat-leaf) parsley
2 tbsps finely chopped
    basil

FOR THE PROVENÇAL COATING FOR THE LAMB

2 tbsps finely chopped
    garlic
4 tbsps finely chopped
    Italian (flat-leaf) parsley

4 tbsps fresh
    breadcrumbs
olive oil
salt and black pepper

TO MARINATE THE LAMB

On the evening before you plan to serve the *carré d'agneau*, prepare a marinade by coarsely chopping the herbs and combining them with olive oil and salt and freshly ground black pepper to taste.

Place the lamb in an earthenware gratin dish, or a roasting pan, and pour over the oil and herb mixture. Place the dish in the refrigerator and allow the lamb to marinate in this mixture for 18–24 hours, turning it two or three times during this period.

At the same time, you can do the advance preparation for the Provençal stuffed miniature vegetables that accompany the lamb in this recipe.

TO PREPARE THE PROVENÇAL COATING FOR THE LAMB

In a small bowl, combine the chopped herbs, breadcrumbs and olive oil and blend to a paste. Spread the roast with this paste and pass it under the broiler until it is lightly colored, about 5 minutes.

TO ROAST THE LAMB

Pre-heat the oven to 475°F. Roast the lamb for 20 minutes per pound.

Transfer the lamb to a heated serving dish and add the lamb stock to the roasting pan. Place the pan over high heat and bring the pan juices to a boil, scraping in all the crusty bits from the bottom and sides of the pan. Strain the pan juices into a clean saucepan, and over high heat whisk in the diced butter until the sauce is thick and smooth. Then add the finely chopped herbs; correct the seasoning and serve the lamb immediately, surrounded by its stuffed vegetables. Serve the herb sauce separately.

Carré d'agneau provençal
with *petits légumes farcis.*

Les petits légumes farcis

Stuffed Provençal vegetables

These little stuffed Provençal vegetables – even-sized small zucchini,
tomatoes, zucchini flowers and new
potatoes – are designed to accompany a roast of lamb *à la provençale,*
as served at the Hôtel Bel Air. The
recipe serves 2 to accompany a baby
rack of spring lamb. To serve 4 or 6
as an accompaniment to a larger
roast, double or triple this recipe.

**2 small zucchini (or, using 1 medium
zucchini, cut a small segment from
each end to form 2 small cups
approximately the same size as the
other vegetables)**
2 small tomatoes
2 small new potatoes
2 zucchini flowers
FOR THE STUFFING
**¾ cup ratatouille (made with 2½
tbsps each finely diced zucchini,
eggplant, onion and tomato,
simmered in a little olive oil until
the vegetables are tender)**
1 thin slice cooked ham, chopped
2 cloves garlic, finely chopped
2–3 leaves basil, finely chopped
4 tbsps finely chopped Italian (flat-leaf) parsley
½ cup fresh breadcrumbs
olive oil
1 generous pinch each dried thyme and rosemary
salt and ground black pepper
pinch powdered saffron (to color and flavor potatoes)

TO PREPARE THE STUFFING
Combine the cooked ratatouille, cooked ham and
garlic in the bowl of a food processor. Add the
finely chopped basil and parsley, breadcrumbs and a

little olive oil. Season generously with dried thyme,
rosemary, salt and freshly ground black pepper
and process until smooth.

TO PREPARE THE VEGETABLES
Pre-heat the oven to 350°F. Cut the tops off the
vegetables; scoop out the interiors of the zucchini,
tomatoes and potatoes. Cook the zucchini in boiling
water until just *al dente.* At the same time, cook the
potatoes in boiling water to which you have added a
pinch of saffron for color and flavor. Stuff the
vegetables with the ratatouille and ham mixture;
brush with olive oil and cook in the pre-heated oven
for 20 minutes. Remove and keep warm.

195

Croustillant aux fruits rouges

—

Summer frut croustillant

—

QUANTITIES FOR 12 PIECES OF *CROUSTILLANT*

1 tbsp fresh orange juice	2½ tbsps butter
grated rind of 1 orange	⅓ cup ground almonds
2 tsps Grand Marnier	2 tsps all-purpose flour
½ cup confectioners' sugar	

FOR THE FRUIT AND *CRÈME CHANTILLY* GARNISH

1 scant cup heavy cream	⅓ cup wild strawberries
1–2 tbsps confectioners' sugar	⅓ cup raspberries
	3 tbsps red currants
few drops vanilla extract	3 tbsps small strawberries

FOR THE RASPBERRY SAUCE

⅔ cup raspberries	lemon juice
confectioners' sugar	

Croustillant aux fruits rouges.

TO PREPARE THE *CROUSTILLANTS*

In a medium-sized bowl, combine the first 7 ingredients; mix well and leave to amalgamate for 2 hours. Then, measure out 12 half-tablespoons of the mixture and form into small balls. Chill again.

When ready to bake, place 4 small balls of the mixture on a non-stick baking sheet and flatten each ball out with a fork which you have moistened in cold water. Leave 1½–2 inches between balls to allow the mixture to spread out during baking.

Pre-heat the oven to 475°F. Bake the *croustillants* in the pre-heated oven for 2–2½ minutes, or until golden brown. Remove from the oven and allow to cool on the baking sheet before removing them with a spatula. Repeat twice more.

TO PREPARE THE GARNISH

Make the *crème chantilly* by whipping the heavy cream until thick; stir in the confectioners' sugar and vanilla extract, to taste, and whip again. Wash and drain the fruits. Mix in a small bowl.

TO SERVE

Place 1 *croustillant* on each of 4 dessert plates; pipe with *crème chantilly*; arrange the red fruits on this bed of cream. Top with the second *croustillant*, add *crème chantilly* and fruits as before; then top with the remaining *croustillant*. Decorate with a few berries and raspberry sauce (see below) around it.

TO MAKE THE SAUCE

Blend or process the raspberries with confectioners' sugar and lemon juice, to taste, until smooth.

A stately procession of trays of fresh figs in the elegant grounds of the Hôtel Bel Air.

The Comtat

DELIGHTS OF NICE, OLD AND NEW

Nice has changed. From its postcard prettiness, with the Promenade des Anglais cut like a long thin ribbon and bordered by the gold of its beaches, its soaring palm trees set against the Matisse-blue sky and its brightly colored houses on the front – a sort of sleeping beauty of the nineteenth century – it has metamorphosed into an ultra-modern city of economic, cultural and aesthetic diversity: symbol of a new Côte d'Azur, a land of brilliant sunshine, wide open to research, industry and high technology.

Gastronomically speaking, Nice has one eye firmly set on the future and the other fixed lovingly on its culinary past. Old Nice (*la vieille ville*), with its narrow, dark streets in the cool shadow of the 'mountain' immediately behind, is an Aladdin's cave filled with wonderful little food shops where you can buy pastas and *charcuterie* of all descriptions; where rock-hard slabs of dried salt cod (and the rarer and more expensive stockfish) snuggle up against colorful displays of herbs and spices and vegetables and salads, and where *socca* and *torta de blea* vendors, ice cream parlors and little restaurants and pizzerias are on every corner.

The little restaurants of Nice – which look like nothing at all and yet are everything that is old Nice – are a must for every visitor. It is here that you can discover the traditional specialities of this food-loving Italian city: *socca* (a huge, soft 'pancake' of chick-pea flour, served by the portion on the street); *torta de blea* (a sweet-savory Swiss chard and pine nut 'quiche' sold in squares); the 'true' *pissaladière* of Nice, a flat onion tart garnished with anchovies and black olives (I say 'true' because there is another version, delicious but not quite authentic, which includes tomatoes and grated Parmesan in its making); *daube de boeuf* (with its traditional accompaniment of ravioli cooked in the juices of the daube); *poche de veau* (calf's stomach or shoulder of veal stuffed with pork and veal, green pot herbs and

# of Nice

aromatics) *morue* (salt cod) or stockfish (a saltier, hardier, rarer and more highly flavored version) cooked with tomatoes, onions, garlic, herbs and black olives or anchovies *à la niçoise*; and red mullet, octopus or squid cooked in the same way.

Names to look out for when you want to enjoy a typical Niçois meal in a typical small, noisy, busy 'no nonsense' Niçois restaurant are: Le Batteleur, Lc Safari, L'Arbolète, Pompon et Marinette, Adrienne at Lou Balico and the Relais des Sportifs. At any of these you will enjoy a truly typical Niçois meal. I like the *ambiance*, I like the atmosphere, I like the noise and I like the cuisine. And then there is the mad luxury of the Hôtel Negresco, bang in the middle of the Promenade des Anglais on the sea front, with its breast-pointed pink cupola.

Other sights to see: the new Musée Matisse in the Villa des Arènes, to view the paintings, drawings, engravings, bronzes and personal objects belonging to the painter; La Galerie des Ponchettes which will soon become a Dufy museum; and the Galerie d'Art Contemporain, to be consecrated to the work of a native painter of the nineteenth century, Gustave Adolph Mossa.

Art is everywhere in Nice. When walking in the narrow streets of old Nice you only have to look up to discover marvel after marvel of baroque and Niçois architecture: l'Eglise de Gésu shows the *piémontaise* influence of the eighteenth century; on one side of the hill is the quarter of the rich at Cimiez; on the other the historical quarter of the merchants, farmers and washerwomen. In recent years, the Place Garibaldi has been repainted in the rich, warm colors of the tradition of Genoa and Piedmont; soon it will be the turn of the Promenade des Anglais – one of the Riviera's most elegant attractions when it was constructed in 1822. The Place Saleya, two jumps from the sea, is the central point of any visit to Nice. There you will find an open-air market of flowers and food products every day except Monday, when it becomes the *foire à la brocante* (flea market). The Place Saleya's long, open spaces are bordered on both sides by crowded cafés and restaurants where it is pleasant to sit in the sun and watch the goings-on in the market.

La vraie pissaladière de Nice

Onion and anchovy tart with black olives

SERVES 4–6

8 oz bread dough
3 lb large yellow onions,
    thinly sliced
2 tbsps olive oil

2 cloves garlic, finely
    chopped
¼ tsp dried *herbes de*
    Provence

FOR THE GARNISH

8 anchovy fillets
2–3 tbsps tiny black olives
    from Nice

dried *herbes de Provence*
olive oil

Sauté the thinly sliced onions and finely chopped garlic in olive oil until transparent and just beginning to turn golden.

Pre-heat the oven to 350°F.

Roll out the bread dough on a floured work surface to a diameter of 10 inches. Place the dough on a lightly oiled baking sheet. Spread the onion mixture on the dough; garnish it with a pinwheel of anchovy fillets radiating out from the center. Sprinkle with black olives and dried *herbes de Provence* and moisten with olive oil.

Bake in the pre-heated oven for 40–45 minutes.

La vraie pissaladière de Nice. Inset: My *pissaladière*.

My pissaladière

Provençal tomato and onion tart

SERVES 6

FOR THE PASTRY

1 cup all-purpose flour
pinch of salt
5 tbsps butter, diced
1 egg

1 egg yolk, beaten with
    equal amount of iced
    water

FOR THE FILLING

6 large ripe tomatoes
olive oil
2 tbsps tomato paste
ground black pepper
3 large yellow onions
2 tbsps butter

¼ to ½ tsp chopped fresh
    rosemary
2 tbsps finely grated
    Parmesan cheese
12 anchovy fillets
black olives, pitted

Pre-heat the oven to fairly hot (425°F).

TO MAKE THE PASTRY

Sift the flour and salt into a bowl; rub in the butter until mixture resembles fine breadcrumbs. Beat the egg yolk with an equal amount of iced water and add it to the flour mixture; knead lightly to form a smooth dough.

Roll out the pastry to line an 8–9-inch fluted tart pan with a removable base. Prick the pastry with the tines of a fork. Chill. Then brush with a little lightly beaten egg yolk and bake for 10–15 minutes, or until the crust is set but not brown. Allow to cool. Reduce the oven temperature to moderate (350°F).

TO MAKE THE FILLING

Plunge the tomatoes into boiling water for a minute to loosen the skins; peel, seed and chop them. Heat 4 tablespoons olive oil in a deep skillet; add the chopped tomatoes, tomato paste and freshly ground black pepper to taste. Simmer over low heat until excess moisture is cooked away, mashing occasionally with a wooden spoon to form a purée.

Slice the onions and simmer them separately in butter, together with the chopped fresh rosemary, until soft and golden but not brown.

Sprinkle the bottom of the pastry shell with grated Parmesan. Add the onions and cover with the tomato purée. Arrange the anchovies in a latticework pattern on top and place a pitted black olive in the center of each square.

Brush the olives and anchovies lightly with oil and bake for about 30 minutes. Serve hot, warm or cold.

Pissaladière aux poivrons

Pepper pissaladière

SERVES 6

1 8–9-inch pastry shell, pre-baked for 5 minutes	2 tbsps freshly grated Parmesan
1 egg yolk, beaten	

FOR THE FILLING

olive oil	4 tbsps freshly grated Parmesan cheese
1 lb ripe tomatoes, peeled and chopped, or a 16 oz can peeled tomatoes, chopped	3 Spanish onions, peeled and chopped
2 tbsps tomato paste	½ tsp dried thyme
½ tsp dried oregano	4 tbsps butter
½ tsp sugar	3 sweet peppers, 1 yellow, 1 green, 1 red
salt and black pepper	

Brush the half-baked pastry shell with beaten egg yolk. Sprinkle with 2 tablespoons freshly grated Parmesan cheese. Leave the prepared pastry shell in its pan on a baking sheet.

Heat 4 tablespoons of olive oil in a heavy pan, add the chopped fresh (or canned) tomatoes and the tomato paste, sprinkle with dried oregano and sugar, and season to taste with salt and freshly ground black pepper. Cook over low heat for about 15 minutes, or until excess moisture has evaporated, stirring and mashing the tomatoes with a wooden spoon to reduce them to a thick purée. Stir in the freshly grated Parmesan cheese. Allow to cool.

Sauté the chopped onions and dried thyme in butter until transparent and very soft. Season with salt and black pepper. Let them cool as well.

Pre-heat the oven to 350°F and light the broiler on its maximum setting.

When the broiler is hot, lay the peppers in the broiler pan and broil them as close to the heat as possible, turning frequently, until their skins are charred and blistered all over. Rub the skins off under cold running water. Cut the peppers in half, remove the cores, wash out the seeds and pat the peppers dry with absorbent paper. Cut each half in three across the width.

Cover the prepared pastry shell with the sautéed onions and spread the tomato purée evenly over the top. Dot with the pepper chunks, using their colors to best advantage.

Brush the top of the tart and the pepper chunks with olive oil and bake for 30 minutes. Serve hot or warm.

La trouchia

Flat green omelet à la niçoise

SERVES 4

This is a lovely flat green omelet made with finely slivered Swiss chard, Italian (flat-leaf) parsley, chervil and basil.

8 eggs	1–1½ cups freshly grated Parmesan cheese
2 lb Swiss chard (green parts only)	salt and ground black pepper
1 bunch Italian (flat-leaf) parsley	cayenne pepper
1 bunch chervil	2–4 tbsps olive oil
1 bunch fresh basil	

In a medium-sized bowl, beat the eggs until frothy.

Wash the Swiss chard, parsley, chervil and basil. Shake dry.

Remove the hard white cores from the Swiss chard and reserve for other use. Cut the green parts of the leaves and the Italian (flat-leaf) parsley, chervil and basil into thin strips crosswise.

Add the slivered greens and grated Parmesan to the egg mixture and mix well. Season with salt, ground black pepper and a hint of cayenne pepper.

When ready to cook, add the olive oil to a large skillet. Pour in the omelet mixture; cover the pan and cook over medium heat for 20 minutes.

Remove the cover and slide the omelet onto a large serving plate; add a little more oil to the pan and reverse the omelet carefully into the pan to brown the other side lightly.

Panisses

Panisses is the Niçois name for thick little pancakes the size of an English crumpet, made in a deep saucer. A typical 'poor man's food' because of their inexpensive base of chick-pea flour and water, these little snacks are quite delicious when cut into thick slices and fried in a little olive oil, dusted with crunchy sugar and served with fruit conserve as a sweet; or, as they are more usually served, topped with generous amounts of freshly ground black pepper as a filling snack; or as the vegetable accompaniment to a daube or fricassee of beef, rabbit or little game birds.

Panisses as a savory snack,
or as a vegetable accompaniment
SERVES 4–6

4¼ cups water	freshly ground black
olive oil	pepper
1 tbsp coarse salt	melted butter
2 cups chick-pea flour	

In a large saucepan, combine the water, 2 tablespoons of olive oil and salt. Bring to a boil. Then sift the chick-pea flour into the water gradually, stirring all the time.

Continue to cook, stirring, for 20 minutes, or until the mixture is thick and bubbling. Then pour it into small cake pans or deep saucers which you have brushed with a little olive oil. Cool until ready to use.

TO SERVE

Remove the *panisses* from their containers and cut into slices 1 inch thick. Sauté these in olive oil for about 3 minutes, or until slices are crisp and golden on all sides. Season generously with freshly ground black pepper and serve with melted butter, or with the sauce from a daube of beef or veal, or with a *poulet à la niçoise*.

Panisses as a sweet

I also like to serve *panisses*, prepared as above, as an inexpensive country sweet. Follow the recipe above, sautéing the sliced *panisses* in olive oil, but instead of seasoning them with ground pepper as above, dredge them with granulated sugar and serve them piping hot with raspberry, blackberry or cherry conserves.

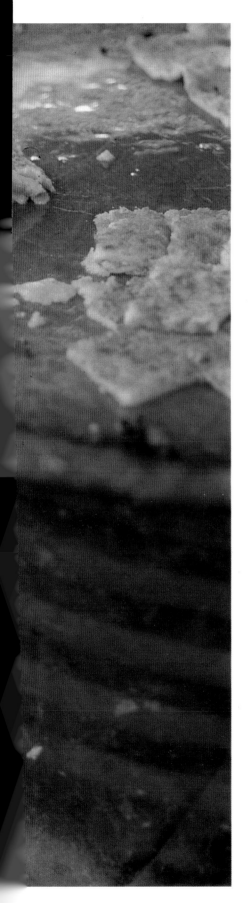

In *la vieille ville* traditional *socca* is still sold by the portion on street corners. In the old days, the *socca* vendors used to wheel this satisfying mid-morning snack from building site to building site in small zinc-hooded carts, keeping it warm over charcoal braziers.

La socca

MAKES 2 *SOCCAS* OF 20 INCHES IN DIAMETER

La socca, a moist baked square of chick-pea gruel, is one of the traditional morning snacks of building workers in the area around Nice. In the old days, the *socca* vendors used to transport their wares from building site to building site in small two-wheeled carts, topped with a large zinc hood to keep the stacked trays of *socca* warm over the charcoal brazier inside the cart. It was the job of the youngest man on the building site to bring steaming portions of hot *socca* to the workers on the site.

A traditional *socca* is still prepared on a large tray, sometimes 2 feet in diameter, and cooked in a large woodburning oven like the ones used for baking pizzas or *tortas* in the streets of old Nice. But for our purposes a thoroughly respectable *socca* can be made in a normal oven, pre-heated for 30 minutes before the *socca* is put in to cook under the broiler.

2 cups chick-pea flour	¼ tsp salt
2¼ cups water	freshly ground black
olive oil	pepper

Pre-heat the oven to 475°F.

Combine the chick-pea flour, water, 2 tablespoons of olive oil and salt in a large bowl and beat the mixture energetically with a large whisk until well mixed. Then strain the mixture into a bowl through a fine sieve to remove any lumps.

Brush 2 baking sheets with a little olive oil. Pour the *socca* mixture to a depth of ½ inch into each baking sheet.

At the moment of putting the *socca* sheet into the oven, turn off the oven and light the broiler. Cook the *socca* near the broiler, pricking the bubbles with the point of a knife as they form.

When the surface is golden, even lightly burned in some places, remove from the broiler; season generously with freshly ground black pepper.

Socca at its best is soft and moist with a robust earthy flavor. The Niçois eat it simply as it is, cut in comfortable 2-inch squares. I like to use it as a rustic base for a Provençal ragout of salt cod, lobster or shrimp *à la niçoise* or a ragout of chicken livers *à la provençale*.

Old Nice, with its
narrow, dark streets,
is an Aladdin's cave
filled with wonderful
little food shops
where you can buy
pastas and *charcuterie*
of all descriptions;
where rock-hard slabs
of dried salt cod
snuggle up against
colorful displays of
herbs and spices and
vegetables and salads,
and where *socca* and
torta de blea vendors,
ice cream parlors
and little restaurants
and pizzerias are
on every corner.

Pan bagnat

Pan bagnat is one of the most famous mid-morning snacks of the Midi. Literally translated, the name means 'soaked bread' or 'bread in a bath' but why translate it when the Provençal name is so appealing? *Pan bagnat* is nothing more nor less than a *salade niçoise*, caught practically between two thick portions of round country bread, so that it can be transported to work or school – for this celebrated salad-cum-sandwich is sold on every street corner.

Originally *pan bagnat* was a combination of cold soup and salad, in which stale bread, cut or broken into bits, was incorporated 1 hour before serving into a salad of lettuce, tomatoes, green peppers, sweet onions, anchovies and black olives. The bread soaked up all the juices of the salad and was a delicious way of using up leftovers in a poor society. It was not long before hard-working farm wives and mothers, wanting to make these bread and salad snacks more portable for their menfolk and children to take to work or school, packed them tidily between two halves of a round loaf. And *pan bagnat* was born.

4 rolls or 1 round loaf of bread	2 green peppers, seeded and sliced
olive oil	2 hard-boiled eggs, sliced
2 cloves garlic	salt and ground black pepper
8 lettuce leaves	
4 large ripe tomatoes, sliced	lemon juice
1 small can pimientos, drained	4 level tbsps finely chopped parsley
2 hard-boiled eggs	16 small black olives
	16 anchovy fillets

Slice the rolls or bread in half lengthwise and pull out the soft center with your fingers. Brush the insides of the crust liberally with olive oil in which you have crushed the garlic cloves.

Place 1 lettuce leaf in the bottom half of each roll, or place a layer of lettuce leaves in the bottom half of the loaf. Cover the lettuce with slices of tomato, canned pimiento, green pepper and hard-boiled egg. Season with salt and freshly ground black pepper. Add lemon juice, to taste, to the remaining garlic oil, then add salt, freshly ground black pepper and finely chopped parsley.

Dribble the dressing over the sliced vegetables and eggs; garnish with black olives and anchovies; top with the remaining lettuce leaves and cover with the top half of the rolls or loaf.

Wrap the rolls in aluminum foil, or cut the round loaf into 4 wedges and wrap; weight with a plate and chill for 1 hour before serving.

Pan bagnat simple

1 round loaf of bread	12 black olives
extra-virgin olive oil	2 stalks celery, thinly
freshly ground black	sliced
pepper	6 basil leaves, cut in
4 large tomatoes, sliced	slivers
1 small red onion, sliced	12 anchovy fillets

Cut the loaf in half crosswise. With your fingers, pull out some of the soft bread from inside the two halves. Moisten the insides of the two halves of the loaf generously with olive oil.

Season with freshly ground black pepper.

Place the tomato slices on one of the loaf sections. Top with onion slices. Sprinkle with black olives, celery slices and slivered basil. Top with the anchovies and sprinkle again with olive oil.

Top with the remaining half loaf; press gently together and serve immediately.

Polenta sauce tomate

Polenta with tomato sauce

SERVES 4–6

3 cups yellow cornmeal	butter
5–6¼ cups salted water	4 tbsps fresh
4 tbsps butter	breadcrumbs
1–1½ cups freshly grated	1¼ cups freshly grated
Parmesan cheese	mozzarella cheese
salt and black pepper	tomato *coulis* (see p. 24)
nutmeg or cayenne pepper	

Bring the water to a boil. Pour the cornmeal in slowly, stirring constantly with a wooden spoon. Continue cooking for 20–30 minutes, stirring frequently, until the polenta is thick and soft and leaves the sides of the pan easily; add a little more water if necessary. Just before serving, stir in the butter and 1 cup of the grated Parmesan cheese. Taste and correct the seasoning, adding a little salt, freshly ground black pepper and nutmeg or cayenne pepper.

Butter a shallow baking dish and sprinkle generously with breadcrumbs and the remaining Parmesan. Spread a quarter of the polenta over it;

cover with a quarter of the grated mozzarella, and dot with 1 tablespoon of butter. Repeat the layers until all the ingredients are used up. Bake in a moderate oven (375°F) for 15–20 minutes, or until well browned. Serve with well-seasoned tomato *coulis* (see page 24).

Risotto provençal

SERVES 4

4 tbsps butter	1½ cups Italian medium-
½ large yellow onion,	grain rice
finely chopped	salt and ground black
3–4 cups hot beef stock	pepper
FOR THE SAUCE	
4 tbsps olive oil	2 cloves garlic, finely
2 tbsps finely chopped	chopped
onion	4 tbsps finely chopped
⅔ cup dry white wine	parsley
6 medium-sized tomatoes,	¼ tsp powdered saffron
peeled, seeded and	½ small green pepper,
chopped	finely chopped
salt and ground black	
pepper	

Melt the butter in a large, heavy-based saucepan over low heat. Add the onion and cook gently for 2–4 minutes without allowing to brown.

Add the rice to the softened onion, increase the heat to medium and cook for 1–2 minutes, stirring constantly. Then stir in the beef stock. Continue cooking, stirring occasionally and adding more stock if necessary, for 20–25 minutes or until the rice is tender. Season with salt and freshly ground black pepper to taste.

Meanwhile make the risotto sauce: heat the olive oil in a small saucepan. Add the finely chopped onion and cook for 7–10 minutes over moderate heat or until transparent, stirring occasionally. Stir in the dry white wine and peeled, seeded and chopped tomatoes. Season with salt and freshly ground black pepper to taste. Stir in the finely chopped garlic, finely chopped parsley and powdered saffron, cover and simmer for 20 minutes, stirring occasionally. Add the chopped green pepper and simmer uncovered for a further 10 minutes or until tender.

Transfer the rice to a heated serving dish and serve the risotto sauce in a separate dish. Serve immediately.

Franck Cerutti

Don Camillo

RIGHT *Thon de lapin*.

Franck Cerutti, young chef-proprietor of the Don Camillo in Nice, is one of the hard-working young Turks of the new *cuisine niçoise*. This is a family-run restaurant – his father-in-law is the elegant *maître d'hôtel*, his mother-in-law and his young wife help with the smiling, unassuming service, and according to Franck even his mother can't be kept out of the kitchen, if only to help with the washing up.

I loved my visits there and can't wait to be a regular of this charming little restaurant behind the Saleya market of old Nice, just one street from the sea. The food is extraordinarily simple, yet at the same time extraordinarily good. Like the great chefs with whom he worked before starting out in his own restaurant – three years as *commis* and then chef with Jacques Maximin, chef with Alain Ducasse and then another three years as a chef in Florence – this young man uses only the finest and freshest ingredients in a region where that really means something. But even though he uses the finest, and thus the most costly, olive oils, herbs and salads and fish, his prices are exceedingly reasonable. This haven of fine food is one of the best and most interesting restaurants on the coast if, like me, you like what Franck Cerutti prefers to call *Alpéen* food, from the country districts of the Alpes Maritimes.

'We are poor,' he is fond of saying, 'Provence is rich.' And that is where he finds his inspiration for homely but superb dishes like his *thon de lapin* (see opposite), his herb-stuffed *poche* of veal, his *friture* of little red mullet (see page 211), or his *poulpes de roche* (little cuttlefish caught among the local rocks, simply boiled and served with boiled new potatoes and fresh green beans). I give you his recipe on page 212 so that you can make this 'real' fisherman's dish – but how can I tell you what a difference the freshly caught cuttlefish make, or the special new potatoes and tender green beans brought in that day from the market gardens just outside Nice? Or how fabulous is his simple seasoning of coarse sea salt, freshly ground black pepper and a very special olive oil imported from Italy, where olive oil is now produced like the finest wines, and costs about as much? And then there is his own version of the famous Niçois Swiss chard, raisin and pine-nut pie, *torta de blea*, to which Cerutti adds zucchini.

Franck Cerutti selects only the finest ingredients.

Thon de lapin

Rabbit 'tuna'

½ **rabbit**	**salt and ground black**
½ **Spanish onion**	**pepper**
1 **celery stalk**	1 **clove garlic, cut in**
1 **small carrot**	**quarters**
1 **sprig thyme**	3 **fresh sage leaves**
1 **bay leaf**	**extra-virgin olive oil**
6 **black peppercorns**	**(about 1¼ cups)**

FOR THE GARNISH

Slices of French bread	*mesclun* **salad (see page**
brushed with olive oil	**102)**
and baked in the oven	

In a large saucepan, bring 9 cups lightly salted water to a boil. Add the onion, celery, carrot, thyme, bay leaf and black peppercorns and bring gently to a boil again; skim the impurities from the surface of the water; add the half rabbit; bring to a boil; skim again; then reduce the heat and simmer for 1 ½ hours.

Remove the casserole from the heat and allow the rabbit to cool in the bouillon. When the rabbit is cold, remove it from the bouillon and place it in a shallow bowl. Then remove all the meat, arranging the pieces in a single layer on a plate, and season them generously with salt and freshly ground black pepper.

Transfer the rabbit pieces to a medium-sized bowl; add the garlic, 3 fresh sage leaves and enough extra-virgin olive oil to just cover the rabbit pieces. Mix the rabbit and oil with your hands to ensure that all the pieces are impregnated with oil and seasonings. Cover with plastic wrap and allow to rest in the refrigerator for 48 hours before serving.

TO SERVE

Remove from the refrigerator and spread the *thon* on slices of French bread which you have brushed on both sides with olive oil and baked in the oven until golden.

Serve with a *mesclun* salad (see page 102).

Torta de blea (blettes) et zucchini

Little Swiss chard and zucchini pies

SERVES 6

FOR THE PASTRY

2¼ cups all-purpose flour	5–6 tbsps water
1 egg	salt
½–⅔ cup olive oil	

FOR THE FILLING

2 lb 4 oz Swiss chard	1 bunch fresh basil leaves
1 lb zucchini	2 eggs
1 tsp coarse salt	freshly ground black
4 tbsps freshly grated	pepper
Parmesan cheese	3–4 tbsps olive oil
1 small onion, finely	
chopped	

TO MAKE THE PASTRY

Sift the flour into a large mixing bowl. In a cup, blend the whole egg, olive oil and water. Add the salt, to taste, and mix well. Then, little by little, add the egg, oil and water mixture to the flour in the bowl, blending all the ingredients together into a smooth, pliable dough. Be careful not to handle the dough as much as you would for a butter-based pastry, or it will get tough. Wrap the pastry in plastic wrap and allow to rest in the refrigerator for 1 hour.

TO MAKE THE FILLING

In the meantime, remove the white stems from the Swiss chard (Provençal cooks use the white stems cut into sticks for a gratin or as a crisp vegetable accompaniment for another dish). Wash the green parts, drain and dry. Chop them as finely as possible and keep in the colander for later use.

Grate the zucchini. Place it in a sieve, sprinkle with 1 teaspoon coarse salt, and then, with your hands, mix thoroughly so that the salt is evenly distributed. After 20 minutes, again with your hands, press the salt and excess liquids out of the zucchini.

In a large mixing bowl, combine the chopped Swiss chard and the grated and pressed zucchini with the finely chopped onion and thinly sliced basil leaves and pepper to taste. Add the well-beaten eggs, grated Parmesan and a splash of olive oil. Do not mix at this point: just allow the flavors of vegetables and seasonings to develop while you roll out the pastry.

TO MAKE THE PIES

Pre-heat the oven to moderate (350°F). Remove the pastry from the refrigerator; remove the plastic wrap and roll the pastry out on a floured work surface to a thickness of ⅛ inch. Cut 6 circles of pastry 4½ inches in diameter and 6 circles 5½ inches in diameter. Then, from the trimmings, cut 6 strips of pastry 1 inch wide and 8 inches long.

Place 6 metal tart rings (4 inches in diameter) on a baking sheet. Place 1 larger pastry circle in each tart ring, pressing the pastry down well with your fingers. Now it is time rapidly and lightly to mix the Swiss chard, zucchini and basil filling. Fill the pastry-lined rings with the mixture, pressing it well down inside. Top with the smaller pastry circles, pressing the pastry down on the filling. Then carefully remove the metal rings from the little pies. Brush the pastry bands with olive oil and place an oiled band of pastry around each pie, fixing the joins in place with your fingers.

Make a little hole in the top of each pie so that moisture can escape and bake in the pre-heated oven for 20 minutes. Serve with a *mesclun* salad (see page 102) or other salad of mixed leaves.

Banaste de pei

Little basket of deep-fried fish

SERVES 4

In the classic Provençal kitchen burning-hot 'deep-fries' of fish are much appreciated, and *banaste de pei* is often found on the simple menus of the small restaurants and bistros along the coast and in the hinterland. The typical *banaste* – often called *brûle-doigts* (burn-your-fingers) or *brûle-gueule* (burn-your-mug) – is generally a fry-up of tiny little red mullet, miniature fresh sardines or a mixture of the little rockfish which are netted along the coast, all served in a napkin in a basket, with half-lemons and sprigs of fresh Italian (flat-leaf) parsley as their only accompaniment.

The fish are also deep-fried and served on their own or mixed with batter-fried vegetables – chunky slices of small zucchini and eggplant – to make a homelier version of the Italian *fritto misto* that is much appreciated in the bars of Marseilles and Nice.

The true secret of this simple dish, according to Franck Cerutti, is to use a large pot and a lot of oil, either peanut oil or olive oil or a mixture of the two. Ten and a half cups of oil for 2½ lb of tiny red mullet to serve six seems a lot to our more puritanical minds: but the results as served by Cerutti are more than worth it. I give you two recipes for *banaste de pei* and you can make up your own mind, using fresh whitebait if baby red mullet or tiny fresh sardines are hard to come by.

1 lb 8 oz very small red mullet (or fresh sardines or whitebait)
1 tbsp all-purpose flour

½ tbsp fine salt
¼ tsp paprika
olive oil or peanut oil, for deep-frying

FOR THE SEASONING MIX

¼ tsp fine salt
¼ tsp paprika

pinch cayenne pepper

FOR THE GARNISH

sprigs of Italian (flat-leaf) parsley

lemon quarters

Do not scale or clean the little fish. Pat them dry with a kitchen towel.

Place the fish in a paper bag with the flour seasoned with salt and paprika, and shake until they are lightly coated.

Heat 1 inch olive oil or peanut oil in a large heat-proof skillet and cook over high heat until sizzling hot. Add the prepared fish and fry, turning from time to time, until they are golden brown on all sides.

Transfer the fish to a clean kitchen towel or absorbent paper to drain, and then arrange them attractively in a folded napkin in a basket.

Sprinkle with a seasoning mix of salt, paprika and cayenne pepper and garnish with lemon quarters and sprigs of Italian (flat-leaf) parsley. Serve immediately.

Friture de petits rougets 'brûle-doigts', Don Camillo

Don Camillo's fry of little red mullet

SERVES 6

2 lb 8 oz little red mullet (or fresh sardines or whitebait)
sifted all-purpose flour

olive oil or peanut oil, for deep-frying
salt

Rinse the fish but do not clean them. Dry them well and dredge them lightly with sifted flour.

In a large heat-proof casserole or deep-fryer, heat

'We are poor,' Franck Cerutti is fond of saying, 'Provence is rich.' It is in the superb produce and cooking of the Alpes Maritimes that he finds inspiration for his own cuisine – extraordinarily simple, yet at the same time extraordinarily good.

Friture de petits rougets 'brûle-doigts', Don Camillo.

the olive oil or peanut oil until sizzling hot; add the lightly floured fish, 5 oz at a time, and deep-fry until golden brown. Transfer the fish to a kitchen towel to drain off excess oil. Season with salt. Continue to fry the remaining fish in the same way.

As soon as all the fish are deep-fried, serve them in separate portions, each folded in a napkin.

Poulpe des roche, pommes de terre et haricots
verts, persil

Franck Cerutti's little cuttlefish with vegetables marinière

SERVES 6

6 little cuttlefish	**salt and ground black**
1 bay leaf	**pepper**
½ lemon	**extra-virgin olive oil**
6 small new potatoes	**juice of ½ lemon**
7 oz slender green beans,	**4 sprigs Italian (flat-leaf)**
trimmed	**parsley, chopped**

Ask the fishmonger to clean the cuttlefish.

In a large saucepan, bring a large quantity of salted water to a boil with the bay leaf and ½ lemon. When the water boils, add the cuttlefish. Bring to a boil again; lower the heat and simmer gently for 40–45 minutes, or until the cuttlefish are tender. Allow the cuttlefish to cool in cooking liquid.

In the meantime, cook the potatoes in their skins in boiling salted water for 20 minutes. Drain and reserve. In another saucepan, cook the green beans in

Poulpes de roche, pommes de terre et haricots verts, persil.

season to taste with salt and freshly ground black pepper; moisten with a dribble of extra-virgin olive oil and the juice of half a lemon; sprinkle with chopped parsley and serve immediately.

Panna cotta Don Camillo.

Panna cotta Don Camillo

'Cooked' cream with red fruits

SERVES 6

2 cups heavy cream	4 tbsps granulated sugar
½ vanilla pod	red fruits e.g. raspberries,
1 tsp gelatin, softened	strawberries, cherries
in a little warm water	

In a small saucepan, combine the heavy cream, sugar and vanilla and cook over low heat, stirring constantly, until the sugar has melted (almost at boiling point).

Remove the saucepan from the heat; remove the half vanilla pod; add the softened gelatin and whisk until the gelatin is completely incorporated into the hot cream.

Pour into 6 individual molds and allow to set.

TO SERVE

Unmold the sweets on to 6 dessert plates and garnish with a mixture of red fruits.

boiling salted water for 6–8 minutes, or until just tender. Drain and reserve.

Cut the cuttlefish into 1-inch slices. Peel and slice the potatoes. In a skillet or shallow casserole, combine the prepared cuttlefish, sliced, peeled potatoes and green beans and warm through in a little of the cuttlefish bouillon.

TO SERVE

Arrange the pieces of cuttlefish and potatoes in heated shallow soup plates; scatter with green beans;

FEAST

Dominique le Stanc

Le Chantecler,
Hôtel Negresco

Dominique le Stanc, originally from Alsace, is one of the most exciting young chefs on the Côte d'Azur. In charge of the prestigious kitchens of the Hôtel Negresco, star of the famous Chantecler restaurant in that hotel, the thirty-four-year-old chef is making culinary history with his lighthearted approach to Provençal food. A fresh new breeze on the Mediterranean, he seems to be reinventing Provençal cuisine single-handed, with a series of special menus devoted to the sea (*menus de la mer*) and to the fresh local products of the kitchen gardens around Nice (*menus dégustation*). Michel Palmer, manager of the Negresco, had the inspired idea of tempting talented young Le Stanc down from his eagle's nest restaurant at the Château Eza in Eze village, on the upper Corniche, when the famous chef Jacques Maximin suddenly left the Chantecler to open his own short-lived restaurant nearby, after putting the Negresco firmly on the gastronomic map.

Le Stanc's cooking at the Chantecler is light and inventive, presenting in the same dish unexpected combinations of rustic and sophisticated flavors which make this gastronome, for one, sit up and take notice. He is perhaps the most creative cook on the entire coast, and yet seems quite unruffled by the demands of his daily responsibilities and completely unspoiled by his immediate and resounding international success.

Le Stanc takes the simplest of vegetables and makes them into staggeringly successful vegetarian first courses. His *vinaigrette de jeunes poireaux en salade, copeaux de parmesan et de truffes blanches d'Alba* is a revelation: the super-fresh, super-young leeks are poached in light stock, dressed with a light vinaigrette sauce and studded with thin slices of fresh Parmesan and white truffles. Friends talk, too, about his *velouté de petits pois aux pointes d'asperges et girolles* (a smooth-textured soup of fresh peas with asparagus tips and tiny wild mushrooms), and of another similar combination of fresh vegetables, his *poêlée* of fat green asparagus spears pan-fried with a cascade of fresh morels. Or try his ragout of fresh Mediterranean vegetables (artichoke hearts, tomatoes and large green onions), dressed with a reduced anchovy-flavored veal stock and brought to your table, amid the grandly decorated surroundings of the Chantecler restaurant, in a 'grandmotherly' black iron *cocotte*: a marvel of both presentation and flavor. On a more rustic note, Le Stanc cooks fresh farm eggs *au plat* as only a French chef can, his secret being a scattering of heavenly golden truffles from Alba and the gentlest of bacon-flavored cream sauces.

One of his most inspired dishes, featuring the local fish of the region, uses the juices of a classic ratatouille to lend excitement to a poached fillet of John Dory (see overleaf). Another dresses the fish with a delicate purée of young artichokes whisked to the lightest of mousses with a dash of extra-virgin olive oil. I also like his *daurade royale* flavored with bay leaves, its light sauce perfumed with anise.

Interesting creations based on meats, poultry and game are much in evidence on Le Stanc's menus: tiny veal kidneys are accompanied by earthy polenta, for example, or a comforting *confit* of shallots, braised lettuces and tiny new peas; and roast pigeon is flavored with cumin in the Arab manner and set with jewel-like baby turnips glazed with honey.

But it is perhaps the glamorous desserts, turned out under his direction by talented young pastry chef Gregory Collet, which are most translatable to our kitchens. His saffron- and honey-flavored ice cream (see page 218) is worth a trip on its own. I suggest you serve it alone (it is delicious) or as an accompaniment to sliced peaches and summer berries; or, as at the

Negresco, with a sparkling jelly of sliced white and yellow peaches and a diminutive rice pudding topped by caramel.

Another delicious dessert is *poires pochées au jus de cassis, glace de verveine et cassis* (pears poached in cassis, then each cut into a five-pointed star and topped with a molded black currant sorbet flavored with fresh lemon verbena). Again, this attractive sweet lends itself admirably to home entertaining: serve the rich red-poached pear 'star' with a simpler sorbet or a scattering of fresh summer fruits – raspberries, strawberries, wild strawberries and cherries – and accompany it with a bowl of whipped cream. I love, too, his *pain d'épice à l'ancienne, glace à la vanille*, a striped *pièce montée* of thin layers of gingerbread and vanilla ice cream, served with a subtle vanilla-flavored sauce; and the notion of his *partition de sorbets aux parfums de l'arrière-pays*, a *millefeuille* of layers of honey, grapefruit, lemon and mandarin sorbets layered with thin sheets of bitter chocolate and served with a citrus-scented *coulis*.

The wine list at the Negresco, under the easy direction of Patrick Millereau, *chef sommelier*, is as impressive as the hotel itself, with no fewer than 500 vintages, ranging from a selection of truly excellent inexpensive small vineyard local wines to the rarefied heights of the best that France has to offer. It is just this down-to-earth search for the very best that the region has to offer that distinguishes Dominique le Stanc's approach, whether it be a simple Côtes de Provence or a dish of consummate distinction based on the earthy simplicity of young leeks, garden peas, creamy fried eggs or polenta.

Fricassée d'artichauts, de tomates et de cébettes en cocotte

Fricassée of vegetables en cocotte, Dominique le Stanc

SERVES 4

For this dish Le Stanc uses garden-fresh little violet artichokes, firm, fat ripe tomatoes from the market, and *cébettes*, full-sized young green onions – a sort of oversized scallion. I suggest you use the largest scallions you can find.

8 small artichokes (the smallest you can find)	2 tsps extra-virgin olive oil
1 small lemon, cut in half	1 sprig thyme
4 firm, ripe tomatoes	1 bay leaf
8 large scallions	1–2 sprigs cilantro
4 tbsps small black olives from Nice	16 leaves fresh basil
¾ cup reduced veal stock	salt and ground black pepper (optional)
2 anchovies in oil	8 small sprigs chervil

TO PREPARE THE ARTICHOKES

With a sharp kitchen knife, turn the artichokes, removing the leaves and chokes. Place the artichoke hearts in a bowl of cold water with half a lemon to stop them changing color. Reserve for later use.

WHEN READY TO COOK

Seed the tomatoes and cut them in quarters. Wash and cut the scallions into 2-inch segments. Pit the olives. Bring the veal stock to a boil; pour the stock into the bowl of an electric food processor; add the anchovy fillets and process for several seconds until the sauce is smooth.

In a large oval enameled iron casserole, heat the olive oil; cut the artichoke hearts in two and sauté in the hot oil for 2 minutes, stirring with a wooden spoon. Tie the thyme, bay leaf and cilantro in a little piece of muslin and add to the artichoke hearts; add a little water; cover the casserole and continue to cook for 10 minutes more. Add the scallions; cook for 2–3 minutes more; then add the tomatoes, the olives and the processed veal stock.

Just before serving, remove the little bag of herbs and add the basil leaves. Correct the seasoning, adding the juice of the remaining half lemon and salt and freshly ground black pepper if necessary; sprinkle with tiny sprigs of chervil and serve immediately.

Fricassée d'artichauts, de tomates et de cébettes en cocotte.

Filets de Saint-Pierre au jus de ratatouille safrannée

—

Fillets of John Dory with saffron ratatouille sauce

—

SERVES 4

—

4 fillets of John Dory **(or red snapper, black bass or sea bream)**	**salt and ground black** **pepper**

FOR THE TOMATO *CONCASSÉE*

1 lb 4 oz ripe tomatoes, **peeled, seeded and diced**	**1–2 tbsps olive oil**
4 scallions, thinly sliced	**salt and ground black** **pepper**

FOR THE SAFFRON RATATOUILLE SAUCE

¾ cup ratatouille juices **(from leftover** **ratatouille)**	**¼ tsp saffron** **4 tbsps butter, diced**

FOR THE GARNISH

eggplant pallets (patties); **or small thin slices of** **sautéed eggplant (see** **right)**	**fresh basil sprigs**

TO PREPARE THE FISH FILLETS

Trim the fish fillets at each end to form equal-sized rectangles. Season the fillets with salt and place on an oiled baking sheet.

TO PREPARE THE TOMATO *CONCASSÉE*

In a small skillet, sauté the thinly sliced scallions in a little olive oil until they are soft. Add the diced tomatoes and continue to cook for 5 minutes. Season with salt and freshly ground black pepper to taste. Keep warm.

TO PREPARE THE SAFFRON RATATOUILLE SAUCE

In a small saucepan, reduce the ratatouille juices with the saffron until the sauce is half its original quantity. Whisk in the diced butter. Keep warm.

TO COOK THE FISH

Pre-heat the oven to 475°F. Cook the fish fillets in the pre-heated oven for 3–4 minutes. Season with freshly ground black pepper.

TO SERVE

Arrange tomato *concassée* in the center of each heated plate. Place a fillet of John Dory on top, pressing the fillet down lightly so that a little of the tomato *concassée* shows all around the fish. Top each serving with a sprig of fresh basil; spoon a ring of saffron ratatouille juices around each dish and garnish – as they do at the Chantecler – with 4 eggplant pallets (patties); or, more simply, with 4–8 thin, small rounds of sautéed unpeeled eggplant.

Aubergine pallets

1 (1 lb) eggplant	**salt and black pepper**
olive oil	**1 small green pepper**
1 cup heavy cream	**¾ cup all-purpose flour**
8 eggs	**4 tbsps butter, melted**

TO MAKE THE AUBERGINE PALLETS

Pre-heat the oven to 375°F. Cut the eggplant in two lengthwise and place it, cut sides down, in a lightly oiled heat-proof gratin dish large enough to hold the two halves side by side. Cook in the pre-heated oven until the eggplant pulp is soft. Scoop out the pulp and process it in a food processor with the heavy cream and 5 of the eggs.

Cut the pepper into tiny dice and add it to the eggplant mixture. Season generously with salt and freshly ground black pepper and mix well. Spoon the eggplant and pepper mixture into a lightly oiled heat-proof gratin dish and bake in the pre-heated oven for 30–40 minutes.

TO MAKE THE *PANADE*

In a medium-sized mixing bowl, combine the remaining 3 eggs, flour and melted butter and beat until well mixed. Then, in a medium-sized saucepan, bring the milk to a boil; pour the milk over the egg and flour mixture, beating constantly until well blended. Return the *panade* mixture to the heat and cook over low heat, stirring constantly until the sauce is thick and smooth. Remove from the heat. Add the *panade* mixture to the eggplant and pepper mousse and mix well. Form into 16 little flat patties (about 1 ½ inches in diameter) and sauté in a skillet in a little olive oil until lightly colored.

Filets de Saint-Pierre au jus de ratatouille safranné.

Glace miel au safran

Honey saffron ice cream

SERVES 4

2 cups milk	**½ cup granulated sugar**
5 tbsps honey	**5 egg yolks**
½ cup heavy cream	**1 pinch saffron**

In a medium-sized saucepan, combine the milk, honey, heavy cream and half the sugar and bring gently to a boil, stirring constantly, until the sugar has completely melted.

In the meantime, in a small bowl beat the egg yolks with the remaining sugar. Pour the boiling milk mixture over the eggs; add the saffron and stir over hot but not boiling water until smooth and thick. Strain into a bowl and bring rapidly to room temperature. When cold, pour the mixture into an ice cream-maker and freeze according to manufacturer's instructions.

Poires pochées au jus de cassis, sorbet de cassis.

Glace miel au safran, as served at the Chantecler restaurant, with its accompaniments of caramelized rice pudding and jelly of sliced peaches.

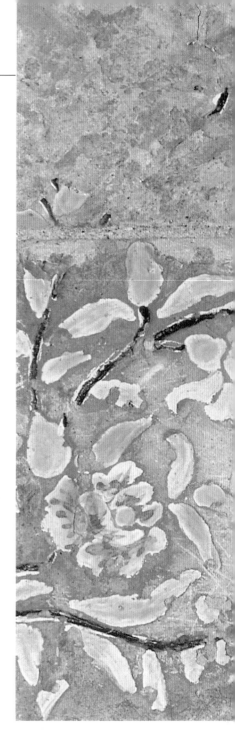

Poires pochées au jus de cassis, sorbet de cassis

Pears poached in berry syrup with berry sorbet

SERVES 4

4 ripe pears	**4¼ cups water**
⅔ cup granulated sugar	**lemon juice**
1¼ cups puréed black currants (or blueberries or blackberries)	
FOR THE BERRY SORBET	
2½ cups black currant, blueberry or blackberry purée	**1⅓ cups granulated sugar**
	1¾ cups water

TO POACH THE PEARS

In a medium-sized saucepan combine the sugar, black currant, blueberry or blackberry purée and water and bring them to a boil.

Peel the pears and brush them with lemon juice to prevent them from discoloring. Add the pears to the black currant, blueberry or blackberry syrup and cook over medium heat, covered, until the pears are tender. Remove the saucepan from the heat and allow the pears to cool in the syrup.

TO MAKE THE BERRY SORBET

In a medium-sized saucepan combine the water and sugar and bring them to a boil; stir in the black currant, blueberry or blackberry purée and allow to cool. Pour the mixture into a sorbet-maker and freeze according to the manufacturer's instructions. Spoon the sorbet mixture into 4 small individual bowls and set to freeze again.

TO ASSEMBLE THE DISH

Cut each pear into 8 pieces and arrange it in a star shape on a chilled dessert plate. Spoon over a little of the poaching liquid. Then place a berry sorbet mold in the center of each pear star and spoon over a little of the poaching liquid. Serve at once.

Index

First published in the United States of America in 1993 by
RIZZOLI INTERNATIONAL PUBLICATIONS, INC.
300 Park Avenue South, New York, NY 10010

Text copyright © 1992 Robert Carrier

First published in Great Britain in 1992 by
George Weidenfeld & Nicolson Limited
Orion House, 5 Upper St Martin's Lane
London WC2H 9EA

ISBN 0-8478-1661-3

LC 92-85369

All rights reserved. No part of this publication
may be reproduced, stored in a retrieval system,
or transmitted in any form or by any means, electronic,
mechanical or otherwise, without the prior
permission of the copyright holder.

Designed by Harry Green
Edited by Barbara Mellor

Typeset by Keyspools Ltd, Golborne, Lancs
Colour separations by Newsele Spa, Milan, Italy
Printed by Printers Srl, Trento, Italy
Bound by L.E.G.O., Vizenza, Italy

PICTURE ACKNOWLEDGEMENTS
The author and publishers would like to thank the following
photographers and organization for their permission to
reproduce the photographs in this book:
MICHELLE GARRETT: endpapers, 2, 5, 8, 10–11, 12–13, 14,
16–17, 19, 20, 21, 23, 25, 27, 29, 33, 37, 39, 40, 42, 44–5, 45,
46, 46–7, 48, 49, 51, 52, 53, 54, 55, 56 left and right, 57, 59
above right, below left (both pictures) and right, 63, 64, 65,
69, 70–1, 72–3, 74, 75, 82 above right, 85, 87, 88, 90, 91, 99,
100–1, 102–3, 105, 106–7, 108, 109, 110 above right,
110–11, 122, 123, 125, 126, 127, 129, 130–1, 132, 132–3,
135, 137, 138, 139 (both pictures), 140–1, 142, 151, 154–5,
156–7, 160, 161, 163 (all except centre), 164, 168 left, 168–9,
172 below, 173, 174, 175, 176–7, 179, 185, 186, 187, 197,
198, 199, 204–5 (all except 204 below right and 205 above
and below right), 206, 208 above and below, 209, 211,
212–3, 213, 214, 215, 216, 218 below left, 218–19.
F. JALAIN: 28, 31, 32, 92–3, 118, 120–21, 152, 159, 162–3
centre, 181, 188, 189, 190–1.
ERIC MORIN: 7 (second left), 30, 34–5, 36, 41, 58, 59 above
left, 66–7, 76–7, 79, 80, 81, 82 below, 83, 84, 86, 94, 96–7,
111 right, 112–13, 114–15, 116, 144, 145, 146–7, 148, 149,
157, 167, 169, 170, 171, 172 above, 180, 182–3, 192 (both
pictures), 193, 195, 196–7, 200 above, 202–3, 203, 204 below
right, 205 above and below right.
JACK NISBERG: 200 below.
TOPHAM PICTURE SOURCE: 1, 15.
Every effort has been made to trace and acknowledge the
copyright owners of the photographs illustrated. If there is
an incorrect or missing credit the author and publishers
apologize most sincerely and will correct the entry in any
future edition.

Albuquerque Academy
Library
6400 Wyoming Blvd. N.E.
Albuquerque, N.M. 87109